# Unlocking the Secrets of Your Childhood Memories

Author of *The Birth Order Book*

# Dr. Kevin Leman
# & Randy Carlson

# UNLOCKING THE SECRETS OF YOUR CHILDHOOD MEMORIES

THOMAS NELSON PUBLISHERS

*Nashville*

Published in Nashville, Tennessee, by Thomas Nelson, Inc. and distributed in Canada by Lawson Falle, Ltd., Cambridge, Ontario.

Printed in the United States of America.

Scripture quotations are from THE NEW KING JAMES VERSION of the Bible. Copyright © 1979, 1980, 1982, Thomas Nelson, Inc., Publishers.

ISBN-0-8407-7631-4

7 8 9 10 11 12 13 14 15 16 17 18 19 20 21 22 23 24 25 95 94 93 92 91 90 89

*To my mom, May Leman, who taught me by*
*example the eternal truths of life.*
*Your love and encouragement have helped me*
*to become the husband and father I am today.*
*I love you, Mom!*

Kevin Leman

*I dedicate this book to the two people who*
*most influenced me during those early*
*memory-making years—my parents, Morry and Dorothy.*
*Thanks for your loving and consistent lives.*
*You helped me to apply many of the concepts*
*found in this book. Your unselfish concern*
*for my well being over the years has been appreciated,*
*even though I seldom have said thanks.*

Randy Carlson

# Contents

# PART ONE

## Why Your Memories Mean So Much

# Chapter *1*

*Years later this same defiant face would appear on a nationally syndicated talk show, proving that the little boy or girl you once were, you still are.*

# "*Now* I Remember...
# So *That's* It!"

We begin this book with a promise: tell us about your earliest childhood memories, and we'll tell you about yourself today.

We can confidently make this declaration because WHO YOU ARE TODAY . . . YOUR BASIC PERSONALITY . . . YOUR PERSONAL LIFE PHILOSOPHY . . . THE SECRET TO YOUR ENTIRE OUTLOOK ON LIFE . . . IS HIDDEN WITHIN YOUR EARLIEST CHILDHOOD MEMORIES.

We all spend much of our earthly existence trying to better understand what makes us tick. We wonder:

"Why doesn't life work out the way I thought it would? Why do I always seem to have bad luck (like spending sixteen dollars to win a goldfish and having it die before I get home from the fair)?"

"Why am I hurting (as in feeling tossed into the manure pile of life)?"

"Why can't I have a satisfying, happy marriage (instead of picking losers)?"

"Why do I have trouble finding real friends (instead of people who need loans and then get amnesia)?"

"Why isn't my job more fulfilling (instead of being so boring I can barely thank God for Fridays)?"

All of these nettlesome matters boil down to one basic question: "Who am I (and does anybody really care)?"

There are many ways to answer the *Who am I?* question. Some try the psycho-safari-search-for-yourself weekend retreat that cousin Muffie's psychotherapist leads once a month in some Rocky Mountain resort with prices higher than the altitude. Others go for the Sesame Street seminars for grownups their companies send them to in order to help them "better understand how to live and work with others."

Occasionally these approaches work, but we've got a much more simple, reliable way to answer your *Who am I?* question. If you stick with us for the next few chapters, you will find that the answer lies waiting to be discovered in your earliest memories. If you stick with us to the end of the book, you'll have a handle on how to strengthen the parts of you that you like and change the parts you don't.

We're not talking magic or mysticism. And we hope you don't think mining your memories sounds like a Freudian trip into the labyrinth of Oedipus and Electra complexes. We will work with just one basic tenet of personality theory: *Your childhood memories—the words you use to describe them and the feelings you attach to them—say volumes about who you are and how you live today.*

## You Can't Go against Your Own Grain

Too often we talk to clients who not only want to change their lives, they want to change their very identities for the better. They have bought into the Madison Avenue messages that tell them they only need to splash on a little Eau de la Muskrat cologne, drink Bozo beer, eat Crispy Critter Crunch cereal, and drive a five-speed, six-liter SX sports car with sunroof and Corinthian leather bucket seats and they can become totally different people. Our answer to all this is a profound psychological term we learned in graduate school:

### BULLCRUMBLE!

The fact is, your basic personality, your underlying identity, is as permanent and unalterable a part of your being as the grain in a piece of oak. You can grow and learn. You can undergo a life-changing conversion, you can adapt and change your behavior in various ways, but your old human nature does not change. You must struggle with it, confront it, and be patient with it all your life.

And that identity starts in the cradle (maybe before). The view of life you picked up back then when you were just a little tyke is nonerasable. As Kevin likes to put it:

## THE LITTLE BOY OR LITTLE GIRL YOU ONCE WERE, YOU STILL ARE!

This isn't just a guess or a half-baked theory. Our counseling practices in Tucson, Arizona, reinforce our thinking five days a week. We know people understand themselves better in the light of their childhood memories, which are like mirrors that reflect their responses to everyday life. Few people realize this, but it's true. Their memories are like a rich mother lode of gold ready for unearthing. Here in this book we will give you the know-how necessary to dig down to your own buried treasure and unlock secrets that will help you reach a new, deeper level of self-understanding.

You say you are not sure you can remember much about "way back then"? Not to worry. We've got some tools and techniques that will help you unlock your memory bank. As we guide you on a search for the secrets in your own memories, we'll also share the recollections of a broad variety of individuals, including our clients, relatives, and personal friends.* We'll even stop to gawk at the private memories of a few of the rich and famous, memories which reveal ever so clearly why they are who they are today.

You'll see that it is no mere coincidence that:

- Donald Trump, real estate entrepreneur extraordinaire, remembers taking all of his little brother's blocks to build a "beautiful building" and never giving them back
- And Lee Iacocca, the management messiah who saved Chrysler from certain doom, hates waste or throwing anything away because he remembers his lean childhood days in the Great Depression

*Except where real identities are clearly noted, the cases and examples we describe are based on composites in which names and other details are changed to protect privacy.

- And Martin Luther King, the great Civil Rights leader, clearly remembers his father telling him when he was very young, "You're as good as anybody."

## If the Memory Fits, Spare It

One of the striking truths about memory exploration is that we all decide at a subconscious level what we will remember and what we choose to block out. Every experience we've had since birth has been recorded and tucked away safely in our brains. Like the most sophisticated computer in the world, the brain retrieves the memories we need when we need them.

Why, then, do we recall some memories and seemingly forget others?

Good question. We touched on the answer when we talked about the basic personality being like the grain in a piece of oak. Part of that grain-producing process includes keeping those early childhood memories that fit—or seem to fit—our present perception of ourselves and the world around us, and blocking out all the others. There is no official term for this sorting out process, but we like to call it the Law of Creative Consistency:

> PEOPLE REMEMBER ONLY THOSE EVENTS
> FROM EARLY CHILDHOOD THAT ARE CONSISTENT
> WITH THEIR PRESENT VIEW OF
> THEMSELVES AND THE WORLD AROUND THEM.

Without Creative Consistency, you'd be in deep trouble. It is your God-given ability to keep the present and past in balance so that you don't fall over the edge into frustration, depression, or insanity. The creative part of it is the way you manage to make sense of all your memory data. The consistency comes into play as you establish crucial reference points for who you are and how you view the world. These reference points *always* match up with your childhood memories.

To begin demonstrating how Creative Consistency works, we want to share a few of our own memories, which clearly reveal some not-very-well-kept secrets about the people Leman and Carlson are today. Because we chose to write this book together, you've already noticed our usual approach is the first person plural—*we*. But at certain points, the first person—*I*—communicates better as we talk about ourselves. So, we'll let Kevin lead off with some revealing reminiscences of his own.

## "Send In the Clowns"

In my very earliest memory (I was about three) I was banging on the front door of my house. I wanted to get in and go potty, but the door was locked. I know it was a Sunday morning because the big thick Sunday paper sat on the front steps. I don't recall why I'd gone outside, but when I wanted to get back in, I found the door locked. So I stood there pounding and calling for someone to let me in. But no one heard me before I messed my pants.

One day when I was seven, as I walked to school I found a brand new, unsmoked Viceroy cigarette lying on the ground. I picked it up and slipped it into my pocket. After school I was walking home when an older kid from our neighborhood came by on his bike. He was twelve and sort of my hero—the Eddy Haskell type. I didn't know how to smoke, but I had that cigarette in my pocket and I wanted to learn. So I asked "Eddy" for a ride, and as I slipped up on the handlebars, I put the Viceroy in my mouth and said, "Hey, 'Eddy' . . . got a light?" And it was on that ride home I smoked my first cigarette feeling very big and tough—just like "Eddy."

I shared the next memory in another book, but I'm retelling it here because it's one of my most vivid—and significant—childhood recollections. I was eight. My sister, as captain of her high school cheerleading squad, had recruited me to be the team mascot. On the particular night in my memory the gym was hot and sweaty, the game close, and the crowd loud. I stood in the middle of the court during a time-out, wearing a sweater with the image of a billy goat pinned on (our team was called the Williamsville Billies), leading the crowd in a cheer. Except I got the words to the cheer backwards and forgot what came next. For a moment I was embarrassed. But as I looked up at those hundreds of laughing faces, I realized I was making them laugh. They were enjoying themselves. Instantly I understood that just by making a mistake I could make people laugh and feel good. And I loved it.[1]

What can you learn about Kevin Leman today by digging through these old childhood memories? Does this memory exploration stuff really work? Well, Kevin will tell you himself that, without even scratching too far below the surface, you can easily learn a lot about who he is and what makes him tick:

> First, let's look at the image of me pounding on the door, screaming loud enough to wake the dead (and sleeping neighbors). In that memory I'm demanding that someone "Let me in"—which is a picture of my entire life. It seems I've spent the better part of my forty-plus years screaming for someone to let me in.
>
> For example, I collected fourteen "No, thank you, we're not interested right now" postcards from the Phil Donahue show before I finally got on as a guest. Actually, fourteen turndowns wasn't that bad. After graduating from high school by the narrowest of grade point margins, I applied to 160 colleges before I got into one—on probation.
>
> My learning to smoke at age seven tells you more. I was the youngest of three children with a sister eight years older and a brother five years my senior. They were the straight-As-and-Bs, quarterback/cheerleader types, and from early on I knew I couldn't outdo them or outshine them. So Kevin became the clown who would do anything to get attention—negative or positive. Smoking my first cigarette while being ridden home on the handlebars of one of the toughest kids in our neighborhood seemed like a perfect way to fulfill my goals at the time.
>
> But my most revealing memory is the scene in that crowded gym when I couldn't remember the words to a cheer. My hitch as mascot for the Williamsville Billies wasn't the only time I've had the goat label pinned on me. I've been a screw-up since I could stand up, and I'm afraid I still am. My attempts at humor are spontaneous and often unrehearsed, and I sometimes fall off of that fine line between the acceptable and what some people might call just a little too much.
>
> Not long ago I appeared as a guest on a nationally

syndicated TV show with two other psychologists to discuss child rearing. One of my fellow panelists started to wax eloquent on the need to be more permissive in order not to damage a child's psyche. As he described how to let your little ankle biters play with your $1,200 stereo if they want to, I got more and more disgusted. Finally, while he was still talking, I turned toward the audience on my side of the set, stuck out my tongue, and made a Joan-Rivers-style gagging motion with my index finger.

Unfortunately, the show's host caught the gesture out of the corner of her eye and said, "Wait a minute! Dr. Leman. Did I just see you stick your tongue out?"

"Uh, well, you see . . . yes, I'm afraid you did. I thought Dr. So and So was giving terrible advice."

Well, that livened up the show and then some! I know I shouldn't have done it, and I didn't mean to show up the other guest. But I can't say I felt too badly about getting caught because I learned very early in life (not too long after my Sunday morning accident on the front porch) that messing up was just one more way to get the attention I lived for.

Kevin's childhood memories are clear and convincing testimony: the little boy he once was, he still is. You can see the recurring themes: feeling left out, wanting acceptance; rebellion against authority; the need for attention and a willingness to take risks. There is also an aggressive cockiness that can roll with the punches and never take no for an answer.

Kevin remembers a producer of "Donahue" asking him if he could handle a full hour as the main resource person for the show. Kevin replied: "Let's put it this way. If Phil gets sick this week and can't show up, why don't you give me a call?"

What about Randy? Anyone who knows us says we're about as different as two people can be. Perhaps that's one reason our daily radio broadcast, "Today's Family," works so well—we are such a contrast. Let's have Randy share some of his early memories and see what we can learn about him.

### "Oops! Oh, No! Be Careful! Ouch!"

I must have been about six or seven when my parents bought me a little used red bike—a *girl's* bike. My dad had to have a bar welded on it because I wouldn't be seen on a girl's bike. One day I remember riding on the park field across the street from our house. Someone called to me from behind, and as I looked back—just for a split second or two—the bike veered into a tree. And I went flying. My overwhelming feeling was embarrassment. I felt far more pain to my ego than to my rear end.

Then there was the time a tornado went across Muskegon, Michigan. Our whole family had to go into our old fruit cellar. I can still hear the rumble of that tornado going over, like a freight train on top of our house. It didn't drop its funnel, but there was wind and rain and noise. I was scared.

One more Muskegon memory: I had two big brothers, one six years and one ten years my senior. They treated me like the "dumb little kid." One day they were both in my oldest brother's bedroom playing with their short-wave radio. I walked in, but I wasn't too welcome. My oldest brother warned, "You better get out of here, Fat Butt" (their favorite pet name for me because I was heavy for my age). Then he added, "You've got three seconds to get out of here, or I'm gonna shoot you with my BB gun." My brother grabbed his air rifle from behind the door, and as I ran out of the room, he cocked the gun and shot me in my ample behind. I felt angry, ostracized, and humiliated.

Now what does this collection of childhood memories tell you about Randy Carlson, the adult? Obviously, he's a very different person from Kevin Leman. Just a quick reading of his memories reveals the recurring themes of pain, fear, and humiliation, as well as the need for security and strong concern about the opinions of others. Like Kevin, Randy admits that all the themes in his early memories crop up in his life today. He says:

I'm a careful, cautious person who longs so badly for security that I sometimes have to force myself to take bold steps and risk humiliation. I often nearly drive my wife crazy with my concern about others' opinions of me and my work.

For example, I worry about the reaction to this book. Will

the reviewers like it? Will the readers like it? One negative review or even a negative letter may discourage me for days. On the other hand, if we should get a trainload of negative mail, Kevin would probably say, "Randy, isn't this great? Do you realize that for every person who writes a letter, there are a thousand more who just bought the book?" Our personalities are that different, and this quick look at his childhood memories and mine clearly reveals the difference.

## Okay, but Does This Work for Everyone?

About now you may be thinking, "This is all very interesting for a couple of psychologists, but I'm not sure I can recall many specific memories, and even if I could, how could I tell what they mean?"

We understand, because in childhood memories seminars, we talk to many clients and students who feel the same way. They start out thinking, "All this memory stuff can't be very practical," but they soon change their opinions as we help them see the striking consistencies between their memories and who they are today.

Don't worry if you don't seem to remember much of your childhood at this point. The memories are in there, and we can show you how to get them out and analyze what they mean. The truth is, this memory exploration business is helpful because it is quite easy to understand. It's simple, but it is not simplistic.

We're not claiming we can answer every question you wrestle with in life. And we're not saying that if you follow our strategy you will gain complete self-understanding, win the Nobel Peace Prize, and become a millionaire. But we do predict you'll learn something new and valuable about yourself by the time you finish this book. In fact, we're practically ready to guarantee that it will help reveal how you think, how you view life, how you relate to others, and how you deal with your emotions. Exploring your memories will explain your attitude toward marriage, toward your children, toward your employer or employees, and even toward your Creator (or your doubts about the existence of a Creator).

As you replay your childhood memories, the lights will come on, the bells will ring, and you'll be saying to yourself, "So *that's* it! *Now* I understand . . . . That's why I can't get a promotion . . . why I've had so many unfulfilling relationships . . . why I can't ever say no . . . why I always feel I have to be in control . . . why I'm afraid to take risks . . . why I don't have friends . . . why it's difficult to communicate with my spouse . . . why my kids know how to press my button. . . ."

Memory exploration does not have to be hidden away in a psychological tool box labeled "For Counseling and Therapy Only." Once you get a few simple rules and techniques in mind, you can use childhood memories to break the ice when you try to talk with strangers. Or you can use memory exploration to learn a little bit more about friends and acquaintances. And there's nothing wrong with using it just to have a little fun now and then. Laughter is the best therapy of all.

But we do have one warning: we are well aware of the truth in David Seamand's book, *Putting Away Childish Things*. He writes: "A lot of folks like to dig around in their past to find excuses for their present behavior. They want to be able to say, 'My mother and dad, my brother, my circumstances, my teacher, or that accident made me what I am today. If only this . . . if only that . . . then I would be okay.'"[2]

We're not interested in helping you find scapegoats from the past to sacrifice on the altar of your anger, your guilt, your depression, or your uncertainties. In fact, by exploring memories, we hope just the opposite will happen. We're going to show you how your own memories can be like mini-videocassettes that you can view to see yourself more clearly than you ever have before. And as the next chapter will show, this works for everybody—the rich and the famous, the ordinary and the average. We all have our memories and they are unerring reflections of who we are today.

# Chapter 2

*Disaster seemed to be Randy's middle name. Childhood memories of failure left him with a fear of taking risks and a longing for security.*

# Why Iacocca Is Still Running Scared

Remember what we said in the first chapter about the significance of certain memories? Why did Kevin remember pounding at that door at three-and-a-half? Or being ridden around on a bike by an older kid at age seven, dragging on his first cigarette?

On the other hand, why did Randy remember a bike incident that ended in disaster or being dry-gulched by his BB-gun-brandishing brother? In all of Randy's memories, disaster seems to be his middle name. Why do his memories have this obvious pattern? You would think Randy would want to forget all that bad stuff.

Neither of us fished up certain memories that we could interpret in a certain way in order to draw a preconceived psychological portrait. The truth is, *the portrait was already painted*. Our memories simply unveiled it. No one just "happens" to pick a particular memory from among the millions of experiences of childhood and adolescence and "forget" all the others. Certain memories come to your mind because the Law of Creative Consistency is always at work. For example, if your early childhood memories are of lean and difficult times, you are probably a saver who knows the current CD interest rates by heart. Security and never wasting anything are crucial for you.

## Why Lee Iacocca Hates Waste

Listen as auto magnate Lee Iacocca recalls early memories of some lean and hungry times of his own:

> For a few years we were actually wealthy. But then came the Depression.
>
> No one who's lived through it can ever forget. My father lost all his money, and we almost lost our house. I remember asking my sister, who was a couple of years older, whether we'd have to move out and how we'd find somewhere else to live. I was only six or seven at the time, but the anxiety I felt about the future is still vivid in my mind. Bad times are indelible—they stay with you forever.[1]

It is no accident that of the millions of childhood experiences young Iacocca had, he chose to recall this small incident with his sister. Note the consistency between that memory and what he writes next about his present view of life:

> The Depression turned me into a materialist. Years later, when I graduated from college, my attitude was: "Don't bother me with philosophy. I want to make ten thousand a year by the time I'm twenty-five, and then I want to be a millionaire." I wasn't interested in a snob degree; I was after the bucks.
>
> Even now, as a member of the working rich, I put most of my money away in very conservative investments. It's not that I'm afraid of being poor, but somewhere in the back of my mind there's still the awareness that lightning can strike again, and my family won't have enough to eat.[2]

But even more Creative Consistency between Iacocca's memories of the Depression and the man he is today can be seen in his next remarks. He admits that no matter how well he is doing financially, the Depression has never disappeared from his consciousness:

> To this day, I hate waste. When neckties went from narrow to wide, I kept all my old ones until the style went back to nar-

row. Throwing out food or scraping half a steak into the disposal still drives me crazy. I've managed to convey some of that awareness to my daughters, and I notice that they don't spend money unless they get a good deal—my goodness, they do go to a lot of sales![3]

It's a little hard to picture a Chrysler Motors mogul scraping lunch leftovers into the sink as he subconsciously wonders if nightfall will find him in line at the neighborhood soup kitchen (as if his neighborhood had a soup kitchen!). His chef probably doesn't even know there is such a thing as "double coupon day" at the supermarket.

Obviously, any anxiety Lee Iacocca might have about stretching the family food dollar is a bit absurd. Yet that anxiety is quite consistent with his early childhood memories. Iacocca's adult perspective (however irrational) makes perfect sense when you consider his memories of being a seven-year-old boy during the Depression.

## The Slat Got His Tongue

For another example of Creative Consistency, let's look at the early memories of Fidel Castro, an even more rebellious lad than Kevin Leman. Anyone who has memories of being boxed in or not feeling free may struggle with being under authority. In fact, that person may turn out to be a manager or leader, strictly for self-protection. Castro's childhood memories paint a vivid picture of a man who struggled with that boxed-in feeling, but who grew up to become leader of Communist Cuba:

I spent most of my time being fresh. . . . I remember that whenever I disagreed with something the teacher said to me, or whenever I got mad, I would swear at her and immediately leave school, running as fast as I could. . . . One day, I had just sworn at the teacher, and was racing down the rear corridor. I took a leap and landed on a board from a guava jelly box with a nail in it. As I fell, the nail stuck in my tongue. When I got back home, my mother said to me: "God punished you for swearing at the teacher." I didn't have the slightest doubt that it was really true. . . .

. . . I had one teacher after another, and my behavior

was different with each one. . . . With the teacher who treated us well and bought us toys, I remember being well behaved. But when pressure, force or punishment was used, my conduct was entirely different.[4]

Castro also recalls that he liked history "very much . . . particularly the story of battles." He admits that he used to invent battles "by taking a lot of little scraps and tiny balls of paper, arranging them on a playing board." He would create obstacles, determine "losses, casualties." He played these games of war for hours at a time.[5]

You don't need a degree in psychology to see the consistency between the memories of young Fidel Castro and the record of the adult revolutionary. Castro is known as much for his venomous tongue and his ranting speeches against Western powers as he is for military leadership. The mouthy little boy he once was, he still is. And as leader of Communist Cuba, he has far more control of life, far more ability to keep from being boxed in.

Spotting the consistencies between the memories and the current lifestyles of the rich or notorious is interesting, but even more helpful are case studies of typical clients we've dealt with in counseling sessions. Often, just one memory can tell us volumes about a person. That was the case with a young woman whose loneliness became so painful that she phoned Kevin for an appointment.

## Meet Ruth, the Weighty Watcher

As we have seen with Iacocca and Castro, the Law of Creative Consistency can work in rather obvious ways. The same was true of Ruth, whose problem was loneliness and depression. If you have childhood memories of being lonely, it is quite possible you will have few friends and to compensate you will be a voracious reader or a couch potato glued to the TV set. You might have a torrid love affair with your personal computer, or you might even be an animal lover.

Twenty-nine-year-old Ruth wasn't an animal lover, which is sometimes a logical source of solace for someone who battles loneliness. Nor did she have anything going with a computer. In fact, she had nothing going with anyone, and her best friends were on TV sitcoms. The first time she stalked into Kevin's office, her very large bell shape was covered by a top that seemed to be made of the kind of camouflage fabric you find at a surplus store.

But somehow it all worked together. Ruth seemed cautious and withdrawn, wanting to hide from life and people—especially psychologists. In an attempt to break the ice, which seemed rather thick at the moment, Kevin asked the woman if she had been hunting.

"No," she replied sharply. "Why?"

"That looks a little like a hunting jacket."

"It's my blouse," she snapped, and Kevin realized it was going to be a long day—or a short client/doctor relationship. We'll let him tell the rest of the story:

> It didn't take masterful insight to realize that referring to Ruth's blouse as a hunting jacket had not gotten us off to a great start. I backpedaled quickly and did manage to learn that she had come to see me because she had been struggling with depression. But I could sense she was already regretting her decision and was probably looking for a reason not to come back for a second session. In fact, she had probably made up her mind to forget me already, and maybe that's why she looked skeptical when I asked her to tell me something about one of her earliest memories.
>
> Her first recollection was from the age of five. She remembered standing in a park, watching other children skipping rocks on a pond. She didn't join them or throw any stones herself. She just watched as the other children played and had fun.
>
> When she finished talking, I told her what her memory said to me about her. I wasn't at all sure she wanted to hear it, but I felt that because we had gotten off on such a wrong foot, I didn't have a whole lot to lose. Maybe I could convince her I had more promise as her counselor than I did as her fashion consultant.
>
> "I'll need a little time to confirm this, but I suspect that the memory you've just shared with me is an accurate analogy of your life."
>
> "How can you tell?" she asked suspiciously. "I'm sure lots of kids have stood by watching the crowd and wishing they could be part of it."

"Yes, I'm sure you're right. What is significant, however, is the scene you fished up out of your memories. Why *that* scene? There's a good chance that what this memory is telling you is that for twenty-nine years you've been standing on the outside, watching other people have fun, longing to get into the action, but afraid to step out and get involved."

Ruth looked at me as though she had caught me reading her diary. "I never have had many friends," she admitted. "It was that way all through grade school, and then high school was hell on earth. I got fat and stayed that way. Now I just sit home watching television and getting depressed."

Ruth stayed for the rest of that first counseling session and came back for several more. Everything I learned about her in subsequent sessions merely fleshed out (no pun intended) the picture of that lonely little girl in the memory. But the more I got to know her, the more I realized there was a gentle, caring, wonderful person hiding behind the fat body, ugly black glasses, and mini-tent wardrobe.

In another session, Ruth shared additional memories. She told of being an only child and hearing her mother tell a friend one day, "Ruth isn't a very pretty girl, but she is obedient." As for her dad, she saw him seldom. He was always working.

"The summer I turned seven he promised to take me to the zoo because I hadn't had a birthday party. I was all ready to go when he called and told my mom he couldn't make it because something had come up at work. I ran upstairs to my bed and cried for a long time. . . ."

The pattern in Ruth's memories was plain: feeling left out, not pretty, rejected. As we worked on all this, I invited her to a party—a party called life. She eventually accepted the invitation, lost weight, bought a pair of contact lenses, changed her hair style, and became a happy, active member of the human race.

Ruth's success story, told here in abbreviated form, sounds simple, almost too simple. But that's the way memory exploration works. Not only did that simple childhood memory of standing there alone watching other kids having fun give Ruth the insight to determine the basic issue she struggled with, but it gave her a concrete image of what she wanted to change. She no longer wanted to be a lonely little girl who stood and watched sadly as life went on by.

When we examine childhood memories, perceptions are all-important. In Ruth's case, her early memory of that day at the pond is consistent with her distorted view of life at age twenty-nine. You may be wondering what was so "creative" about Ruth's perceptions, but keep in mind that creativity can be negative as well as positive.

At age five, Ruth perceived that experience of standing apart and being left out as something that fit—for her. She told herself, "I can't join in. I'll just watch." Her perception made sense to her at the time and became a building block of her personality. It wasn't a positive factor, but that is not the point. Twenty-four years later, her memory of the incident supported her perception of life, and her perception of life was consistent with that first childhood memory. The Law of Creative Consistency always balances one against the other.

## Jane Was a Loner—and Liked It

To see how perceptions can differ, let's look at Jane, who spent a lot of time alone growing up but, unlike Ruth, never felt lonely. In her first counseling session with Randy, Jane shared three early childhood memories, all of which matched who she was as an adult:

> I remember sitting alone in my room. I must have been about four years old at the time. I was practicing my alphabet.

> When I was five, I remember the day I got lost in the store. It took me fifteen minutes to find my mother. But I did it.

> I think I was five in this one also. I remember walking by myself to the store to buy some candy. Then I walked home all by myself—without any help.

These memories are no mystery. Jane preferred being a loner, which helped explain her recent divorce. During counseling she admitted she had always had a hard time sharing, cooperating, or opening up enough to communicate—even with her husband.

What is amazing is that she even came in for counseling, which is totally out of character for a loner. It says something about how desperate she felt. She admitted she was fifteen hundred miles from her family and felt close to no one in her church or her divorce recovery group. She felt she didn't have a single friend she could share any problems with.

## Susan Feared the Bottom Would Fall Out

In our work we talk with many clients who have childhood memories of painful and scary times. It often turns out that for these people taking risks is not their cup of tea; being careful and "taking care" is. They are often cautious planners of every move, and they don't like surprises. When Randy met a young woman named Susan, the consistency between her current outlook on life and a vivid childhood memory wasn't that obvious to her at first. Randy was leading a seminar on memory exploration at a family retreat in New Mexico when Susan shared this story:

> When I was two or three, my mother and I were taking a trip on a train. I needed to use the bathroom. When I got there, I noticed there was no bottom to the toilet—it opened straight down to the tracks that were rushing by below. My mother tried to put me on the seat, but I wouldn't let her. I kicked and screamed, "No! no!" until she let me go. I was afraid of falling through.

As he assessed Susan's memory, Randy speculated there might be times when the adult Susan would be fearful about the bottom of life falling out. Susan vehemently denied this, and from the look on her face, Randy feared she might walk out.

Later, however, Randy saw Susan edging her way forward during break time. She asked him if they could speak privately, so they sat down a row or two away from the others.

"You know," she said, "even though I thought this memory analysis stuff was a crock when you said what you did about my memory, I've been thinking about it, and I guess you're right. You just hit me where I hurt, and I couldn't admit it. I actually do fear the bottom of life falling through. My husband has reminded me of several times in past months when I've been gripped by fear. I now realize I must work on this area, so thanks. I really learned something valuable today."

It's not too hard to understand why Randy's simple explanation of the bottomless toilet seat incident made Susan angry at first. As an adult, Susan is much too mature to scream, "No! no!" every time she faces a new experience that is threatening or challenging. But when those experiences come along, her memory tape begins to roll in the back of her mind, asking, "What if the bottom falls out?" And each time it does, she gives herself permission to feel fearful and insecure.

It was easy for Randy to spot Susan's problem because he can empathize with anybody who feels insecure. His own memories feature crashing on a bike, cowering in a storm cellar as a tornado roars overhead, suffering pain and humiliation at the hands of his sadistic brothers. Randy's struggle with a don't-take-many-risks approach to life today is consistent with the experiences he remembers from childhood.

## Are You a Consistent Giver or Taker?

Creative Consistency can even reveal if you are a person who habitually gives or takes. In their fascinating book *The Givers and the Takers,*[6] Cris Evatt and Bruce Feld observe that every person is predominantly one or the other. In other words, the world is divided into givers and takers.

For example, takers are more assertive while givers are less assertive. Takers tend to be more attractive while givers are less attractive. Takers break away while givers hang on. Givers seldom break off a relationship, but takers often do. Takers are less service oriented while givers are more service oriented. Takers are in control while givers have less control.

A heroic giver was Corrie ten Boom, the Dutch woman who survived Nazi concentration camps and told her story in the best-selling book, *The Hiding Place,* which also became a major film. Corrie was sent to prison by the Nazis for helping to hide Jews in the ten Boom home. As early as ages five and six, long before the Nazis came, Corrie can remember praying for unfortunate people in her town. One of her memories is from her first day of school: "When we arrived at the school, I saw a little boy being carried into Master Robyns' classroom in his father's arms. . . . He was crying so lustily, even louder than I was. He looked so ugly that I felt sorry for him."[7]

Corrie's memories, which are recorded in several different books, clearly reflect a person who would risk her life for others, and that is exactly why she wound up in a concentration camp.

Corrie ten Boom was the classic giver. A classic taker is a man we'll call Duane, one of Randy's clients. Duane's early memories include being four years old and stealing strawberries from the neighbor's yard, then hurrying back to his garage to eat them. At age six or seven, Duane remembers getting into a fight because the other boy wouldn't let Duane play with his basketball.

Duane's classic taker mentality carried over into adulthood. He came for counseling because his pursuit of money and things caused him to lose his family, his friends, and most of his warm feelings toward the human race. Even his newest relationship with a woman was built on "what's in it for me." His attendance at his church was based on the same motivation—new contacts he could use in business dealings.

## Consistency Is Never Coincidental

All the examples in this chapter clearly show how a person's memories match up with that person's current view of life and way of operating. The Law of Creative Consistency never depends on simple coincidence. And it has nothing to do with conscious choice on your part. You don't consciously choose to remember one thing and forget many others.

As we have tried to demonstrate, there are very good reasons that you remember certain experiences or events. Very often, your parents are involved. For example, if you have early childhood memories of being criticized by your mother or father or both, it's quite likely you usually run behind schedule because you procrastinate. You may often bite off more than you can chew, and it's not unusual for your desk to be very messy. All these are traits of the perfectionist (yes, even the messy desk—that's for *discouraged* perfectionists!). In the next chapter, you will meet a discouraged perfectionist and see how she traced her problem right back to a day when her mother called her stupid.

And if you're getting interested in exploring your own memories, we'll give you a simple six-step plan that explains how it's done. There is no time like the present to look into your past just a little bit. Maybe it will change your future!

# Chapter 3

*A revealing question is whether you remember feeling in control or feeling controlled by others.*

# Pick a Memory—
# Any Memory

Perhaps you're a bit frustrated at this point. We've done all this talking about early memories, and you can't remember anything before the age of eight or ten, maybe even twelve or older. We've worked with people who thought they couldn't get back beyond their high school prom.

If you seem to get a mild case of amnesia when trying to recall your childhood, this chapter should give you a few specific starting points that will spark a chain reaction of memories. We will also go over six simple rules of memory exploration and some techniques we use with our clients to open windows to the past.

Whether or not you remember anything at the moment, don't worry. It's all there. Everything you've ever seen or done is stored on a video memory tape somewhere in your mind. For most people, it's only a matter of plugging into one or two memories and they are on their way. There are a few exceptions, however—extreme cases for whom there is a deep psychological reason for the lack of memories.

People who suffer traumatic experiences often protect themselves from painful memories by blocking them out. Sexual abuse, parental neglect, acts of violence, serious automobile accidents, and other shocking or jolting experiences may cause a person to throw up barriers to keep out the painful memories.

If that kind of horrible memory is buried in your past, keep in mind that this book is not intended to be a substitute for a trained therapist. If you appear to have total memory block due to a traumatic experience or you uncover a particularly painful memory that is persistently disturbing, we suggest you seek competent psychological help.

## Cracking Your Memory Safe

Serious memory block is rare, however, and chances are that all you need is a little prodding and practice to get your memories going. So if you're thinking, "I really can't remember a thing," try relaxing and going for it to see what happens. There are dozens of ways to get at memories that you think you've forgotten. Following are just a few questions and ideas that we've used with many people who thought their minds were "blank." Read this list slowly, and let your mind wander a bit. Chances are you'll hit a question or a thought that will get the memories flowing:

- Can you remember an early birthday party?
- Can you recall any of your teachers when you were young, especially in kindergarten or first or second grade? Did you get along with them? Did you ever have problems?
- What were your teachers like? Do one or two stand out? Why?
- What kind of vacations did your family take? Can you think of a special one? Where did you go?
- Can you remember the day you learned to ride a bike? What happened?
- What about Christmas times? Can you remember a special Christmas or Hanukkah—a special present you received at holiday time?
- What did your family do for fun? Can you remember any special picnics or other kinds of outings?
- What did you do at bedtime when you were little? Can you think of any special incidents?

If you're still drawing blanks, try to take an imaginary walk through the house where you lived as a young child. Or maybe there will be several houses. Did your family move much? It's always good to associate your memories with historical events like moving, your first polio shot, your first day of school, and so on.

We suggest putting the book down for a moment and just letting your mind wander back over some or just one of these questions. It's our guess that the memories will start to flicker into focus on your video screen. Sometimes early childhood memories are nothing more than brief glimpses into the past, bits and pieces from your personal ancient history. All you may get is a smell, a word or two, or perhaps a visual image that was burned deep into your mind but forgotten until now. Some memories may be crisp and clear while others are like shadows. Any of these might reveal something interesting, helpful, or even startling.

As you begin to tune in on your memories, you'll need to decide which ones deserve more thorough exploration. That's where the six rules of memory exploration come in. Come with us into one of Randy's counseling sessions, and we'll show you exactly how it works.

## Meet Andrea—Up Close and Consistent

When Andrea walked into Randy's office for the first time, she acted as if she had it all together. Looking much younger than her forty years, she gave every impression of being self-confident, secure, and controlled. As they got acquainted, Randy noted that Andrea liked doing the proper thing at the proper time. Her three children, two of whom were teenagers, were neat, well-behaved, and doing well in school. Andrea admitted, "I guess most of my friends envy me at least a little bit, but . . ." and her voice trailed off.

"But what?" Randy probed.

"I'm dying inside. I doubt that my husband really loves me anymore, and I'm even beginning to wonder if he's not having an affair. And I know a lot of those envious friends of mine talk behind my back."

As Randy talked with Andrea further, it soon became clear she had no real evidence to back up any of her doubts and suspicions. She was putting herself through tremendous stress for no apparent reason—at least no reason he could see on the surface. In an attempt to get to the heart of her crisis, he asked Andrea to tell him one of her earliest childhood memories. In memory exploration, it's always advisable to try to go back to the earliest childhood memory you can, below eight years old, if possible. That is not to say that memories above eight aren't useful, but Rule No. 1 says earlier memories are usually more significant.

## 1. The Earlier the Memory, the Better

There are at least two good reasons why early memories are more valuable. First, almost all psychologists agree that children make many important decisions in their first five or six years. Researchers have found that "within those first few years, children will have created their own idiosyncratic answers to: Who am I? What is life? What must I do? What is good? What is bad? Children create their own unique private logic, which, to some extent, will make each of them different from any other human being."[1]

You begin working out this thing called your private logic from the moment you are born. Through trial and error you test everything to see if it fits your emotional need to belong in life. If it does, you make a mental note and keep that behavior and those feelings for later use. If what you do or feel doesn't fit your need to belong, you throw it out.

In the process of all this picking and choosing, small pieces of your childlike personality fall into place. These small pieces are most clearly visible in the earliest of childhood memories because they are far less cluttered with all those defense mechanisms and rationalizations that you have learned to use as an adult.

Look at it this way: as an adult, when you remember something from last week or even last year, you filter that memory through all of your powers of adult logic and reasoning. Recent memories are more likely to reflect what you'd like to be or the person you think you are, rather than the real person who was molded so long ago in your childhood.

The other reason early memories are best is that they follow the Law of Creative Consistency, which we discussed in chapters 1 and 2. When you reach back over the years to childhood, you come up with certain memories and leave out literally millions of others that are tucked away in your mind. *Why only those memories?* Because the Law of Creative Consistency says you remember only those events from early childhood that are consistent with your present view of yourself in the world around you.

In other words, your early memories can't be fooled. They don't picture who you think you are or who you'd like to be. They picture the *real you,* how you actually perceive life and live it, whether you realize it or not. Andrea's early memories did just that, but she did need a little encouragement to make her first trip into the past. "Early childhood seems so long ago," Andrea said. "I can't remember much from back there."

Randy assured her the exercise would be helpful and that she should relax and see what would happen. As a daydreamy look came on Andrea's face, Randy knew she was rerunning her old memory tapes. Mentally passing by millions of early childhood images and pictures, she insisted she had no specific recollections of her girlhood years.

To help Andrea recapture a memory, Randy prompted her: "What do you remember about your house when you were, let's say, five years old?"

"Not much," she replied. "Though I do remember our living room had red and blue carpeting. I also remember I slept in the same room with my little sister."

"Anything about the people in the house that you remember?"

As she thought for a few more seconds, her gaze dropped to the floor. Tears began to stream down her cheeks.

"What do you remember?" Randy encouraged.

"Well, I must have been about four or five at the time. . . . Maybe I was six, I'm not sure. I recall it was a rainy day, sort of a downer day. The house was a mess, and I think company was coming over for dinner. Apparently my mother felt I wasn't helping out enough. I remember she gave me that critical look she always had and said, 'Can't you see I need your help here? Why can't you be more responsible? Are you blind or just stupid?'"

Andrea looked up and quickly added, "My mother was good at calling me stupid—I could never do enough to please her. I always felt like a failure around her." She paused, "You know, I haven't thought about that incident since the day it happened thirty-five years ago."

"Oh, I think you may have thought about it more than you realize," Randy said. "Do you have any other memories now that you've sort of gotten rolling?"

At this point Randy was bringing another rule of memory exploration into action. Not only should memories be as early as possible, but it helps to have more than one.

## 2. The More Early Memories, the Better

You can learn a lot from a single memory, but in most cases you can learn even more from several. Early childhood memories are like threads woven together to form the fabric of self-understanding. The equation is simple: the more early childhood memories, the more threads; the more threads, the stronger the fabric; the stronger the fabric, the more personal insight.

That first memory of her critical mother had brought tears to Andrea's eyes. Randy suspected she could have a secret fear of failure, but he wanted more evidence. She thought for less than a minute, then said: "When I was about five, I recall playing with my sister in her bedroom. As I remember it, the room was painted a light yellow with yellow curtains. I remember Mother yelling up the stairs for me to get my own room picked up—and fast. I felt sad we had to stop playing together and angry at my mother for making us stop."

Andrea barely paused to breathe before continuing with a third memory: "I also remember my mother and grandmother trying to teach me the alphabet. I guess I was five, or had just turned six. They used these white cards with the letters printed in black—one letter per card. I can remember my mother scolding me whenever I made a mistake with a letter. She was big on that. I felt like a failure again."

With three memories to work on, Randy had all he needed to help Andrea understand that she struggled with a fear of failure. In addition, Andrea's memories met another important requirement. They belonged to her and no one else.

## 3. The Memories Must Be Yours Alone

In other words, traditions or family stories that have been repeated so many times they become like memories are not usable. A parent, grandparent, or even older sibling might have told you, "I'll never forget the time when you . . ." so many times that you are no longer certain whether you remember the incident yourself or just remember having it told to you.

For example, when Kevin was only eleven days old, his father picked him up and said with prophetic insight: "He looks just like a little bear cub." Everybody chuckled, and from that day forward Kevin was known as Cub or Cubby.

As he grew up, Kevin heard the story of his nickname so many times he could almost picture his dad looking down and likening him to a bear cub. It would be easy for him to call this a "childhood memory," but, of course, it isn't because he doesn't actually remember the incident.

But here's one memory he does associate with the nickname "Cubby" and you can easily see why: When he was nine, Kevin joined the Cub Scouts (naturally), and at one den meeting at a friend's home, the den mother served a snack. Being inexperienced or maybe a bit naïve, she put the cookies on one of her most valuable china plates. As she set the cookies on the table, Kevin jumped up and lunged to get the biggest one. The food went flying, and Kevin clearly remembers that horrible helpless feeling as he saw the family heirloom cookie platter fall to the floor and shatter.

"Cubby Leman!" the distraught den mother screamed. "Every time you walk in this house, something gets broken!"

She was exaggerating, but not much. The memory is fixed vividly in Kevin's mind and is indeed his, not someone else's, story.

A simple test to separate real memories from vivid familiar stories is this. Close your eyes and ask two questions: What did I feel? What did I see? If you can remember feeling a specific emotion and seeing a specific picture of the memory in your mind, it is probably yours. If you can't, don't use it because it's probably just a story you've been told by others.

There was little doubt that Andrea's three memories involved painful or discouraging experiences she clearly recalled as happening to her. In addition, they met a fourth requirement because they were specific occurrences that she could single out and picture in her mind.

## 4. The Memories Must Involve Specific Events

When digging for memories, it is often easier to remember generalities rather than specifics. For example, you might say: "Every day when I rode to school I would . . ." or "My kindergarten teacher always . . ."

To get a real memory you must focus on a specific event or a specific day. For example: "I remember one day I was riding the school bus when this car came through the stop sign and hit us. . . ." or "One time my kindergarten teacher asked me to leave the room because . . . ."

As for Andrea, her three memories were all specific happenings. Had she simply said, "My mother was sort of critical and disciplined us a lot," it wouldn't have been nearly as helpful. Focusing on particular situations clearly illustrating her mother's critical nature made all the difference:

- Andrea's mother bustled about and became impatient enough to call her stupid.
- Andrea's mother brusquely interrupted her play time with her sister and ordered her to clean her room.
- And when Andrea tried to do alphabet cards, her mother criticized every mistake.

In each case, the memory passes the simple "I remember the time when . . ." test. You should be able to locate a legitimate childhood memory as a certain time or a certain day—a certain occasion when something happened.

## Have You Picked A Memory Yet?

Let's quickly review the four rules of memory exploration that we've looked at so far and see how they might apply to one of your own memories:

1. The earlier the memories, the better.
2. The more early memories, the better.
3. The memories must be yours alone.
4. The memories must involve specific events.

Have you come up with a memory that fits these four requirements? We're assuming that by now you're getting something on your own memory transmission screen. If it's still a little snowy, here are some additional memory joggers:

- What was your usual mood as a young child? Happy? Sad? Why?
- Did you ever feel sorry for yourself? Why?
- What were your brothers and sisters like? Did you get along with them? Why or why not?
- Did your parents have much time to spend with you?
- Did you always believe your parents? Can you think of a time

when you argued with either of them? Or a time when you realized that they weren't perfect or invincible?
- Did you get spanked much as a child? Why?
- Could you manipulate or "bluff" your parents? How?
- What frightened you as a child? Can you remember some of your "scariest" experiences?
- What were some "most embarrassing" experiences? Who and what were involved?
- Did you ever feel lonely or rejected? Why?

Many of the above questions may not press any buttons for you, but some of them should. As we suggested earlier, let your mind wander a bit.* If a memory starts coming into focus, stop right here and record it on the lines below. Remember, it doesn't have to be something outstanding, exciting, or unusual. It just has to be yours. As the chapter title says, pick a memory—*any* memory.

MY FIRST CHILDHOOD MEMORY IS: _____

_____

_____

_____

_____

_____

Now that you have something written down, let's go on and look at the other two rules of memory exploration, which are the most important of all.

*If you are having trouble coming up with a childhood memory, we have several suggestions. 1. Try something from your teenage years, which is usually easier; 2. Go back to the memory jogger questions on pages 42 and 43 and go over them again to see if something clicks; 3. Instead of getting bogged down, ask your spouse or a friend to give you a memory and use it as your first example. Your own will come later.

## 5. Focus on the Clearest Part of the Memory

Many memories are stories that have several parts. For example, it's typical to remember a mishap on a bike. Hypothetically speaking, you might say:

> I remember getting a new red bike when I was seven. One day I was riding it after school and I hit the curb and crashed. My arm really hurt and I started crying. My mom ran out of the house, picked me up, kissed the skinned spot on my elbow, and helped me back on the bike so I could try again.

This memory fits several necessary requirements: It's early—you're seven years old. It's yours alone—because you can see yourself riding that new red bike and falling down. There's no mention of "My mother often told me about the time I . . ." And, the memory zeros in on a specific event—you aren't using "I used to ride my bike a lot after school" or some other generality.

But what you need to do now is zero in on the clearest part of the bike disaster. How do you do that? You ask this question: *If this memory were a movie, which moment of action or frame of the film is the most vivid or memorable?* Is it the moment of falling or feeling pain? Is it when Mom arrives to give comfort? Or maybe it's the help she gave you to get started again.

The bike mishap is only a hypothetical example to help you see what you're after. Now focus on the clearest part of your own memory video and see what you come up with.

THE CLEAREST PART OF MY FIRST MEMORY IS: _____

_____

_____

Establishing that clearest "freeze frame" of a memory is extremely important because it sets you up for the most significant part of the six-step sequence. What do you remember feeling when this event happened?

## 6. Attach a Feeling to the Clearest Part of the Memory

Continuing with the hypothetical bike wreck, if the clearest part of the memory for you is falling down, you might attach a feeling of fear, hurt, anger, or embarrassment. If the clearest part of that memory is Mom's giving you comfort, you could attach the primary feeling of security. If the clearest part is the encouragement she gave you, the primary feeling might be determination—"I'll never quit."

Not only will people focus on different parts of a similar memory, but they can have entirely different feelings about remembering a similar experience. Remember, the Law of Creative Consistency is always at work. The memories that come into your mind are the ones that reflect your view of yourself and your world around you today. The feelings you associate with those memories are proof of that. That's why two people can remember a similar incident, but have totally different feelings about it.

For example, Kevin remembers being the cheerleader mascot and making the crowd laugh by fouling up a cheer. (He thought it was great!) Randy has a similar memory of being embarrassed in front of a large crowd in a gymnasium. He was participating in a third-grade spelling bee. All the classes from all the different grades in the school sat around the perimeter of the gym. The teacher in charge went from child to child, calling out the words. Those who spelled their words correctly would keep their seats, and she would give a new word to the next person. But those who missed were out. The very first word she asked Randy was *gang*. Somehow he misspelled it! He remembers to this day the overwhelming feeling of "Dummy me!" He was totally humiliated when that happened in front of all those people.

Here are similar memories that took place when Randy and Kevin were approximately the same age—around eight. Both were set in gymnasiums, in front of large numbers of people. Both memories involved making a public mistake. Yet the emotional reactions were totally different: Randy felt humiliation while Kevin enjoyed a feeling of acceptance and approval.

And both of these memories clearly describe who we are today. Randy is cautious, still working very hard as an adult to avoid humiliation and embarrassment. Kevin is a go-for-broke risk taker who will try just about anything to get a laugh and the approval of the crowd.

## Superwoman Gets the Point

In Andrea's case, the last two rules of memory exploration helped her make a real breakthrough with her own problems. The clearest part of each of her memories was her mother's critical look or tone of irritation and anger. In each case, the feelings she attached to those memories were those of rejection, sadness, that she was a failure and could never please her mother, no matter how hard she tried.

After hearing her out, Randy told Andrea gently: "Andrea, I want you to think about something with me. Could it be that every time you have an opportunity to succeed, these memories flash on the screen in the back of your mind and tell you that you're not only stupid, but inadequate, irresponsible, and unable ever to measure up? To counteract these feelings, you work extra hard at "being perfect," and while you have been successful, the stress is wearing you out. Is it possible you've spent a lifetime trying to be the little girl you think your mother wanted you to be?"

Andrea looked at Randy for a long moment and then the "So that's it!" look dawned on her face. She admitted that she had been feeling overwhelmed by a constant sense of inadequacy. That sudden freeze-frame glimpse of the little girl being called stupid got past the Superwoman façade to the very heart and soul of a hurting person. Once Andrea identified her problem, she made fast progress in dealing with her crippling feelings and misconceptions of her husband and her friends.

Attaching a feeling to the memory that you've been working with in this chapter is the last crucial step in your own exploration process. You might want to close your eyes and refocus on the clearest scene in the memory. How did you feel at that moment?

THE FEELING I ATTACH TO THE CLEAREST PART OF THE MEMORY IS:

_____

_____

Now take a closer look at that feeling. Does it recur with any kind of consistent pattern today? Under what circumstances? Does that feeling have any effect on the person you are today?

## For Still More Insight

For many clients like Andrea, all they need is to identify the clearest part of a memory and how they remember feeling when it happened. That alone gives them the insight to make some needed changes. There are, however, many other techniques that we use to help clients weave a tapestry of self-understanding from their memories.

For example, we might ask if there is a recurring location where the memories take place—school, the home, or maybe a special hiding place that might say something about their interests or personalities.

It also sometimes helps to ask if the memories are full of people or things. Recurring people are quite common. The recurring person in Andrea's memories, for example, was her critical, impatient mother. Where was Andrea's father? He doesn't seem to be visible. Why not? And if Dad wasn't there for Andrea when she was a child, what does that mean to her today, especially in regard to her relationship to men?

Sometimes it helps to note if the memories reveal the client as an observer or a participator. Observers look in from the outside while participators are in the middle of the action. Ruth, the weighty watcher of life described in chapter 2, was obviously an observer and would have stayed that way if she had not come to see Kevin and learned that she too could participate and enjoy if she chose to do so.

Another revealing question is whether or not you see yourself as the one in control of the situation or the one who's being controlled by others. A quick look at the memories of Kevin and Randy leaves no doubt as to who was in control and who felt he was being controlled. Kevin started kicking down doors at the age of three and went on from there to be the one who was always the center of the action, causing things to happen and making people laugh.

Randy, on the other hand, always seemed to be in the clutches of other powers: his bike went out of control and he crashed into a tree; a tornado rumbled over his house and he felt totally at its mercy; his brothers peppered him with BBs and laughingly called him "Fat Butt." He missed a simple word in a spelling bee and was humiliated.

Other questions we might ask someone about a memory are: "Did you feel secure or fearful?" "Were you alone or with others?" "Were you a giver or a taker?" Not all of these questions apply to every situation, but any one of them can reveal telltale patterns or habits.

## Attitudes Are Also Important

While there are many ways to look at memories, we always come back to their effect on the client's feelings and emotions. Look back over your memories for recurring emotions, such as anger, fear, confidence, or successfulness. If you have trouble assigning an emotion to your memories, it could mean you have difficulty getting in touch with your emotions as an adult. This is simply that Law of Creative Consistency coming into play once more. A lack of emotion can mean you are a rationalizer, the type of person who intellectualizes everything and seldom wants to confront or share feelings.

Attitudes are crucial also. Look for a recurring physical posture in your memories. Were you always standing, sitting, running? What was your attitude toward authority? You could get some clues about your attitude toward authority as an adult. Here is another place where we notice big differences between our own memories. While seven-year-old Kevin was copping smokes to show the world he could do as he jolly well pleased, seven-year-old Randy was desperately trying to please spelling teachers, older brothers, and anyone else who might happen to notice.

For Randy, "performing as expected" is very important today. He dresses for conservative success and always tries to do and say the right thing—what people expect. Kevin, on the other hand, expresses his attitude toward authority and societal convention by taking frequent airplane flights around the country dressed in the same casual garb he wears while tooling around Tucson in his light blue '64 Oldsmobile: casual shirt, shorts, and his ever-ready Nikes.

Recently he walked out of a big city hotel in search of the limo scheduled to whisk him off to an important radio interview. The driver took one look at Kevin's plaid shorts and Arizona Wildcats baseball cap and refused to open the door. Finally Kevin convinced him he was, indeed, the intended passenger and the limo driver relented. As Kevin slid into the back seat, the driver handed him a copy of that day's *Wall Street Journal*, but Kevin just handed it back, saying, "No, thanks, it doesn't have many pictures." Then he settled back in the cushions, chuckling over the poor fellow's dumfounded look.

Attitude has to do with more than reaction to authority. What about recurring pain or hurt in your memories? Perhaps you've developed an attitude of self-pity or martyrdom because you've been hurt or think you've been hurt.

## The Best Clue Is the Simplest

While memory exploration can include many avenues, in this chapter we have touched on only some of the more basic ones to get you started. Keep in mind that you don't need dozens of clues to find the one that describes you best. The clue you need is usually right there in plain sight. One of the most significant clues to look for is a *key word or phrase* used in the memory.

While on a plane flight, one of Kevin's clients began chatting with a seat mate. Trying a little memory exploration of his own, he asked the young man to share one of his early memories. The fellow looked at him a bit curiously, but went ahead and said:

> I remember when I was about four—that was back when they delivered milk in bottles. I went out on the stoop, picked up the bottle, and tried to bring it into the house. But I dropped it, and it smashed all over the place. I felt terrible.

Kevin's client, who had no more training than two counseling sessions, said: "It's just a guess, but I'm wondering if you aren't a very responsible person today—you simply wouldn't ever want to be caught dropping the ball or failing on a responsibility."

The young man did a double take and admitted that that was true. It turned out he was a youth pastor who was known for shooting straight from the hip with youth groups and being very strong on always fulfilling his responsibilities.

## What Have You Learned So Far?

Before moving on, take a few minutes to draw together what you've learned from your memories in this chapter. Identify the key threads that seem to pull your memories together. List any new insights you may have gotten about yourself. Be sure to record feelings that were usually present in your early memories. And, if possible, try nailing down the main truth in your memories with a key word or phrase that seems to stand out.

Don't be too concerned if you don't come up with a neat, tidy package that answers every question or problem. No system can do that because human beings are just not that simple. As the Old Testament puts it, you are "fearfully and wonderfully made."[2] The next two chapters will explain how your memories developed, starting from the moment you were born. Out of the making of those memories came your particular lifestyle and personality. To understand how all this happened, you have to go back to life with Mom and Dad during your very first years on this planet.

# PART TWO

## Memories: Where It All Began

# Chapter 4

*Conscientious, orderly, cautious—with six and ten years between
Randy and his older brothers, Randy reflects more traits of a
first-born than of a baby. Birth order, as well as family
atmosphere, strongly influences who you are today.*

# "I Remember Mama—
# and Daddy, Too"

According to Shakespeare, "All the world's a stage, / And all the men and women merely players. . . ."[1] That's all too true, and the curtain goes up very early in life. Like everyone else you accumulated your childhood memories on a very special stage—your family setting. To unlock the deepest secrets of your memories, you need to get a better understanding of how that setting affected you.

Mom and Dad were the king pin and queen pin of your family theater troupe. They set the stage, and each family member had a part in the play. The scripts were written as you went along, and the entire improvised production of "Days of Your Childhood" was under the direction (good or bad) of your parents.

While you acted out your roles on your family's stage, you learned early what would work and not work for you. Studies have shown that learning can occur even while a child is in the womb, and once an infant hits life's stage and gets that first "hand of recognition," he or she learns very fast indeed.

Actually, we don't give tiny babies enough credit. They're anything but the helpless little darlings we make them out to be in ads for Pampers or Michelins. For example, a normal baby with deaf/mute parents soon concludes that making noise to get his way doesn't work, so he becomes an expert at "crying" in pantomime, contorting his little red mug, pumping his arms and legs like little windmills, but never making a sound! Later he may learn to stomp on the floor during tantrums so his parents can "hear" the vibrations.[2]

One psychologist did studies that showed it's possible to teach a toddler to read with comprehension, take dictation, and even operate an electric typewriter.[3] Tiny tots aren't quite ready to bail out that poor boss in the television commercial ("She can't type!"), but they are ready to take an active role in creating their own personalities. That's exactly what you did when you were born. As you sorted out what worked and what didn't, you created a life "plan" that developed into a unique style of living—yours.

We'll look more closely at lifestyles in chapter 5, but here we want to focus on the family stage where you played your own starring role. It is here that your memories were made. We will look at that stage from two perspectives: (1) The "climate control" set up by your parents, who created a certain family atmosphere that influences you to this day; (2) your birth order, the limb where you landed on the family tree.

Although we know generalizations can be dangerous, research has shown that individuals with similar personalities and problems tend to come from similar family atmospheres. This is as true for those who come from encouraging, nurturing families as it is for those from critical, chaotic, and abusive environments. To see how family atmosphere dovetails with memory exploration, let's look at the emotional climates of typical homes and the life-molding memories they produced.

## "As Long as You Live in This House . . ."

Carl was the only child of immigrant parents. The family lived in an apartment behind the family-run business they all (kids as well as Mom and Dad) worked in. Carl recalls this memory from when he was eight:

> Early one morning, just before time to leave for school, my father handed me a box of merchandise and told me to hurry and put it all out on the store shelves. When he came to check on me a few minutes later, I'd stopped to look at a book; only half the box had been emptied. My father was so angry he took

me into the storeroom and ordered me to stand in the corner until he came back.

The hours ticked by but I never moved. It seemed as if my dad was gone for *days*. When he finally did come back, it was three o'clock in the afternoon! He'd forgotten all about me! And I'd missed school. I'd had to go to the bathroom so bad, but I hadn't dared move because I was afraid my father would come back and whale the daylights out of me.

What kind of family atmosphere was this? Carl obviously grew up in an *authoritarian* home, where the parents—especially his father—were the boss and no questions were asked. Carl's dad was from the Old Country. He had grown up in an authoritarian atmosphere, and his own home was exactly the same.

Carl told Kevin this early memory when he came in for counseling after he became miserable in his high-paying job in microbiology. He had gone to postgraduate programs for seven years to obtain science degrees. Now his job was good, but his life was in the pits. His wife had just left him because she couldn't handle his perfectionistic ways any more.

Carl was so prescriptive in his thinking that before his wedding he read several books on "how to be married." Unfortunately, they didn't cover "Thou shalt not nit-pick thy wife." She managed to put him through school and hoped things would be better once he got his degree, but they weren't. Finally his constant criticism caused her to pack up her belongings and their two children and leave.

When Carl and Kevin explored that early memory together, the light went on. He realized that he had sweated through college and graduate school to do something, not for himself, but for his authoritarian father who wanted him to get the education and high-paying job he never had. Carl decided to quit that high-paying job and totally change careers. Today he is a well-adjusted—and contented—operator of a salvage yard. On Kevin's advice, he is taking his time about remarrying and is trying to be more aware of his habit of nit-picking and criticizing as he develops new relationships.

Carl is a good example of a child who grew up in an authoritarian atmosphere and knuckled under. By sharp comparison, a client named Bruce knuckled up. He came to Randy for consultation because he was having so much trouble dealing with those who had authority over him at work. Together they discovered a series of Bruce's childhood memories that all centered on how he rebelled against his father's authoritarian ways:

> My dad would use his belt on me all the time, even when I was small. By the time I was eight or nine, we were practically at each other's throats. We just never got along. I remember one day my dad thought I had done something wrong and he wouldn't listen to me when I tried to explain. All he said was, "None of your mouth—you can spend the rest of the day in your room without lunch or dinner." I was so mad I crawled out of my bedroom window and went over to a friend's house to play for the afternoon. I wasn't about to submit to my dad's punishment.

Bruce also remembered loving rock music by the time he was eleven or twelve and playing it "just loud enough" to set his dad off. And he clearly remembered the time his father told him, "Son, your grades are lousy. If you don't pass this next test, you're grounded for a week." Bruce deliberately failed the test and recalls thinking, "It's worth it just to show Dad."

As we counsel with families, one of the most serious causes of chaos and misery that we deal with is authoritarian parenting. Research shows that children from authoritarian homes display the following characteristics:

- Often rebel in later life or when free of authority
- Likely to be inconsiderate of others, quarrelsome, unpopular, emotionally unstable
- Often very sensitive to praise and blame
- May be polite, "respectful," and proper, but shy and timid
- Often unable to solve problems without the help of an authority
- Often lack creativity, spontaneity, and resourcefulness
- May resort to passive-aggressive strategy such as lying and stealing
- Can "go wild" when shifted to a more permissive atmosphere or when living on his or her own[4]

Look again at the list of characteristics above. Do any of them fit you today? Look back on your own family atmosphere. Was either of your parents authoritarian? In what ways? Mine your memories a little to see if you can come up with some brief videotapes that may shed light on your habits or hang-ups.

## "Let's Be Sure We Get It Right This Time!"

Perhaps you're saying, "My parents weren't really hard-core authoritarians. I got a few spankings, sure, but what I remember more is the criticism—the constant demand to measure up."

If your childhood memories center on those constant demands to measure up or jump a little higher, you probably grew up in a *perfectionistic* family atmosphere. Victims of this kind of environment are also frequent visitors to our counseling offices. For example, first-born Brenda, discouraged and finally broken by years of feeling like a failure, finally sought some help. Here are two samples of her early childhood memories that told Randy a lot about her childhood family atmosphere and why she's having problems today:

> At six I was a big girl—bigger than the others in my class. I was also clumsy. I always wanted to play with the other girls on the playground, but no one would pick me for their team. In fact, I remember one day a girl telling me I wasn't good enough to be on her team.

> Another time, my dad took me to watch my younger sister play softball. I must have been nine or ten at the time. I recall his words as though it were yesterday. "Brenda, maybe someday you'll learn to try as hard as your sister does." I was crushed.

Brenda's parents, like most perfectionistic parents, set high standards to encourage their children to succeed. But Brenda ended up feeling she could never measure up. While her younger sister and baby brother always seemed to exceed the goals set for them, Brenda always landed a few feet short in the broad jump of life. The harder she worked, the farther behind she fell.

It didn't help Brenda any to be first-born. She already had one foot in the perfectionist's swamp of despair, trying to measure up to all those high standards Mom and Dad set for their first child. People raised in a perfectionistic atmosphere show many highly recognizable characteristics:

- That feeling of never measuring up, always believing they could do much better
- Low self-esteem
- Feeling like a failure with no real hope of ever being a success
- Strong feelings of self-criticism, lashing themselves for even the slightest error or mistake
- Biting off more than they can chew and never being able to finish on time
- Procrastinating because "there isn't enough time to do it right anyway"

Like a bad penny, your family atmosphere follows you through life. Whom did Brenda marry? A flaw picker, of course. (We'll explain why people seem to marry their fathers or their mothers in a later chapter.) Brenda's husband, Gary, was also a first-born whose job as an accountant called for meticulous attention to every percentage point. At home, every burnt piece of toast, every cold cup of coffee, every wrinkled shirt was held up to his unwavering, critical gaze. But while he commented on all of Brenda's flaws, he seldom noticed or praised any of her strengths or successes. So Brenda wound up playing the same familiar role in her marriage that she had played on her childhood family stage.

Do you struggle with perfectionism? Look over that list of characteristics above, and then flip on your memory video to see if anything starts to make sense. You may find memories where you're being unfavorably compared to a brother or sister. Or perhaps you will recall the sting of a remark made when you failed a test or struck out in the last of the ninth in the Little League championship game. Maybe your video will show you being frustrated, feeling hopeless.

On the other side of the coin, perhaps your memories center on personal achievements and successes. Maybe you build your life around how well you perform, and so far you've gotten away with it. But the performance treadmill gets old. You may already be getting a bit tired. We'll take a closer look at perfectionism when we talk about the self-defeating behaviors of pleasers and martyrs in chapter 5. You can't change your perfectionist grain, but there is a lot you can do to counter the demands of those critical parents who flicker across your memory screen.

## "Well, I Guess Just One More Time Won't Matter . . . ."

At the other end of the spectrum from authoritarian and *perfectionistic* atmosphere is the family where the climate is *permissive*. Barbara, thirty-eight-year-old mother of three and last-born in a family where she had three older brothers, came to see Kevin. She complained of frustration, friction with her husband and children, and being discriminated against at work by being passed over for promotions while men who weren't as capable got better jobs.

As she and Kevin probed her early childhood memories, several scenes came up, all of which featured Barbara, the baby princess at the center of attention. But Barbara's most revealing memory of all was this:

> Neither one of our parents was much for discipline. My three older brothers were terrors, but when I came along, they really let down all the fences because they had wanted a girl so very badly. I got whatever I wanted and can still remember the time we were all headed out for burgers and fries—something my brothers really loved. But I stamped my feet and insisted that we go to Guiseppe's for pizza. They all tried to talk me out of it, but I wouldn't budge. I wanted pizza, and that was that! My parents gave in, much to my brothers' disgust, and we all went out for pizza. But on the way home they did stop and buy all the guys milkshakes—and one for me, of course. Our parents were always giving in to us like that.

As Kevin probed a little deeper, Barbara's problem became plain. She had always gotten her way, and now, as a married mother of three, she was running into problems. She wanted to be permissive with the children, but her husband, Jim, had come from an authoritarian atmosphere and had radically different ideas. They clashed constantly on how to discipline their two sons and daughter.

As for friends, Barbara had few at work or at church. People tended to stay clear of her because of her quick wit and biting tongue. "My office is filled with male chauvinist pigs," she said bitterly. "I'm twice the salesperson any of the men are, but I know two cases where men were moved up to manager and I am still where I started."

Kevin worked hard with Barbara to show her how her parents had raised her in a permissive atmosphere that had never helped her learn self-discipline and compromise. Not surprisingly, none of her memories revealed her having to give in to anyone. She always got her own way. Now, in her late thirties, Barbara revealed characteristics that are standard in a person reared in an overly permissive family:

- A lack of consideration for others
- Compulsive behavior, like overspending, overeating, or overdrinking, typical of someone whose family atmosphere lacked direction and boundaries
- A quick and caustic tongue that doesn't spare the feelings of others
- The inability to delay gratification, the overwhelming drive to "want what I want when I want it, which is now"
- An ability to be charming on the surface, but lack of ability to maintain lasting friendships

If your memory videos reveal these characteristics, you probably were reared in a permissive family atmosphere. Maybe it didn't seem too permissive to you at the time because you never knew what toeing the mark was like, but a look at some early childhood memories will be consistent with the difficulties you are having today.

## "I Knew It Wouldn't Work Out . . ."

A family climate that leads children to see life with the glass half empty is the *martyred* atmosphere that Nels grew up in. His parents lived through the Depression years and lost, within a few weeks, the savings and accumulations of a lifetime. From this traumatic experience, they concluded that all they could expect from life was to be taken advantage of by "the system." Naturally, they passed this attitude along to first-born Nels as we can see in this typical memory he shared with Randy:

I recall the time my third-grade teacher gave me an F on a work paper because I forgot to do the problems on the back side—which I hadn't noticed when I was working on the assignment. Now that didn't seem fair to me.

Children like Nels, raised in a martyred atmosphere, often:

- Conclude life doesn't hold much promise for them
- Become self-righteous and judgmental toward others
- Try to control others through guilt and manipulation

You can see some strong similarities between the martyred child and the overprotected one. The martyr isn't just timid and afraid of risks. He is basically pessimistic. He knows life just isn't going to work out and the glass is always half empty, never half full.

While martyrs feel pessimistic about their own roles in life, they still look down on others, whom they blame for all their suffering. Often this blaming shifts to control or manipulation. They say, "Just look at all I've been through. Surely you can see I need you to help me out, or at least feel sorry for me or be impressed by my noble suffering."

Do any of the above traits fit you at all? If you're in the habit of throwing pity parties for yourself today, you might want to look through your childhood memories for any scenes that came out of a martyred family atmosphere, scenes that taught you pessimism, negativism, prejudice, or a judgmental attitude.

It isn't comfortable to admit that you might be something of a martyr, but be honest. To be a martyr for a worthy cause may get you into history books; to be a martyr without a cause may get you into counseling.

## Atmospheric Conditions Can Overlap

After looking at several examples of family climate control (or more correctly, families where the climate is out of control), you may be unsure that the family of your childhood could be described by any of these labels. Because families include human beings, they seldom fit totally into nice neat categories. Whenever we speak about a category like "authoritarian family," we are pointing only toward certain trends or characteristics that may be prevalent. And there are many other nuances or idiosyncrasies in families that could be called "atmospheres."

In *the overprotective or pitying atmosphere,* excessive sympathy is given to the misfortunes and losses of the child. These atmospheres are close cousins to families that are permissive, but the emphasis is on going overboard to help the child, comfort him when he is hurt, and give him the best care possible.

In *the competitive atmosphere,* one family member's performance is compared and contrasted to the others in a constant attempt to see "who can be the best." It is similar in many ways to the perfectionistic atmosphere and, in some cases, the authoritarian. Some fathers, for example, are frustrated jocks who drive their kids to see the world as a competitive battleground where nice guys finish last.

In *the neglecting atmosphere,* the parents are so preoccupied with their own problems or interests they have no time for the child. The neglecting parent is often pictured as a criminal or drug addict. Sometimes that is true. Very often, however, neglecting parents are workaholics who are so busy with their jobs or their duties they have little awareness of or interest in their child's needs.

In *the materialistic atmosphere,* the acquisition and control of things, money, and power are sought after.

In *the hurried atmosphere,* all family members are caught in the fast lane of life, and the children are exposed to adult lifestyles and adult pressures that force them to become older than their years too quickly. This can start as early as preschool where the kids get shoved into kiddy college, while Mom and Dad hurry off to high-pressure jobs, a commuter's hour or so away. Obviously, the materialistic or hurried atmospheres can help contribute to making children feel neglected.

If you're getting the idea that family atmospheres can overlap, you're right. Many family atmospheres are variations of the ones we've described or combinations of two or more.

## Can a Family's Atmosphere Be Changed?

While this book is not intended to be a parenting guide, you may be getting obvious hints about some changes you need to make in your own parenting style. As you explore your own memories and remember the family atmosphere in which you grew up, it's natural to ask yourself: "How can I build healthier childhood memories for my kids?" We'll look more closely at that question in chapter 12 where we talk about the good-time memories that come out of an atmosphere of mutual self-respect.

One other question may have popped into your mind as we have described some examples of family atmosphere: "If a family atmosphere is such a strong determinant of a person's personality, why can children from the same family atmosphere turn out to be so different from each other?"

A big part of the answer to that one lies in the fact that two children reared by the same parents in the same house can each perceive and/or respond to the family atmosphere very differently. For example, take Greg and his younger sister, Peggy, who grew up in what could be judged an overprotective family. Yet, there's an obvious difference in their memories. Greg recalls:

> One day when I was four, I wanted to go across the street to the park, but my parents said no. I would have to wait until one of them could go along. It made me mad that I wasn't allowed to do something by myself. That happened a lot. I felt my parents never trusted me.

Greg's sister, Peggy, however, has a series of memories that show the family "protective" atmosphere in another light. For example:

> Our parents were always concerned about taking care of us and protecting us from danger. I remember one day when I was five or six. I was riding my bike in the street by our home when my dad yelled at me to get off the street "NOW!" I wasn't allowed to ride my bike for a week. I felt terrible that I had disobeyed my dad.

First-born Greg viewed his family atmosphere as oppressive, and he responded by resenting it and wanting to break loose. His younger sister saw the same atmosphere as protective and responded by feeling guilty if she did not abide by her parents' wishes.

All of this simply says that it's not just the family atmosphere that shapes a child's personality. The child's perception of his family—how he sees himself fitting into the atmosphere of his home—has a powerful impact. And a lot of it has to do with the child's birth order—his or her particular limb on the family tree.

## Memories Are Born as Well as Made

We could spend a whole book chronicling the impact your birth order has on who you are and why you do what you do. In fact, that's just what Kevin does in *The Birth Order Book*. So we're not going to go through all that in great detail, but we do want to cover it briefly to show how it ties in with family atmosphere to mold your early memories.

Birth order theory holds that the order of your arrival in your family strongly influences who you are today. Basically, there are four birth order categories: only child, first-born, the middle child, and the last-born or baby. Each group commonly exhibits distinct characteristics.

## First-Borns Get Too Much Attention

First-born children are guinea pigs without cages for novice parents to experiment on. They're usually the recipients of high expectations, too much attention, considerable criticism, and other examples of over-parenting.

But it's not all bad by any means. First-borns discover right from the start that the world is a challenging place and everything they do is a "big deal" to Mom and Dad and the grandparents. They quickly learn the ground rules for fitting into the forest of adult kneecaps around them. They tend to take life seriously and grow up to be reliable and conscientious—seekers of approval who want to win as many good citizenship awards as possible.

## Lonely Onlies Are a Special Breed

A special breed of first-born is the only child. In fact, an only child is simply a first-born in spades, diamonds, clubs, and hearts. Lonely onlies can often be critical of everyone, including themselves. They grow up with few friends or playmates, and their most frequent contacts are with Mom and Dad. When they get older, they often have a hard time relating to their peer group. They get along far better with people who are much older or much younger.

If you're a first-born or only child, your early childhood memories are likely to reflect:

- Mistakes, goof-ups that really bothered you
- Times of achievement (in school or athletics)
- Self-discipline (being the "good" one)
- Concern about the approval of others
- Being afraid—especially of being hurt or falling
- Doing things right
- Authority figures
- Lots of detail
- Stressful or lonely times

Because only children and first-borns get huge amounts of attention, glory—and pressure—they share a common burden: the tar baby of perfectionism. If things don't go just right, the first-born or only child can get very uptight. We call perfectionism "slow suicide," and so it is. You don't have to be a first-born or only child to be a perfectionist, but our case loads often bear out this characterization.

## The Middle Child Is Much More "Iffy"

Predicting the path for middle children is a much "iffier" proposition than it is with first-borns or babies. The personalities of middle children are less predictable because they are subject to pressures coming from more than one direction. To understand the middle child, you usually have to look at who is above and below.

One of the few rules you can cite for middle children is that they are likely to be the opposite of their first-born brother or sister. If big brother is an A student, the middle child may opt for athletics. She reasons: "Why fill a spot that is already taken? I'll carve my own niche in life."

Because they feel squeezed between the older and younger ones in the family, middle children get that "fifth-wheel" feeling. They go outside the home to spend time with friends more than anyone else in the family. In fact, friends are very important to middle-born kids. It's among friends that the middle-borns find recognition and feelings of acceptance.

Another typical characteristic of the middle child is the ability to negotiate. Many middle-born children are excellent diplomats who grow up to be mediators and go-betweens. They can also be quite manipulative, skilled in the art of compromise and working out conflicts through negotiation because they have to deal with both the older and younger siblings.

If you're a middle-born, your early childhood memories may well reflect:

- Feelings of not belonging
- Having lots of friends, and hearing Mom call you home from next door because you're late for dinner, again
- Feeling sensitive about being treated unjustly
- Compromising—being good at negotiation and "working things out"

Randy recalls counseling a thirty-three-year-old mother who specialized in smoothing the waters for her entire family, especially keeping peace between her husband and the in-laws. She clearly remembered the time when she was eight, and the entire family was going out for ice cream. Her older and younger sisters began pushing and fighting in the back seat, and her father threatened to cancel ice cream for everyone if they didn't shape up.

Marian clearly remembers saying, "Hey, if you knock it off, you can play with my Barbie dolls when we get back home." Because both sisters loved that Barbie doll collection, they quickly settled down and a good ice cream time was had by all.

## Babies Love the Limelight

Last-born children, "babies," are often the attention-getters and comedians in their families. They love to be the life of the party— carefree, vivacious, and outgoing. Babies of the family love the limelight and can become self-centered because they want all the attention.

Kevin's early memories paint a clear picture—maybe it's a clear caricature—of a typical baby of the family. After he got the nickname "Cub," he made the most of it with attention-getting behavior that ranged from cute and amusing to boisterous and obnoxious.

If you're a baby of the family, your early childhood memories may well reflect:

- Being cute, getting attention with your antics
- Celebrating birthdays and Christmas and receiving gifts
- Having other people do things for you because you were "too little"
- Wanting to show those bigger, older kids you could do it, too
- Feeling that you always had to prove you could be trusted because you were youngest or "littlest"

Randy recalls counseling a last-born gentleman who clearly remembered being told when he was about six: "You can't climb up that ladder. Be sure to stay away from the ladder." Naturally, the little last-born waited until no one was around and went scampering up the ladder to the roof, where he screamed, "Hey, look at me." His parents came rushing out and almost had dual heart attacks on the spot. Naturally, the little last-born had to be rescued, something else that babies love.

## Birth Order Is Only a Partial Picture

This brief sketch of birth order may have left you feeling a bit confused. You may be a first-born who acts more like a middle child, but there are usually very good reasons for that. Every family tree grows with different branches. The correct psychological term is *constellation*, but family tree is more descriptive. (In some homes, family zoo comes even closer.) Different factors affect the assembly of each family, especially *spacing*, the number of years between each child. One important birth order rule of thumb says any gap of five or more years between children starts the entire system over.

Suppose, for example, you had this kind of family combination:

First-born male

Four-year gap

Second-born male

Six-year gap

Third-born male

Does this family of three boys with several years between each child sound familiar? You may remember Randy had two big brothers— one six years older and the other ten years ahead of him. Yes, Randy was last-born in his family, but instead of reflecting baby characteristics, he comes across with many first-born or only child traits. He's conscientious, serious, organized, cautious, and orderly. He wouldn't think of coming to work without his coat and tie, while Kevin often shows up to tape our radio show wearing tennis shoes, shorts, and a sport shirt. He would probably come in even less, but the station put up a sign just for him: "No shoes or shirt, no show!"

It's not hard to see why Randy came out more first-born than baby. With six and ten years between his older brothers and himself, he didn't spend that much time with them. In fact, he admits that he grew up as something of a loner, trying to avoid trouble and embarrassment. He recalls being the funniest child in the family, but not to get attention. Instead, he did it to keep the peace or relieve tension.

A subtle but important thing to remember about birth order is that the entire family changes with the birth of each child. Besides spacing, birth order can be affected by other forces:

> The birth order of parents can make a real difference. For example, if two perfectionistic first-borns get together, they're going to rear their children a lot differently than two babies would.
>
> A handicapped sibling can flip-flop everything and make a younger or older sibling do a complete role reversal to help care for a child who is handicapped.
>
> A traumatic event or the death of a sibling can have a strong effect. So can physical differences like height, weight, and looks. For example, little first-born Dickie, who is ten years old, an even five feet tall, and ninety pounds dripping wet, is going to have his hands full with his second-born brother who is half a head taller, thirty-five pounds heavier, and answers to the name of "Moose."
>
> And stepsiblings are an entirely different ball game. Many of today's Brady bunches are finding that they have at least two family constellations to work with, sometimes more.

Birth order is just part of the personality puzzle. The more pieces you can find that fit, the better you will understand yourself. And childhood memories are critical to your finding more pieces to the puzzle. As Kevin says, "Childhood memories are even more reliable than birth order as an indicator of 'why you are the way you are,' since these memories are the tapes you play in your head, which determine your response to everyday living."

Remember the analogy picturing a family enacting a drama on a stage? As you play your own role, you discover, by trial and error, what works and doesn't work—for you. It is here that your memories were made, and out of the scenes that made your memories, you developed your own unique style of living, or what is called your personality.

In the next chapter we will look at several common lifestyles and how they developed. You may find yourself among the controllers, drivers, or getters. Or perhaps you will fall into categories like victims, martyrs, or pleasers. And it's possible you'll discover a new style that is all your own. How did you develop your own style of life, which affects everything you think, say, and do today? Whatever the case, the key to your lifestyle is hidden there in your memories waiting to be unlocked.

# Chapter 5

*Kevin the charmer still likes making people laugh and being the center of attention.*

# Why Donald Trump Makes His Deals

Your answers to three questions tell a great deal about who you are today:

I AM_____?
OTHER PEOPLE ARE _____?
THE WORLD IS _____?

You began answering these questions back there in your early childhood, when those two powerful forces described in chapter 4 came into play: your family atmosphere and your order of birth.

Psychologists are known for arguing about a lot of issues, but most of them agree that the human personality forms in the first few years of life. Generally speaking, it's entirely formed by age six or seven. As you grow out of babyhood, you form your personality through trial and error. You learn what behavior works for you and helps you reach your desired goals in life.

As Kevin would put it, even while cooing in your crib or toddling along after Mom, you were "a powerful little buzzard." As you coped with your world, which basically revolved around your family, you constantly used your considerable powers of persuasion to figure out how to get what you wanted. You kept what worked and tossed out the rest. Your behavior was reinforced until it became ingrained in what is called your personality.

As you coped with real and imagined difficulties and challenges, you developed a life "plan" that helped you make sense out of things. As your life plan took shape, so did your lifestyle, which has nothing to do with choosing to drive Porsches or Hyundais, or deciding to wear Levi's 501s instead of Dockers. As your lifestyle developed, so did your idiosyncrasies. The word *idiosyncrasy* is often used incorrectly to refer to someone's odd quirks or habits. Actually, we all have idiosyncrasies, which are simply the personal behavioral characteristics that make up our lifestyles.

To emphasize what we said earlier, a lifestyle is a *style of living*—the way you do things to reach the goals that fit in with that life plan you formed so very long ago. And your lifestyle is very resistant to change. That is why we keep saying that the little boy or little girl you once were, you still are. The grain of your wood is set. You can experience education, spiritual rebirth, counseling, or psychotherapy, but the tendency to go back to those early behavioral patterns is always there beneath the surface.

As you examine your early memories, they enable you to put a handle on your own lifestyle and some of your unique private logic—your personal overview of life, others, and yourself. While lifestyle is always consistent with early childhood memories, we admit there is one problem: Defining lifestyles has to be done in broad categories that don't totally fit individuals. Each person has his or her own unique lifestyle, which is a combination of several general categories that we see over and over as people come to us for counseling. So as we describe controllers, drivers, pleasers, victims, martyrs, charmers, and others, keep in mind that most people are blends of different lifestyles. One general category may predominate, but others are usually involved as well.

## Controllers Just Can't Let Go

As a rule, *controllers* don't come for counseling as often as the people they tend to drive a little crazy. For example, the typical marriage counseling situation features a husband who is a controller and a wife who is a pleaser. *She* is the one who comes for help because she feels put down and walked on. *He* stays home, at least at first, saying he's sure that he has no problems and "If anyone has a problem, it's *her!*" When controllers do agree to counseling, it's a mixed blessing. The first challenge for the counselor is to keep the controlling husband from trying to take over each session and tell everyone how to shape up.

Controllers see the world as a pretty serious place and often have difficulty with relaxing and just enjoying life. They just can't let go. Much of their energy is spent trying to keep others in line with their own expectations of what is good, right, and needed.

Often in their obsession to make sure everything goes right (*their* concept of right), controllers set unrealistic expectations for themselves and others. This often leads to real problems in relationships—especially with spouses and children. A controller's private logic goes something like this:

I AM going to do things my way.

OTHER PEOPLE ARE not to be trusted to do things as well as I can.

THE WORLD IS a mess and it needs to be set right— with my help.

## Controllers Come in Two Categories

There are two basic kinds of controllers: offensive and defensive. Defensive controllers are a special breed who control out of fear of being dominated or crushed. They are often women who have been "kicked in the teeth" by men. We'll look more closely at defensive controllers in Part 3 when we talk about self-defeating behaviors that various lifestyles can produce.

Offensive controllers act upon life and people around them. They love to make things happen and, in some cases, to create chaos.

Kevin has some offensive controller traits, which are evidenced in his strong desire to get attention by making things happen. He also doesn't mind creating a little chaos—on talk shows, for example. One of his memories from his teenage years is a vivid clue to that controller/manipulator part of his lifestyle today:

One year at church summer camp the director decided that perhaps he could curb my misbehavior by honoring me with a "responsible" assignment. He called me, along with a friend, into his office one morning and asked us if we'd be willing to collect the offering during the evening service. We took one look at each other and promptly agreed.

That afternoon we sneaked into the chapel and pilfered the offering plates from beneath the pulpit. That night, during the service, when the time came to collect the offering, the director asked the ushers to come forward. And then, as my friend and I stood innocently before the altar, the man reached under the pulpit for the offering plates. Then he bent down to look. Finally he began searching all over the platform. The longer and more frantically he searched, the more restless his congregation of campers got. My friend and I just stood there grinning and enjoying the commotion we had created. We were in control.

That story is vintage Leman, but it doesn't label Kevin a complete controller. His main lifestyle is "charmer," which we'll look at later. He is a good example of a blend of basic lifestyle categories. You will probably find yourself to be a blend as well.

Do you have any controller traits in your lifestyle? Look at the following list. If you agree with three or more of these statements, you are a controller to at least some degree.

- It is hard for me to function if I am not in charge.
- I prefer to work alone.
- I enjoy competition—especially winning.
- I place high expectations on others.
- I like to make things happen.
- I have a temper.
- I don't enjoy surprises; I want to know when, where, why, and how.
- I often find myself wishing other people would take life a little more seriously.

If any of these statements sounds like you, look back into your memories for situations that match. Do you recall times you were frustrated by what seemed to be disorder or a lack of organization? Were you a loner? Did athletics or other forms of competition play a major role in your life? What about the times you lost your temper?

## The Heart of His Deal

Donald Trump, the real estate magnate mentioned in chapter 1, is a classic controller, and his childhood memories bear it out. His father, Fred Trump, a hard-driving builder and manager of huge apartment complexes in New York City, succeeded through toughness and tenacity. He named his first-born son, Fred, Junior, and expected him to follow in his footsteps, but it was not to be. Freddie's complacent nature just couldn't cope with Dad's tough ways and the rough-and-tumble negotiations with contractors and suppliers. Middle-child Donald (fourth of five children) was not intimidated by his dad or anything else. He soon moved in to replace Freddie as the family standard-bearer.

Early on, Donald Trump started letting people know exactly what he thought and how he felt. In second grade he blackened his music teacher's eye with one punch because "I didn't think he knew anything about music, and I almost got expelled."

Fortunately, Donald grew up to be a controller who used his brains more than his fists. He remembers being a leader in the neighborhood and loving to create mischief: "For some reason I liked to stir things up, and I liked to test people. I'd throw water balloons, shoot spitballs, and make a ruckus in the schoolyard and at birthday parties. It wasn't malicious so much as it was aggressive."

But the capper story is the one about borrowing his younger brother's blocks to create a masterful edifice in their playroom. Donald had promised his brother that he would give back the blocks, but once his building was up and looked so beautiful, "I liked it so much that I glued the whole thing together. And that was the end of Robert's blocks."[1]

While still in his playroom, Donald Trump became the entrepreneur, which is typical of middle-borns. One study shows that entrepreneurs are most likely to come from the middle, not the front or end, of the family. They are much more inclined to take risks than first-borns, and they are more able to mediate and negotiate than babies.

## Drivers Will "Finish or Bust"

First cousin to the controller is the *driver*. You may know the type (you may *be* the type!). For many drivers, their life motto is: "The finish line or bust!"

Donald Trump is a driver as well as a controller. His autobiography, *Trump: The Art of the Deal*, records one drive after another for real estate pay dirt, most of them in New York City, which has some of the highest-priced territory per foot in the world. Just a few of Trump's deals include:

- Developing the site for the Jacob Javits Convention Center
- Transforming the deteriorating Commodore Hotel into the $30-million-a-year Grand Hyatt
- Building the Trump Tower, flagship of the Trump organization, located at Fifth Avenue and 56th Street, and described as sixty-eight stories of some of the most exclusive residential, retail, and office space in New York, including a six-story marble atrium and an eighty-foot waterfall
- Constructing the $320-million Trump's Castle Hotel and Casino in Atlantic City

What drives Donald Trump to make one incredible deal after another? He says, "I don't do it for the money. I've got enough, much more than I'll ever need. I do it to do it. Deals are my art form. Other people paint beautifully on canvas or write wonderful poetry. I like making deals, preferably big deals, that's how I get my kicks."[2]

Donald Trump is a very wealthy driver, but he shares the same private logic of all those with traits of the driver lifestyle. As drivers work out their life plans, they conclude:

I AM goal-oriented and will do whatever it takes to reach my objective.

OTHER PEOPLE ARE obstructions who will interfere with my reaching my goals if I let them.

THE WORLD IS full of things to be done.

## Drivers Race Everywhere with Few Pit Stops

Drivers tend to run their families and businesses by the clock. They can easily ruin a family vacation for everyone but themselves. For example, it's tough being the son or daughter of a driver dad, especially if you're two hundred miles from the motel and he's driving! Your walnut-sized bladder is about to burst, but dear old Dad smiles and says, "Just hold it a little longer, honey. We'll be there soon."

Drivers race through life trying to cover the most miles with the fewest possible pit stops. They're always looking ahead to the next possible accomplishment. No matter what they're doing, drivers want to win.

The dedicated driver is so competitive that he would check the bottom line of his profit and loss sheet on his deathbed. For him, winning isn't everything; it's the *only thing!*

Is there any of the driver in your lifestyle? If so, you'll answer yes to several of the following:

- I don't have enough time to fool around with this stupid quiz.
- I work from a daily checklist.
- I have to get through that daily checklist.
- I feel that reaching my goals is more important than spending time with people.
- I prefer to win. Nice guys finish last, and results are what count.
- Most of my memories include times of accomplishment and feelings of pride and satisfaction about my successes.

If some of the above statements sound like you, you may look back to memories of being impatient, not wanting to wait. Perhaps you will think of things that you built or projects that you finished with a great deal of hard work. And it won't be surprising if many of your memories focus on things rather than people. Drivers are task-oriented. As much as they may like people or train themselves to like people, the job, the project, the game, come first.

It's not too hard to see that drivers are first cousins to controllers. Now let's take a look at the other end of the spectrum. Following are several lifestyles that describe the "controllees" of this world.

## Pleasers Have an Avis Complex

We mentioned earlier that many marriages are made up of a controller and a pleaser. Although women can be controllers, most of those who come to our offices for counseling are *pleasers*, women who simply can't say no to the men who control them. In fact, we'll go out on a limb and say that true pleasers are almost always women.

As Kevin likes to put it facetiously, we have done an informal survey that turned up nineteen male pleasers in the continental United States. Oh, yes, in case you are wondering, we cannot release their addresses or phone numbers for fear their communities will be overrun with women who would like to be pleased instead of controlled for a change.

We're simply saying that it is possible for a man to exhibit pleaser characteristics, but we haven't seen too many of them. The men we counsel fall more consistently into other more assertive lifestyles.

Pleasers have an Avis Complex. Burdened by low self-esteem, they are always willing to try harder so that others will like and accept them. For one example, here's a memory shared by a woman named Sharon:

> My earliest memory is from age four. I recall one day trying to help my dad wash his car. After the car dried, several spots I had missed showed. So Dad had to go over it and correct my mistakes. I felt terrible that I had let my dad down.

Sharon's private logic as a twenty-eight-year-old mother is consistent with the logic she worked out when she was only four. That logic says:

> I AM trying but I never quite do enough (I remember those spots that four-year-old left on the car).
> OTHER PEOPLE ARE relying on me to do a little bit more (Dad expected a perfect job).
> THE WORLD IS full of people I am responsible to make happy, and if I don't, they won't like me (I felt bad when I let Dad down).

As early as age four, Sharon began establishing the behavioral patterns and the lifestyle of a pleaser. She grew up to be a twenty-eight-year-old mother of two toddlers with more responsibilities than the old woman who lived in a shoe. We'll tell you more about her self-defeating behavior in chapter 8.

## Pleasers Are Their Own Worst Enemies

Pleasers feel their value does not come from within but from without. They feel they have worth only when they perform well and others accept them. They live their lives on a yo-yo, dependent on the moods, emotions, and opinions of others.

Pleasers are quick to blame themselves and go through life saying, "I'm sorry. It's my fault. How stupid of me. . . ." When pleasers make a marital match, they usually find someone they can please and then take over the relationship to make it work. A pleaser may be so adept at taking over that on the surface she can look like a controller, but what she's really doing is trying harder to gain acceptance from her husband.

Sometimes the pleaser wife becomes a "Martha Luther," as she follows in the footsteps of the great church reformer, trying to fix, change, improve, make over, rehabilitate, or rescue her husband, other members of the family, or her friends. Pleasers often turn up in the helping and caring professions, such as social work, nursing, and preschool teaching. They are the care givers of this world.

The pleaser often sees God as a big policeman in the sky who is ready to zap her for the slightest infraction, mistake, or shortcoming.[3] The pleaser often makes remarks like these:

- I wish I had more confidence.
- Sometimes I feel as if I'm walking on eggs to keep the peace.
- If the clerk shorts me a penny or two, I don't challenge it.
- I feel I really can't do most things right.
- I feel overpowered by my spouse and my kids.
- I can't say no and will often appear to agree with people when I really don't.
- Giving in is easier than standing up for my rights.
- I wish I could run my own life for a change.

If you answered yes or even partially yes to several of the above statements, the pleaser lifestyle is definitely part of your life plan. Actually, there is nothing wrong with being a pleaser as long as you keep your schedule halfway under control and don't feel walked on or totally unloved and unappreciated. When that happens, you start moving toward two other lifestyles that border on pseudo-masochism. Some people may not admit it, but they actually prefer being kicked around a little and abused.

## Pleasers Can Turn into Victims and Martyrs

When a pleaser's lifestyle gets out of hand and the controllers move in like sharks for the kill, she becomes a *victim* or a *martyr*. We'll put these two lifestyles together because of their strong similarities. First, here's a representative memory from a fellow we'll call Victor the Victim. He gave Randy the following account of a day at Disneyland that turned out to be anything but fun in the Magic Kingdom:

> I remember my first family vacation. I was eight, and we went to Disneyland for a day. Everything went wrong. My parents lost me in the crowd. I got sick on the cable car and threw up all over my dad. And, finally, as if that weren't enough, I slipped off the curb watching the Main Street Parade and sprained my ankle. It was a terrible day for me.

Victor's memory is a classic confirmation of the old cliché, "The victim is a disaster waiting to happen." The victim loves words like *me*, *my*, and *I*, usually followed by a list of laments that would make Job feel like the luckiest man alive. The private logic of a victim goes something like this:

> I AM surely the most unfortunate of human beings.
> OTHER PEOPLE ARE going to have to take pity and make allowances for my terrible plight.
> THE WORLD IS surely out to get me, and it's succeeding.

Do any of these statements sound familiar? Go back to chapters 1 and 3 and the childhood memories of one Randy Carlson. Again and again he comes up the victim: of an embarrassing bicycle crash, of a tornado that scares him to death, of failing in front of his whole school on a simple word in a spelling bee, and maybe most poignant of all, of an older brother's unerring aim as he said, "Out of here, Fat Butt!"

Are there strains of the victim in your own lifestyle? Be honest as you check the following victim statements. Are any of them true for you to some degree? Admitting a lifestyle is the first step toward modifying it for the better:

- I seek sympathy or pity from others.
- I have a lot of aches and pains that I complain about, but they seem to come and go.
- I like to be the center of attention.
- I feel others often take advantage of me.
- My early childhood memories include recurring threads of suffering.

If several of these fit you to some degree, you can join Randy in realizing that the victim is at least a part of your lifestyle. If that's the case, congratulations! Self-knowledge is the first step toward self-improvement.

## Martyrs Always Need a Cause

A very close cousin to the victim is the *martyr*. Unlike victims, who suffer through anything and everything, martyrs need a cause of some kind. For the woman martyr, her cause usually is the family, particularly the man she married, who may use or abuse her.

Because martyrs have a poor self-image, they seek out a mate who will reinforce that image. For example, a martyr is often married to an alcoholic, a drug user, or a deadbeat who is always out of work but still planning to make the big killing that will put them all on Easy Street. These kinds of men are a perfect match for the martyr because she can make excuses for him and take care of him until he "gets his act together." To quote the titles of a couple of best-selling books of the last few years, martyrs are "women who love too much" and/or who have had the misfortune to hook up with "men who hate women."[4]

The logic of the martyr differs somewhat from that of the victim. The martyr thinks:

I AM someone who needs to suffer—by putting myself out.

OTHER PEOPLE ARE there to be helped and served.

THE WORLD IS unfair, but I don't deserve anything better anyway.

This logic isn't very sound, but it is such a consistent part of the martyr's memory patterns that it holds the martyr in a viselike grip. In many instances, if the martyr's alcoholic husband finally does get on the wagon, she will divorce him. Why? Because she is no longer needed. She must find someone who can be her project, someone she can nurse and support.

## Charmers Love the Spotlight

*Charmers* are people who get by in life relying on being cute or funny. Their memories include times of being accepted by making people smile and laugh, times of cutting up and goofing off, and times of being upset if they didn't get their way. It's not unusual for charmers to be the baby cubs of the family, with all those accompanying traits.

It's no surprise that Jackie Gleason, the Great One of the entertainment world, was the baby of his family. From his biography come these early childhood memories:

My mom kept me in the house all the time. I could never go on the street and play with the other kids. I used to watch them with my face pressed against the window. I think this is how I developed my Poor Soul look.[5]

That brief statement from Jackie Gleason's own lips almost sounds like the self-pity of a victim or a martyr, but actually it's a charmer wanting his chance to perform. Gleason obeyed his mother and stayed in the house most of the time, but occasionally he and his dad would go to the Saturday matinee at the Halsey Theatre in their neighborhood. There he would watch the two-reel silent comedies of Charlie Chaplin and Buster Keaton. They became young Gleason's idols.

Also on the bill at the Halsey were five or six live vaudeville acts, and they intrigued Jackie the most. He clearly remembers standing up while a vaudeville act was going on and turning to see all the other people laughing their heads off. His father made him sit down, but not before he told his dad that "he could do what that guy up there on the stage is doing."[6]

Many other comedians have been the babies of their families: Eddie Murphy, Billy Crystal, Goldie Hawn, and Charlie Chaplin, just to name a few. Note that even their names are charmingly diminutive. It's Jackie, not Jack; Eddie, not Edward; Billy, not William; Charlie, not Charles.

Is there any charmer in your lifestyle? Ask yourself these questions about your early childhood memories:

- Did you like to make people laugh?
- Did you rely on charm to make others like and accept you?
- Did you enjoy being the center of attention?
- Did you pout if you didn't get your way?
- Do any of your memories involve times of entertaining others with your charm, cuteness, and humor?

Once a charmer, always a charmer. If charmer is part of your lifestyle at all, you still like making people laugh and being the center of attention. We have already mentioned a few controlling strains in Kevin's lifestyle because he likes to make things happen, but his predominant trait by far is that of charmer. That little guy of age eight, who learned that crowds love someone who can make them laugh, went on to become an expert in the art.

Kevin loves his work as counselor and therapist, but when the call comes to appear on a talk show or speak to a live audience, he is ready to answer. Recently, as he left a group of businessmen rolling in the luncheon aisles, Kevin thought: *Here I am, in my forties, and I can still do it, and I love it—I'll never get enough!*

## Lifestyles Come in Assorted Flavors

Obviously, it would be easier to admit you are a charmer rather than a victim or a martyr. Keep in mind, however, that no lifestyle is necessarily "good" or "bad." They all simply serve to show us how we perceive the world and how we act in order to make it make sense—for us. There are many other lifestyles:

*Getters* are not-too-distant cousins to charmers and, in some ways, controllers. All tiny children are by nature getters, but some develop a getting lifestyle that lasts into adulthood. They are sure the Bible has a misprint and that it is really more blessed to receive than to give. Their logic tells them things like, "I am more important than others . . ."; "Others owe me, and I deserve everything I get . . ."; "The world is a place where you can get big payoffs with small investments."

*Rationalizers* are intellectuals who do everything they can to avoid or deny any emotions. They love theoretical talk but bury their true feelings below layers of facts and opinions.

*Goody-goodies* are first cousins to perfectionists and pleasers. They strive to be just a little more competent, useful, or holy than the others. The goody-goody lives by the book—the rule book—and believes that only by excelling in the particular area of moral perfection that he believes is right can he truly be accepted and belong.

As we've already mentioned, we seldom see someone who is a pure anything as far as lifestyle is concerned. We are much more likely to see blends, but in most cases one particular lifestyle will dominate the others in a person's personality.

Within the broad parameters of that lifestyle, you work out a personal life theme that is uniquely yours. For example, Kevin is a charmer/controller whose life theme could read: "I'll never get enough of making people laugh." Randy is a blend of that rare species called male pleaser and victim. His life theme says: "Watch out; take few risks; don't make waves; keep people happy." Donald Trump, the driver/controller, who makes multimillion dollar real estate deals for kicks, could state his life theme, "I do it to do it."

Keep in mind that a lifestyle doesn't take a lifetime to develop. The broad strokes are there by the time you are two or three. By the time you are four or five, the grain of your wood is set. The childhood memories that you think of today consistently confirm the perception of life that you fashioned for yourself so long ago. If you don't like some things about your particular grain, what can you do? While you can't change your grain, there are many things you can change, and you can begin by cutting your memories down to size.

# PART THREE

## You Can Cut Your Memories Down to Size

# Chapter 6

*The kid who deserted his own birthday party learned to get attention in ways that have helped thousands of people.*

# Letting the Air Out of Inflated Memories

When you were a member of the ankle-biter battalion, all the important stuff was just out of reach. The light switches, counter tops, stereo, cookie jar, and ice cream freezer were all above your head. Things at eye level included dust balls under the bed, the garbage pail, and knickknacks on the coffee table, which sometimes got you into big trouble.

During these early years, surrounded by the kneecaps of parents, teachers, and neighbors, you made the memories that molded your life. And sometimes you gave your parents memories that will stick for life also.

Kevin and his wife, Sande, will never forget taking their three children out to eat at Coco's, one of his fast food favorites. He and Sande ordered, as did Holly and Krissy, and then they turned to see what Kevey would like. There he sat, happily chewing a big wad of gum. Kevin and Sande looked at each other and he asked, "Did you give him gum?"

"No, I never give him gum. I thought you did."

"Where did you get the gum?" Kevin asked his four-year-old.

Kevey didn't say anything. He just pointed under the table and smiled innocently while chewing several assorted flavors with gusto.

87

## All Those "Firsts" Turned into Fiction

As far as Kevin and Sande know, that used gum wad at Coco's was a "first" for little Kevey (and hopefully a last). The early years of childhood are full of "firsts": the first time you ever ate too much candy or ice cream; the first time you couldn't get to a bathroom and had an "accident;" the first time you didn't get your own way; the first time you put a rock or baseball through a window; the first time you got lost in the store and your name came over the PA system; the first time you were applauded for your efforts on the training potty; the first time you could tell Mom was really mad because she added your middle name when she yelled at you.

You may not remember many of those "firsts," but you experienced them, nonetheless. Images and impressions were coming at your little mind so fast you couldn't keep up. You had to make decisions about life and people based on your impressions, and while you had excellent observation skills, you didn't have the maturity to handle all that information correctly. As you made your decisions, you kept telling yourself, "I only count if . . ." Because you had nothing to go on but your own inexperience, you decided that only if you acted in certain ways would you count or belong in your own little world.

As you coped with real and imagined difficulties, you developed certain goals and a certain direction in your life, and out of this came your lifestyle—your basic orientation toward living. That's how you became a controller, a driver, a pleaser, a victim, or one of the other broad categories.

As you grew and learned in those first years of life, the grain of your wood developed according to your own unique pattern. As that grain was becoming well established, you made a lot of choices, but you never made them casually or at random. They were absolutely essential to your early survival and sanity because they gave you something to build on. Without your fast-developing lifestyle, you would have had to start from scratch with each new experience that came your way. You would have had no way to progress toward the unique person you are today.

While this process was going on, you were making plenty of childhood memories. The ones you recollect today seem accurate enough, but they are not telling you the whole truth for several reasons.

For one thing, because you accepted the mistaken belief "I only count if . . . ," you started telling yourself lies at an early age. Truth or reality didn't matter. All that mattered was feeling accepted—that you belonged in your particular family atmosphere. You were willing to tell yourself anything—just so it worked—or seemed to work.

As this process went on, you gained a distorted view of reality. You built your life on a fictional foundation; perhaps we should say "semi-fictional." It didn't seem very fictional to you at the time; in fact, it was all very real. Nonetheless, it was distorted.

## Your Self-Talk Never Stops

Today your memories present a consistent testimony to what you decided was true for you way back when you were small. Are your memories lying? Not exactly. They are small video episodes of the experiences that molded your lifestyle. And today the Law of Creative Consistency guarantees that your memories are consistent with your present view of yourself and your world.

Whenever you recall early memories, an important tool comes into play—your self-talk. The term *self-talk* has become popular in recent years, but it is simply a euphemism for the belief system that influences the way you think all day long.

Self-talk can involve external speech (talking to yourself out loud), but it usually centers in your thoughts. Most people speak aloud at the rate of 150 to 200 words per minute, but research suggests that you can talk privately to yourself by thinking at rates of up to 1,300 words per minute. Your self-talk is a powerful force in your life and works according to several basic principles:[1]

1. *Your thoughts create your emotions.* The idea that thoughts and emotions go together isn't anything new. As King Solomon said several thousand years ago, "As [a man] thinks in his heart, so is he."[2]

That's why we counsel our clients to work on their thinking. Get your thinking straight and your emotions will follow.

2. *Your thoughts affect your behavior.* If thoughts affect your emotions, it follows that they affect your behavior. Let's use shyness as an example. If you believe you are shy, you will behave like a shy person. And then you will add for good measure, "Well, that's just the way I am, I guess."

If shyness has plagued you all your life, your early childhood memories will support this unhealthy view of yourself. You have incorrectly bought into a lifestyle that tells you the best way to get along is by being shy, and so you act that way.

3. *Your perceptions affect your thoughts.* In other words, it's not what is happening around you that makes the difference; it's the way you *perceive* what's happening. Here is *the most important building block* in developing your lifestyle. As a small child, you have certain perceptions of your family atmosphere. You may decide, "This is a place where I need to be in control." Or you may say, "This is a dangerous place that is full of threats and insecurities. I'd better be careful."

During his talk show travels, Kevin has had the privilege of meeting Sid Caesar, whom he considers one of the funniest (and cleanest) comedians in the world. From Caesar's autobiography comes a very early memory of a time when his older brother, Dave, put him in his baby carriage and wheeled him outside their house in Yonkers, New York. The house was on a very steep street and Caesar recalls:

> . . . I was comfortable in the carriage, with Dave's nice, safe hands on the push-bar. To my infant mind, those hands represented love and protection. But then, suddenly, the hands were gone. Dave, a ten-year-old boy bored with baby-sitting, had concocted a little game to amuse himself. I learned later that he had tied a rope to the carriage and let me roll down the hill, to the very end of the length of the rope. He did it over and over again. It amused him, but it apparently terrified *me*. The scene comes back to me this very day— especially at times when *other* loving, protective hands are suddenly removed without explanation.[3]

From what you have learned about memory exploration, what do you suspect Sid Caesar has battled as an adult? If you guessed the fear of rejection by friends and family, we agree. Unquestionably, his perceptions of that interesting "ride" he got as a tiny child were not the kind that told him the world was a safe, secure place! The Law of Creative Consistency followed him into adulthood where his feelings of personal insecurity constantly plagued him.

When his television series, which had once been a hit, was canceled in the late 1950s, he was so devastated that it led him into the abuse of alcohol and drugs. The way Sid Caesar saw life as an adult was reflected in that early childhood memory. The hands of his brother on that carriage bar represented the loving hands of friends and family he knew as an adult. And when love and support were removed, the same terror he felt in the baby carriage engulfed him.

As Sid Caesar's story shows, your lifestyle begins with your perception of the world around you when you are very small. And those first impressions are critical. Once you make them, you simply reinforce them over and over, and that's how the grain of your wood is formed. Your early perceptions literally set your course for life.

Kevin once had a teenage client whose earliest perceptions of life overshadowed any later, positive memories. A Vietnamese girl with scars from cigarette burns on her arms, she had been abused as a baby and then adopted at age four by an American couple. Her adoptive home was one of the most loving environments any child could possibly ask for, but she had a chip on her shoulder and saw the world as a hostile, hateful place. Those cigarette burns had scarred more than her arms.

4. *You think irrationally.* Don't take this principle personally. Everybody does. We all say things we don't mean, worry about things that aren't even there, do things that don't make any sense.

Randy and his wife, Donna, were having a good, old-fashioned argument—the kind that both of them knew would soon end, but they both wanted to get all their points in before it was over. Randy finally realized he was wrong and apologized to Donna for what he had said. But his quick apology caught her off guard, and he could tell by the look on her face that she didn't want to accept it just yet. She said, "Wait a minute. I'm not done being mad yet."

Rationally, Donna knew she should accept Randy's apology and forget the argument. But part of her wanted to continue to argue a little longer. Was it simply a matter of still being a bit angry and not cooled down enough yet? That's part of the answer, but Donna is like anyone else. The child you once were, you still are. And that little child usually shows up in times of stress, like an argument with your spouse. The truth may be very plain, but you don't want to accept it because you prefer to cling to what makes sense to that little child deep within, even when the adult part of you knows it doesn't make much sense at all!

5. *You can gain control of your thoughts and change them.* Changing your thoughts is part of the process of cutting your memories down to

size. In a way, a lot of your memories are "larger than life," and you need to let the air out of them. As you bring them down to size, you will be able to reconstruct your perception of the past and develop a healthier adult outlook on life today. You will remain a controller, pleaser, driver, or whatever lifestyle you have developed, but you will come out of it with healthier perceptions and healthier self-talk that will enable you to capitalize on your strengths and shore up your weaknesses.

## The A-B-Cs of Truth Therapy

To help our clients counter the negative self-talk they have been feeding themselves for years, we developed a simple "truth therapy" approach. One of the biggest lies people tell themselves is, "I can't really change—this is the way I am." While it is true you can't change the basic grain of your wood, there is a great deal you can do to change the way you live with that grain. You can reshape that grain by using the A-B-Cs of truth therapy:

- *A*ccept the fact that your memories can be lying—at least a little bit.
- *B*elieve the truth instead of the lies that are ingrained into your lifestyle.
- *C*hange your behavior by using different self-talk.

We know this sounds too simple, but as we have seen time and again, it's the simple things that work best. The A-B-Cs of truth therapy are no guaranteed formula. Instead, they can help you challenge that slightly skewed view of reality you have had since you were small. We see truth therapy work for pleasers who have been living in a frustrating pursuit of perfection, thinking that unless they do everything flawlessly, no one will accept them or like them.

We use truth therapy to help victims and martyrs who think that life has dealt them a bad hand, that everyone is out to get them, and that the only way they can be happy is to suffer.

We see truth therapy work with drivers and controllers who can't get along at home or at work because they think they have to be in charge, can't trust anyone, and must reach their goals no matter what it does to themselves or others.

## Truth Therapy Even Worked for Us

But the major reason we're so high on truth therapy is that we've seen its principles work in our own lives. Kevin, the pesky little kid who decided the only way he could count was to be as off-the-wall as possible in order to be funny, was headed nowhere when he finally realized he needed to change. Eventually he took the little kid he once was, shaped him up, and taught him to get attention in productive, helpful ways that have touched thousands of people.

And then there was Randy, who grew up "keeping his fat butt down," just in case his brothers were lurking about. Randy's self-talk told him the only way he could achieve security was to try to please everyone, never make waves, and *never, never* take risks. He could have faded into the woodwork and gone carefully through life as a victim who never got a break. Instead, he learned to help other victims and became a leader who realized he didn't need everyone's approval to feel comfortable.

We think our stories are worth telling, but not because we are extraordinary. On the contrary we were both very ordinary kids, but we have a hunch you will be able to identify with many of our experiences. As usual, we'll let Kevin, the demanding little door-kicker, lead off. Randy will get his turn in chapter 7.

### The Cub Caught On Fast

Remember Kevin's early memories that he shared in chapter 1? His family atmosphere included being born baby of the family and having a brother five years older and a sister eight years older—both very capable, smart, and popular. In many families, a five-year gap between children can be enough of a variable to start the whole birth order sequence over again. Kevin could have taken on first-born or even only-born characteristics, but his particular family atmosphere didn't allow that to happen.

His older brother, Jack, became the first-born *son* of the family, and there never was any question about who the "baby" was. Dubbed "Cub" when he was only eleven days old, Kevin caught on quickly. Perceiving the lock his older brother and sister had on so many areas of achievement (and gaining attention), he redoubled his efforts to be charming, full of antics, surprises, and occasional deviltry. It's no wonder, then, that in his earliest memory he sees himself kicking at the door to get what he wanted. When you're a baby of the family, what you want can become very important.

At his sixth birthday party, Kevin clearly remembers abandoning all the little guests who had come to share cake and other goodies and riding around his neighborhood for forty-five minutes on his brand new Roadmaster bike. When he got back, Mom was in the driveway wondering where he'd been and wanting him to get inside to be with his little friends.

Why Kevin took off on the bike is no mystery. He wanted to please himself and nobody else. He had wanted that bike very badly for a long time, and when he finally got it, he couldn't wait to ride it.

Just about a year later there was the other scene on a bike, when he learned to smoke while riding home on an older kid's handlebars. You may recall he felt "big and tough," which expressed the rebellious streak that had become part of his lifestyle. Babies of the family love to say, "I'll show you," and mixed with Kevin's desire for attention through being cute and funny was an equally strong desire to show the world he was someone to be reckoned with. This combination often led Kevin across the line from what was charming to minor vandalism—or worse.

## Little Old Ladies Were in Danger

One of Kevin's calamitous memories, which happened when he was seven or eight, really wasn't funny at all and could have ended in terrible tragedy. He recalls it this way:

> I could never catch a break—like one winter day when I was bombing traffic with snowballs. I'd crouch in the bushes and wait for cars to come along. A blind curve in the road in front of our house made things more sporting; I couldn't see an approaching car til the last minute, so I had to let the snowballs fly the moment I saw it. A perfect shot would smack a door panel with a BANG loud enough to startle the poor driver and echo across the yard as the car disappeared down the road.
>
> I heard a car coming, and the moment I saw the hood (it was a tan '51 DeSoto), I sent my snow bomb sailing—right at the driver's window. Or right at where the window should have been if it hadn't been rolled down. Bingo. The snowball splattered right on the temple of the seventy-year-old lady driver.

By the time that DeSoto finished swerving all over the road and skidded to a stop, I'd fled into the house.

Hiding in the basement, I listened gratefully as my older brother, Jack, answered the door and tried to appease a very angry old lady with a large red welt on the side of her head. Of course, my brother felt responsible to inform my parents when they came home. And they in turn felt responsible to impress upon me (particularly my backside) the error of my ways.

I, however, though genuinely sorry for inflicting a souvenir Leman lump on the old woman's head, didn't feel all that responsible. After all, I wasn't the one driving around in the dead of winter with my car window down.

As an adult and a psychologist who is supposed to be helping other people "grow up," Kevin looks back on this story with no small amount of chagrin. But he shares his feelings in this memory to underline the lack of a sense of responsibility that many babies of the family can have. Sure, he felt sorry for the old lady but it really wasn't all his fault! She shouldn't have had her window down! This is the typical reasoning of a baby who sees the world as a place that caters to him and should always fit his parameters.

## The Ornaments Never Had a Chance

To some people, the world is their oyster. For Kevin, the world was his target. One of his memories concerns some priceless, hand-painted Christmas tree ornaments brought from Norway by his grandmother who came to America when she was only twenty-one. She had handed the ornaments down to her daughter (Kevin's mother) and they were used every year on the Leman Christmas tree. Eight-year-old Kevin found an old BB pistol somewhere, and that Christmas the temptation was just too great:

When no one was around, I would sit out in the hallway on the stairs, shooting through a crack in the living room door at the ornaments on the tree. I became a crack shot and could pick them off at up to thirty feet by learning to aim just a little high and allow for trajectory because my pistol only had so much power.

Somehow Mom and Grandma never figured it out. They always thought the shattered balls were the work of "Puff," our family cat, who already had a bad name because he loved to swat at things and had once even climbed our Christmas tree and toppled it over.

My big brother, Jack, liked to join me sometimes in turning those tree ornaments into a shooting gallery. But every time he did, he would get mad at me because I was a better shot!

## The Cub Didn't Care for Religion

Kevin's rebellion extended to church, where his mother took him regularly each Sunday, whether he wanted to go or not. Kevin didn't like Sunday school, and he particularly didn't like the little old ladies of the church. He remembers:

I'm sure those ladies meant well and were fine people, but when they would bend down to pinch my cheeks and tell me how big I was getting, I wanted to run. They had moles on their faces with hairs sticking out of them, and I could smell their mothball breath. Another ordeal was shaking hands with "ol' Ebert" every Sunday. Shaking hands doesn't sound like much of a hardship, except that Ebert had only three fingers on that hand, and I used to tell my mother, "He gives me the heebie jeebies."

But baby Cubs have their ways of fighting back. When I was quite small, my mother made me sit with her in her regular pew. When she wasn't looking, I would occasionally crawl away and tickle the feet of the women who had removed their shoes for comfort during the sermon.

When I grew older—around nine or ten—Mom would let me sit up in the balcony with my friends while she remained in her regular seat, four rows back on the right.

Every Sunday we would go through the same routine. Just before the sermon, everyone would stand to sing a hymn, and my mother would turn around to check on me. There I would be in the balcony, singing lustily and looking quite angelic. She would turn back to her hymnbook, sure that all was well. But as soon as the last verse of the hymn started, my buddies and I would duck out the back door of the balcony, down the steps, and over several blocks to a place called the Lacto B-Bar, which specialized in ice cream, milk shakes, and hot fudge sundaes.

I'd spend my offering on a hot fudge sundae or a shake, and then we would all hustle back to church, timing it so perfectly that we would get back in our balcony seats just as everyone was standing to sing the closing hymn. As she stood, my mother would turn around again, and there would be her little Kevin, singing away with fervor. We always knew when we had to be back. The ladies of the church had roasts in the oven, and the pastor didn't dare go past twelve noon!

That little church seemed huge to Kevin when he was busy slipping out of the balcony to spend his offering on ice cream. When he went back and attended there a few years ago, he couldn't believe his eyes. What had seemed like St. Patrick's Cathedral to a small boy turned out to have about ten or twelve rows on each side—about the size of a small chapel. It helped Kevin realize that his distorted memories of the size of the church went along with the distorted view of God that he picked up in those early years. It took him many years to come to a mature faith and shake his bad memories of God and God's house.

## The Cub Loved to Con His Teachers

Most of Kevin's antics went on in front of as many people who could appreciate him as possible. His life-molding memory of making the crowd laugh when he couldn't remember a cheer took him on to junior high and high school wanting to make a name for himself as the class cutup. He loved the first day of school each year when all the other kids would nudge each other with anticipation as they learned they had "gotten into one of Leman's classes."

One of his favorite tricks was pretending to gaze out the window and daydream while the teacher was explaining an important concept. The teacher would spot Kevin looking as if he could care less about the lesson and then try to embarrass him by asking him to repeat whatever she had just said. As the teacher waited righteously for an answer, Kevin would pause for dramatic effect and then give her the answer, word for word. He had been listening all the time, and instead of Kevin's being embarrassed, the teacher was red-faced because everyone knew she had been had by the class clown again.

Kevin the Clown went on his merry way, entertaining his schoolmates while he drove the teachers a little bonkers. One even retired early and freely admitted that it was mostly Kevin Leman who was the cause. But when he hit his senior year, Kevin was brought up short by a very effective force that many people understand: the fear factor. As most of his schoolmates made plans to go on to college, he realized he was going on to nowhere. He had gotten As in entertaining people, but his grade point average was so low there wasn't even a heart beat. He went in to see the counselor about trying to get into college and was told, "Leman, with your record, I couldn't even get you into reform school."

Kevin had to admit the counselor was right. As a senior in high school, he had been assigned to a class called "consumer math," in which he was becoming proficient at "guz-in-das"—five guz-in-da ten, twice; five guz-in-da twenty, four times. Kevin realized his life wasn't adding up. He had liked all the attention from clowning around, but now it looked as though he had sold himself down a river to oblivion.

Despite his counselor's encouragement to forget college, he applied everywhere. He tried every college he knew of and many he was sure no one had ever heard of, including a refrigeration repair school. Finally, after several refusals, the denominational school connected to his family's church relented and let him in on probation. Perhaps it was his letters containing biblical admonitions to forgive that swayed them, or maybe it was a hastily scratched note in pencil by his older brother, Jack, already a college graduate, who assured the admissions officer, "I believe in Kevin and I know he can do it."

Whatever it was, Kevin did get into college. For two semesters he reformed and managed to establish a grade point average somewhere above rock bottom. Proudly, he wrote home to tell his parents about getting Cs. But eventually his old grain came to the surface. Walking the straight and narrow wasn't that much fun, and as is often the case, the fear factor lost some of its power.

He knew his fun-loving, rebel lifestyle had been self-defeating, but he reverted to that same old life theme: "Do anything to get attention." After all, it had always gotten him laughs, and at that point laughs were still more important than succeeding in what he had tried desperately to accomplish—getting into college and then earning a degree.

Kevin started slipping in his studies and had soon pulled a couple of Fs. The final straw snapped when he and a friend ripped off the Ice

Cream Conscience Fund and bought pizza for the entire floor of their dorm. The dean didn't see much humor in this. He called it petty larceny that really wasn't that petty, and Kevin wound up in Tucson, Arizona, where his family had recently moved. He got a job emptying trash and cleaning urinals for $195 a month at the Tucson Medical Center.

Kevin's story to this point is similar to that of many people whom we counsel. As they try to use the A-B-Cs of truth therapy, they have a little success, but the final C eludes them. They simply cannot sustain changes in their self-talk or their behavior.

Kevin came home from college with a modest GPA, but not much of a future. His old self-talk told him, "What's the use? You tried to play it straight, and it didn't work. You might as well be a goof-off and get attention that way. You're still funny—all your friends say so. You can show them."

But emptying trash and cleaning urinals all day every day makes a long week. Once again the fear factor came into play, and Kevin did some intense soul searching:

> Somewhere deep inside a voice kept saying, "Is this what you want to do all your life? You know you can do better."
>
> While I had been turned off by the church all my life, I still wanted a relationship with God. Sermons and Sunday school lessons made Him seem austere, judgmental, and far away. I knew there had to be more to God than that and more to my life, too, but I didn't know how to find it.
>
> And then one day part of the answer walked into my life, outside one of the rest rooms I was cleaning. Her name was Sande, and she was a nurse's aide at the Medical Center. Sande was not only beautiful; she had a sweet and different wholesomeness about her I couldn't quite pin down until we started dating. I quickly learned she had a strong faith in God that was personal, not theoretical. When she invited me to go to church with her, I said I had been brought up in the church and heard the "Good News" for years, but it hadn't done me much good. She said she understood, but would I try it anyway?
>
> And so we went on Sunday evenings. One Sunday night the pastor started talking about people who "know all about

God" but all they have is head knowledge. "These people are just straddling the fence," he said. "They have no joy or peace and no real faith. These people are tortured because they know better—they've heard the truth."

At that moment I felt as if everyone in the place had cleared away and I was sitting there alone listening to him preach only to me. I didn't "walk the aisle" that night, but I did make a decision that changed my life direction forever. I finally understood that God wasn't an authoritarian judge watching my every move but that He was my Savior and Friend.

But getting on better terms with God didn't solve all Kevin's problems. He enrolled in a night course at the University of Arizona and promptly flunked it. Now he was really scared. He tried again—a lot harder. This time he passed with the highest grade in a class of six hundred students. He was on his way and didn't stop until he got a doctorate.

On the way to his degree, he discovered terms like *lifestyle, family atmosphere, birth order,* and *early childhood memories.* He realized he had used his own brand of truth therapy to turn things around. The driving, fun-loving rebel had been telling himself lies for years. "Do anything for a laugh. Make them notice. Don't worry about rules. Break a few rules. Show them you're not afraid."

Ironically, the driving force behind much of Kevin's cocky rebellion had been insecurity. When he looked up to a brother and sister who were so much older, stronger, and smarter, he always felt littlest, scrawniest, and least capable—in a word, inadequate. In high school he became a master of the put-on and clowning around because he felt inadequate in any other role. And he *was* inadequate at the time. A high school senior doing "guz-in-da" math problems is not someone who rates "most likely to succeed" in the class yearbook. As Kevin puts it, "I was a perfect candidate for 'most likely to sink without a trace.'"

But Kevin the Clown changed and became Dr. Leman, the psychologist with a sense of humor. He changed his self-talk from lies to truth. He learned he could count in life without always being the center of attention. He learned to tell himself: "Look for the humor in things, but don't be so obnoxious. . . . Be helpful and entertaining, but have respect for the rules."

## Truth Therapy Has Another Name

The best thing about our brand of truth therapy is that it is not an esoteric psychological formula. You won't find this term in any psychology textbook. It's one we coined ourselves to put a handle on the oldest and most positive weapon known to humanity—common sense.

While a senior in high school, several years away from knowing anything about psychology, Kevin took that first crucial step: He realized almost instinctively that his lifestyle had betrayed him. Once he made that initial discovery, he was on his way to meaningful change.

What do you need to change? What habit or hang-up dogs your footsteps saying, "You can't help it. It's the grain of your wood. You'll just have to live with it"? That's a lie, of course. The grain of the wood is there, yes, but *how you shape that wood* is up to you. In the next chapter, we'll show you how Randy also used the principles of truth therapy to conquer the lies that had kept him insecure and defeated for much of his life.

### Worth Remembering . . .

No matter what your memories may tell you,
no matter what your lifestyle,
you are not stuck with self-defeating behavior.
The little kid you once were you still are,
but you can live happily ever after anyway.

# Chapter 7

*The timid victim with the chubby behind grew up to take risks and confront life in a positive way.*

# What You and Joe Friday Have in Common

"**G**ive us the facts, Ma'am, just the facts."

With those terse words, uttered in a droning monotone, Sergeant Joe Friday carved himself a niche in television history and the hearts of "Dragnet" fans everywhere. When he played the starring role on "Dragnet," which is still seen in reruns all over the world, Jack Webb was trying to catch crooks. But his famous phrase, "Just the facts," is also good for catching yourself in the lies that keep you operating at less than 100 percent.

Some of our clients don't like to hear that they have been telling themselves lies. They prefer to think they have problems because other people have been lying to *them*.

"How can my memories be telling me lies?" Allen asked Randy during a counseling session. "Are you saying my memory is bad? The memories I gave you are as clear as the day they happened. I'll never forget them."

"Not at all," Randy explained. "You aren't deliberately blowing some of those memories out of proportion. You are simply remembering *what you experienced and how you felt at the time* those memories happened. But that doesn't mean your perceptions were 100 percent accurate. Still, you took those perceptions of what went on and built your lifestyle. The grain of your wood came out a certain way that is uniquely you. What you need to do now is work with that grain and make the most of it."

## Allen's Life Was Out of Control

Allen had come to Randy struggling with the shambles he had made of his life, which featured a dominating controller/driver lifestyle. When asked to share his earliest memories, Allen mentioned two emotionally packed episodes with his authoritarian father, both of which happened when Allen was six years old.

> My dad was a very successful builder in our town, and I remember going to a job site with him one day when I was about six. I found a few boards and nails to play with. My dad gave me a hammer, and I spent the next hour building my own project. I remember when it was time to go, I yelled, screamed, and kicked, trying to get my dad to let me stay and finish what I was working on. Finally he gave me a whipping to make his point.

> I also remember taking my bike and trying to run away from home. My dad had told me that I couldn't play at a friend's house down the street, but I did it anyway. When he found out, he came down to where I was and gave me a whipping that I can still feel. He yelled and screamed and actually dragged me home and locked me in my room for the rest of the day.

As we counsel families, and especially children, we see all kinds of reactions to authoritarian parenting. Some kids quietly take it, walking softly while Mom and Dad carry their big stick. They may never rebel, or they may wait until they're out of the house and away from the authoritarian thumb of their parents. Other kids, however, perceive an authoritarian upbringing differently. They fight back and learn to be controllers, drivers, or other aggressive personality types.

Allen took the controller/driver route. His childhood and early teenage years were a battle royal with his parents, and he finally left home at seventeen to get out on his own. Before he was twenty-one, he had lost his first wife and several jobs, due to his run-roughshod approach to everyone. When he came to Randy for help, he had remarried and found his first good job as a supervisor for a construction firm. But things were coming apart again at home and on the job.

At work he ran into a boss who was a replica of his own inflexible, demanding father. Allen was butting heads with the boss and coming up short. To compensate, he took it out on his crew by setting unrealistic production goals, openly ridiculing those who made errors, and threatening dismissal for anyone who couldn't live up to his standards. The result was chaos, and he had been told to shape up or ship out.

At home, Allen was in similar straits. His second wife was sick and tired of his controlling, dominating ways and authoritarian (naturally) treatment of their three-year-old son. In fact, it was she who got him to come in to see Randy for help.

During Allen's second visit, Randy started him on truth therapy. Beginning with step A, Allen accepted the possibility that his early childhood memories were a distortion of the real world and that those memories reinforced his destructive lifestyle. Because he had been controlled by a demanding, authoritarian father, Allen had become a controller himself. His life theme said, "Things must be done my way or I might as well do them myself." That theme came out of the destructive self-talk he fed himself all day long: "Never mind; I'll do it myself and do it right . . ."; "I don't need any help—you can't trust people anyway . . ."; "People aren't worth listening to—I'm one jump ahead of them anyway . . ."; "I can do it, but I have to be the one in charge."

One thing that helped the light dawn for Allen is that he really didn't like the way he was. He told Randy, "I seem to always run into a brick wall every time I try to get started with people."

Once he saw the meaning in his early childhood memories, Allen realized that he had built his life on distortions of reality. Yes, his father had been strict, but Allen had to admit that much of the blame for the tension was just as much his fault as his dad's. *He began to see that memories of childhood can be perceived in different ways.* A real breakthrough came when he realized his dad's inflexible, demanding approach was actually his clumsy way of showing love.

Next Allen moved on to tackle the B phase of truth therapy—his beliefs. For over twenty-five years he had been lying to himself about everything and everybody. He realized his self-talk was riddled with lies and distortions, such as "I must stay in charge at all times. People only respect me if I'm tough and powerful."

Allen learned to counter this lie with the truth: "I don't have to be in charge all the time to be okay. While I desire the respect of others, I can get along without it if for some reason I don't live up to their expectations or my own."

A lie Allen had been constantly telling himself about others was: "You can't trust anyone. People will do the job right only if you stay right on top of them. People will slow you down if you let them."

Allen learned to counter this lie with the truth about others: "People can be trusted. Even if they do mess up the job, it's not the end of the world. Delegating to other people and trusting them will speed up the work, not slow it down."

As Allen made progress with the A and B of truth therapy, he also started working on the C: Change your self-talk—and your behavior. As Allen began challenging the old lies with the truth, positive things began to happen in his life. As he lightened up on others, they became much more responsive, cooperative, and productive. He realized that there were much healthier ways to think and more productive approaches to the world around him.

"You know," Allen told Randy in one of his last counseling sessions, "this truth therapy stuff really works."

Offensive controllers like Allen are easy to spot because they always want to sit behind the steering wheel of life. They want to act on other people and on things. Some people, however, control themselves and others defensively instead of offensively. They see life working on *them*, and they try to control people and things out of fear that they will be dominated or even crushed.

## Is Donahue a Defensive Controller?

It's possible that talk show host Phil Donahue is a defensive controller of sorts. In his autobiography, he confesses to being a combative kid who was always getting into fights with bigger, stronger opponents who usually left him in a bloody heap. He recalls the day he suffered two defeats, the first at the hands of another Phil who met him in a vacant lot to have it out over an angry exchange of words that had happened earlier.

Donahue brought his best friend, Tommy, for moral support and went at it with his opponent. He remembers that he was landing punches and "doing okay." Suddenly he found himself coming to, in a sitting position with Tommy asking about his condition. Shaking the winner's hand, Donahue left with Tommy, and on the way home suffered his second "KO" of the day—this one to his ego. His friend said, "I had an idea that was gonna happen."

Says Donahue in his book: "I may not always remember yesterday's show guest, but I will never forget those back to back 'KO's' on that day in Cleveland in the mid-forties."[1]

But why did Phil Donahue continue to find himself in losing conflicts with bigger, stronger opponents? He writes:

> I believe I fought because I was scared. Fighting proved to others that I wasn't scared. The only way I could show the other guys that I wasn't scared was to fight. Apparently losing was better than having my fear exposed. A real dilemma with this strategy was that after I fought and lost, and possibly convinced others that I wasn't scared, I was left with the knowledge that I was still scared. I realize now that what's important is not what others think, but what I know. And believe me, I knew I was scared. It would have been so much easier just to accept being scared and forgo the bloody nose.[2]

In a very real sense, Phil Donahue has applied the principles of truth therapy to himself quite accurately. He realizes that he thought he had to fight to prove he was not scared (the lie in his lifestyle). Today he counters that lie with the truth and believes it is not what others think that is important, but what he knows.

## Fred Was a Shy Controller

Some defensive controllers use subtle tactics, often so subtle the last thing people would call them is controller. See if you can spot a defensive controller strategy in the memory of a man named Fred, who came to see Kevin complaining about being too shy. It was not only making things difficult for him at home, but it was really limiting his opportunities to advance at work. One of the memories Fred shared was this:

> I was about four when I was invited to a birthday party for one of my friends. All the other children were going in, but I was shy, so I stayed outside until everyone else was there and my mother finally took my hand and escorted me into the room.

Because Kevin works with many children who use shyness to control adults, he perked up his ears when he heard that story. As he probed deeper, he found he was right. Fred was a defensive controller. Very early in life, he had learned to get people to pay attention to him by acting shy. They had to approach him on his terms. For example, he would make adults bend lower and lower to hear what his "shy, faint little voice" was saying.

Please bear in mind we are not saying all the shy people in the world are controllers. Shyness is a burdensome, sometimes painful, condition that can spring from many sources and become part of different lifestyles, like pleaser, martyr, or victim.

Note, however, the way Fred recalls that scene at the party. As he remembers it, looking back through the clouded lenses of adult perspective, he describes himself as "shy." But this is a cover-up for his real problem: he has difficulty opening up and sharing his feelings. He maintains control by holding all of his emotional cards close to the vest.

But Fred's behavior has created problems for him at home and at work. His wife is tired of his turtle-shell lack of communication. On the job, he is being passed over for higher-paying management positions because his employers "doubt that he can handle people."

In a real sense, Fred is a victim who became a defensive controller because he feared the world would take advantage of him. He came to Kevin for help with his shyness, but what he really wanted was sympathy. When Kevin suggested some truth therapy, Fred balked. He was too comfortable with the cocoon of shyness he had built around himself, and leaving that cocoon was just too threatening. The bottom line was that Fred chose not to change, even though he clearly saw how his lifestyle was crippling him. He preferred to remain a victim, who could control his world by acting shy.

## How "Fat Butt" Learned to Take a Risk

If anyone could have taken the same path Fred did, it was Randy Carlson, whose early childhood memories are littered with painful experiences, disasters, embarrassments, and the incessant teasing of two older brothers who liked to call him "Fat Butt" and use his chubby behind for target practice at the same time.

Randy has already shared some traumatic memories of fleeing tornadoes, crashing on bicycles, and suffering humiliation in spelling bees. But the Law of Creative Consistency guarantees that he has still more. Your memories always match your basic lifestyle, and Randy's memories are chock-full of trauma and tragedy that gnawed away at his feelings of security as an adult.

Although he functioned as a visibly secure and capable person, insecurity plagued him for many years. Deep inside, Randy's life theme could be set to the tune of "Please Fence Me In," and the more protective the better.

From his early childhood memory file, Randy can recall:

> Throughout my early childhood years we had a huge and hairy English sheepdog named Stony. When I was six, Stony tried to jump a picket fence, but she didn't make it and practically impaled herself on some of the sharp points. She was bleeding badly and had to be taken to the vet. People came running to try to help Stony. All I could do was run inside and hide in the closet in my room. I just knew Stony was going to die. (She didn't.)

Randy realizes today that he picked up the tendency to want to hide from anything threatening or overwhelming when he was very young. It was easier to pull away, hide himself in his bedroom, or maybe in his office, and hope the problem would go away. Then he didn't have to deal with it—out of sight, out of mind.

But when life closes in with stressful situations, you can run but you can't always hide. Life was always stressful for young Randy, particularly in second grade:

> I remember having to play Abraham Lincoln in the school play. I had a black hat and a black coat, and I had to memorize a little poem about Lincoln and his virtues as president. Memorizing the poem and saying it at home for my mom was easy. But when I walked out on the platform and saw all those parents staring at me, I was petrified. I clearly remember being

afraid I simply couldn't repeat the poem, which I didn't think
was true anyway. (Nobody could be that good.) I was just so
fearful I would make a mistake or not even be able to finish.

The most interesting thing about that memory is that I
don't know how it ended. I guess I finished the poem, but I
can't remember feeling good or relieved or much of anything
else. Perhaps that experience is symbolic of what I do today. For
example, I enjoy speaking, but I am always concerned about
how I will be accepted. I want to do it right and get it done, but
I don't sit around afterward enjoying my work and saying, "I
did a great job; I deserve a pat on the back." I envy Kevin for
his ability to do just that. As for me, I just can't stop and be
satisfied.

Randy's parents were warm and supportive, but his feelings of security took a real beating from his two big brothers—Warren and Larry,
ten and six years older, respectively. It was Warren who dubbed him
"Fat Butt," and the name stuck. Randy remembers some of his many
adventures with his brothers as follows:

Warren hardly knew I was alive. By the time I was out of
diapers and into Lincoln Logs, he was into the throes of puberty
and dating. He had about as much interest in me as he would a
fly speck on the wall. My other brother, Larry, showed a little
more interest, but usually the wrong kind. He loved to scriggle
his nose at me and say, "I'm going to get you, Fat Butt." I used
to run crying to Mom and she'd have to make him stop it.

I remember clearly a camping trip the whole family took to
the shores of Lake Michigan when I was only five. We stayed in
a cabin that hadn't been used in a while and was full of
cobwebs. I had been assigned to sleep in one of the rooms by
myself, and my older brothers, especially Warren, took great
delight in telling me about the big black spiders that would be in
that room with me all night long.

"They're going to bite you right on your little fat butt,"
Warren said gleefully. As usual, I ran howling to Mom who

dispensed proper justice by making Warren sleep in that room instead of me.

Of course, not every memory I have from childhood is traumatic. For example, I recall attending Sunday school and singing my favorite hymn, "Trust and Obey." I wanted to be secure, and what better way than to trust Jesus to take care of me, always to obey and stay out of trouble (and please, God, keep Larry and Warren away from me!).

## From Victory to Defeat

Randy's early childhood memories clearly paint a portrait of a blend of victim and pleaser lifestyles. Although his big brothers teased him unmercifully, Randy desperately wanted their acceptance and would do anything to get it. One of his great days of triumph occurred at Sheldon Park, just down the street from his house in Muskegon. Both his brothers were there, along with several other kids.

In the group was a twelve-year-old boy named Byron, who was the Peewee Herman of the neighborhood. Warren and Larry started teasing Byron and saying, "I'll bet even our little seven-year-old brother can beat you at arm wrestling."

And so Randy and Byron squared off at a picnic table. With super-human determination, fueled by a desire for approval and acceptance, Randy won the arm wrestling match, much to his brothers' delight. They teased Byron mercilessly as he slunk away in disgrace. But Randy's arm wrestling triumph was his sole thrill of victory as a young athlete. His other venture into the wide world of sports met with the agony of defeat:

> As the youngest in the family, I wanted to find fresh soil into which I could plant my dreams—some area that hadn't been staked out by my two older brothers. Warren was an electronic whiz and Larry had captured the corner on music. So I thought, why not try sports? By then I knew I wasn't making it on the report card front.
>
> Summer was fast approaching, and I decided to try out for the Pirate Little League baseball team. The day for tryouts

finally came, and I was there early—ready to make a good impression on the coach. He sent me out to first base to see if I had the stuff to become a Pirate. As my victim's luck would have it, the first ball hit at me was a ninety-mile-an-hour grounder—or so it seemed. This was my big chance and I went for it. Stumbling over first base, I fell to my knees in time and stopped that ball!

There was only one problem. I stopped it with my teeth, not my glove. As the blood flowed out of my mouth and nose, I knew an athletic career didn't hold a lot of promise. There just wasn't enough security, and I ran home to see how many teeth I had lost.

## Joe Friday to the Rescue

With a memory library like Randy Carlson's, you would expect him to wind up a very fearful, insecure adult, who would go through life playing it safe, keeping his nose clean, and staying off slow-pitch softball teams. But that didn't happen because he took a hard look at the facts and became aware he could change things.

After graduating from high school, he went on to get a B.A. in business at the University of Arizona and then decided that he would try for a master's degree in counseling as well. It was during his training to become a marriage and family counselor that he discovered the power in early childhood memories and the way to cut those memories down to size. He realized all those negative memories were telling him lies and decided to take the Joe Friday approach—"Just the facts, Carlson, just the facts."

Randy's first steps toward change involved using a major premise taught in his counselor training classes:

YOU ARE RESPONSIBLE FOR YOUR OWN CHOICES AND FOR THE CONSEQUENCES OF YOUR CHOICES.

That brief sentence told him he couldn't blame his parents, his brothers, his second-grade teacher, or that Little League coach who hit him a ninety-mile-an-hour grounder. He alone was responsible for his insecurities and had to answer the question, "What are you going to do about them?"

His counselor training gave him a helpful tool called Conflict Resolution. Often used to work out disagreements between two or more parties, Conflict Resolution is also useful for self-change in the individual. Conflict Resolution involves three steps:

1. Identify the problem.
2. Identify how you are contributing to the problem.
3. Identify what you are willing to do (and not do) about it.

Identifying the problem sounds simple. It's amazing how many people can't pinpoint their real problem, which is centered in the lies and beliefs that keep them trapped. All they know is they feel depressed, angry, anxious, or some other symptom of stress and discomfort. Or they may try to hide their symptoms, which is what Randy tried to do until he entered counselor training. He recalls:

> My peers and professors confronted me and helped me see
> I had developed a confident front, complete with lots of clichés
> to hide my insecurities. My real problem was being afraid to
> take any kind of risk or make any kind of waves for fear I would
> jeopardize my security.

The second step in Conflict Resolution involves identifying how you contribute to the problem. Many people are convinced that whatever is wrong, it's not their fault. Instead their spouse, or the boss or the weather is to blame—anyone or anything but them. Randy says:

> As my classmates and professors bored in on me, I saw my
> lifestyle clearly for the first time. I wasn't just a poor little Fat
> Butt, who had been run over by the freight train of life (with
> those two older brothers at the throttle). I was contributing to
> my own problems by letting the little kid part of me run the
> show. There was a battle going on between my rational self and
> that little child who was still a very real part of me.
>
> The third step I had to take was the big one. What was I
> willing to do about this? And, equally important, what was I *not*
> *willing to do?* I had contributed to my own problems by letting
> my rational adult side become lazy and unassertive. The little kid

I once was had taken over and held the upper hand. In a sense I had been saying, "Let little Fat Butt do it"—and he was.

To put my rational, adult self back in charge, I started taking tiny steps by changing my self-talk. Instead of always telling myself, "You had better take care," I started saying, "Why not take a risk?" When I got a bad meal or bad service in a restaurant, I would confront the waiter or waitress and politely point out the problem. And at work (I held a full-time job at the radio station throughout my graduate studies), I became much more definite in decision-making situations where I knew I should express my opinion.

My new approach even extended to casual conversations where people might express opinions that didn't sound right to me. In the past, I had always just sat quietly and listened, afraid to offend people by asking them just exactly what they meant or to explain their reasoning. Now I started to challenge them and discovered that conversation was a lot more fun.

The bottom line was that Randy, the timid little victim with the chubby behind, started taking responsibility for becoming an adult who was willing to take risks and assertively and positively confront life. To his counseling case load, he added working on this book, helping develop a national radio network, and going out frequently to do speaking. All these "risks" are part of his change process, and as he says, "I can do it. I can stand in front of a group and not have to be accepted. Everyone doesn't have to like me, and I can still enjoy what I'm doing."

## But Fat Butt's Battles Aren't Over

While he has made huge strides toward overcoming the life theme that bound him in insecurity, Randy's struggles are not over. He still battles his "fat butt" image and the lie that sings its siren song from deep within the refrigerator. He fights a battle familiar to millions—the battle of the bulge. In the next chapter, he will share a technique he calls "rewriting your early childhood memories," another weapon that can help win the battle against self-defeating behavior.

## Worth Remembering . . .

You are responsible for your own choices
and the consequences of those choices.
You must identify your problem,
the part you play in that problem,
and what you are willing to do about it.

# Chapter 8

One lie Randy started telling himself early was, "You can eat your way to happiness." Parents and grandparents can help perpetuate lies that make long-term change difficult.

# Permanent Change Is Possible If...

If most people are honest, they realize they engage in self-defeating behavior of some kind, at least some of the time. Under the veneer of their public selves are the hidden pockets of private and personal weakness—the habits and hang-ups that are counterproductive. Over the years we've heard all kinds of confessions from our clients:

- I can't keep my temper—I'm always blowing my cool.
- I always forget to think before I speak.
- I know I should stop drinking—it's killing me.
- I'm always putting things off—procrastinating, I guess they call it.
- I worry about everything—I lose a lot of sleep.
- I know the divorce was my fault.
- I'm too strict with my kids—I get too rough on them.
- Yes, I work fourteen hours a day, and I'm never home—but it's for Mary Ann and the kids!
- I can't stay away from food—it's my pacifier.

The above list of admissions is only the tip of a huge iceberg of self-defeating behavior, but it is representative of negative theme songs that mature, educated people pick up along their way to becoming adults. Their early memories give them glimpses of how they started learning these destructive tunes that now constantly play in the back of their minds. Why don't they just change those tunes to something more positive? It can be done if they are willing to confront the lies they've been telling themselves and replace them with truth.

## Temporary Change Is Easy, But . . .

Reaching the place where you can confess a certain habit or hang-up is a good start on truth therapy. You accept the fact that at least parts of your lifestyle are not helping you at all. You are able to spot the habitually negative self-talk that you have been feeding yourself daily at the rate of over one thousand words a minute. You understand that this kind of self-talk is full of lies and you want to believe the truth about yourself and other people.

So far so good, but the last step—the C of truth therapy—is the giant leap that makes the real difference. Can you change your self-talk and your usual way of behaving, both of which keep you snarled in self-defeat? Temporary change is not that difficult, but long-term change is another matter. Those lies you have been telling yourself over the years do not die easily. They have a way of coming back and whispering in your ear all over again.

Randy admits his own struggles with long-term change in an area he can't hide—his weight. One lie he started telling himself when he was very young was, "You can eat your way to happiness." While Randy has no memory of going on food binges, he does have general recollections that his mother always kept him well fed—too well fed. When little Randy fell victim to life's incessant slings, arrows, and BB guns, Mom was right there with a cookie, a piece of cake, a sandwich—something to give comfort and solace. Even today she operates on the same principle. When Randy and his family visit, the first words out of Mom's mouth are, "Would you like something to eat?"

Randy's mother tells him he was a stocky child, but Randy already knows that. Your older brothers don't dub you "Fat Butt" for nothing. It's what Randy did with that nickname, however, that helps explain his weight battles today. While he didn't like being shot at with BB guns or being teased, Randy did find a positive side to his nickname. At least it gave him a sense of belonging and a role he could fill. Warren, ten years older, was a ham radio operator, Larry was a master of the piano, and Randy was Fat Butt. The nickname, unpleasant as it sounds, stuck because it fit. It not only fit the perception that Warren and Larry had of Randy, but *Randy's perception of himself.*

And when his security was threatened—which was often—Randy told himself, "I can eat, and then I'll feel better." With brothers so much older, Randy spent a lot of time playing alone, and he found food a pleasant companion. Food didn't talk back; it was dependable and consistent. It never shouted at him, never called him dummy, and gave instant gratification. "Food," admits Randy, "was a silent partner in my battle to belong."

## Good Little Fat Butt Almost Flunked

As Randy went through grade school, his experiences only confirmed the victim/pleaser lifestyle he had chosen. He suffered defeats like the spelling bee failure and then found relief just a swallow away in the refrigerator. He became discouraged with school and just didn't try. He was never a behavior problem because he was just too afraid.

One teacher told his mother, "I wish I had a whole room full of Randys—he's such a good little boy." Of course, that only confirmed his careful, "Don't make waves" approach to life. Yet when Randy reached sixth grade, he was in serious academic trouble. The principal called in his mother and told her, "Randy is practically failing all his subjects. We'll have to put him in remedial classes or he'll never make it." To remedial classes Randy went, and while it didn't help his ego, it did get him into seventh grade.

The summer he was twelve, Randy went to a church camp and discovered God for the first time—or so he thought. He'd been brought up in Sunday school and church, and while he had never disagreed with it, he had never felt it had a lot to do with him. But camp that year changed all that. Randy realized that a relationship with God was personal, not simply a heritage from his family or church, and he made a choice to pursue this relationship. This decision helped him begin to piece together some answers to big questions: "Who am I?" "Where am I going?" "What do I really want to be like?"

## The Perfectionist Decides to Crash Diet

Also beginning to surface in Randy's lifestyle was the perfectionist who had quietly hidden beneath discouragement during his grade school years. When Randy turned thirteen in seventh grade, he was 5'7" and weighed 205 pounds. In grade school he hadn't minded being the chubby butt of many jokes, but things were changing, including his perception of girls. He decided his flab had to go.

Randy went at losing weight with the all-or-nothing attitude typical of the perfectionist. He began a one-apple/one-glass-of-milk-a-day diet, went out for track, and dropped over fifty pounds in three weeks. His diet had "worked," but he paid a big price. In his run-down condition he contracted rheumatic fever, which put him out of action for over a month. But he bounced back and zealously pursued his new image by participating in track and basketball and starting to study for the first time. He also had a sudden growth spurt and shot up to his full height—6'1".

In high school, Randy still ate like a wolf, but his activity rate helped keep his weight around 150. He graduated with a B average and went to work as an announcer with the Family Life Radio Network. He continued to hold that job while he attended college where he earned a 3.7 grade point average.

But his insecurities and victim/pleaser lifestyle were not eradicated. Randy still battled insecurity and lack of being assertive enough. He and Donna (his high school sweetheart) were married when he was a freshman in college. Quiet, consistent, and sure of her beliefs, Donna frequently proved to be a strong pillar for Randy. When they bought their first house—a tiny two-bedroom fixer-upper—for $12,500, scraping up the $2,500 down payment was difficult enough, but signing that note for a $10,000 loan kept Randy awake nights for weeks. The payments would be $97 a month for thirty years! What if he lost his job? What if he got sick? The "what if's" never stopped and Randy headed for the refrigerator to find comfort.

## The Pounds Began to Reappear

It was about then the weight started to come back—just a few pounds at first, but nothing to worry about. After all, it was typical for a hungry young husband to gain some weight, particularly when his wife was a good cook and he liked cleaning up those leftovers every night. All those fat cells Randy had developed in his boyhood were waiting to fill up. And fill up they did.

When Randy entered graduate school, he continued working full time while maintaining a 4.0 average (his perfectionism again). As the pressure increased, so did his anxieties. No longer as active as he had been in high school, he put on the pounds slowly but surely, and the lie he had told himself years before came back more persuasively than ever: "When things get tense or tough, eat your way to peace of mind."

And another strain in his life theme told him, "So you're a little heavy—it's not that big a deal." He told himself the typical lies that enabled him to excuse his eating patterns:

- I need this Snickers bar for energy.
- I didn't have dessert at lunch, so a little at dinner is okay.
- We ate early tonight, so I need a bowl of cereal for a bedtime snack.
- It's not a really *big* candy bar. . . .

At one point the doctors sent Randy to a stress reduction class, and Donna decided to attend with him. They went faithfully every Tuesday night where they did exercises and learned to relax. Feeling he had earned a reward, Randy always insisted that they stop off on their way home at his favorite ice cream parlor.

Randy battled weight into his mid-thirties, hitting over two hundred pounds, crash dieting, and then gaining it all back. Learning to take more risks and do something with his life had its pros and cons. A masters in counseling gave him opportunities to help other people. His job responsibilities increased at the radio station, and eventually he was put in charge of over one hundred employees. But when the pressure mounted, he told himself it was okay to head for the refrigerator or the snack bar.

When traveling or on any tight schedule, he found it oh-so-easy to stop at McDonald's for a shake or at the candy machine for his favorite, a Snickers bar. After all, Snickers are full of peanuts, and peanuts are nutritious, right?

And when he was home, naturally he would head for the refrigerator with automatic regularity. He stills remembers the night he was missing a very important file, something he had to have at the office the next morning. He started tearing the house apart and even accused Donna of stealing the file or throwing it out in one of her cleaning binges. After ten or fifteen minutes, he found himself in the kitchen where Donna asked, "What are you doing?"

"I'm looking for the file, of course. What else?"

"Well," said his wife, "I am positive it is not in the refrigerator."

Out of sheer habit, Randy had opened the refrigerator door. The familiar theme song had clicked in: "The answer to the problem is in the fridge."

## Randy Decides Fat Butt Has To Go

The day of reckoning came not long ago when Randy skied to 210 pounds (again) and his doctor told him, "Your blood pressure is way too high and your sugar level is up. You need to lose thirty pounds and keep it lost or you're headed for trouble." This time the old lies didn't sound so convincing. Besides, it was getting embarrassing. A counselor who couldn't solve his own eating problems! For shame! Was Randy stuck? Would the grain of the wood be too difficult to reshape? All the childhood memories had pointed him in one direction—seeking security. The refrigerator had turned out to be a friendly refuge. What could he do? "What you can do," he told himself, "is use the techniques you tell other people to use. Rewrite your memories by changing your perceptions."

It's ridiculous for a thirty-seven-year-old man to still remember missing the word *gang* in a third-grade spelling bee. It's silly to remember how your brothers teased you and called you Fat Butt, or is it? Have I ever really dealt with that? I got used to it, I guess. I accepted it, but do I really like it? It's not a compliment. I don't need to be Fat Butt to belong today. The truth is, I have to be more considerate of my health, my family, and my future and stop believing the same old lie that it's okay and a little bit of weight won't hurt me. Weight is hurting me and I've got to change.

During that inner conversation with himself, Randy realized he had never put overeating in the context of something truly negative. He had used food to belong as a child, and although he had managed a few years of staying thin in high school, he hadn't dealt with the real issue. Responding to the Law of Creative Consistency, his lifestyle lured him back to "eating his way to happiness." Randy knew he could go on another crash diet, but that wouldn't really solve his weight problem. *What he had to change was his perception of his childhood memories.* They were still controlling those trips to the refrigerator.

Yes, his memories were full of disasters, but none of them were big enough to control his life unless he chose to let it happen. As for being "Fat Butt," he didn't need that name any more. By changing his perception of the past, Randy was able to change his perception of the present—and the future.

He didn't need food to belong. In fact, while Donna didn't nag him, he knew she didn't like him fat. It was time to really change and move beyond the A and B of his own truth therapy principles. He needed to take action:

> I had to quit telling myself I could eat my way to happiness or at least out of my anxieties. That old lie just wasn't working. In fact, the eating had become a source of even greater anxiety than the stress that sent me to the refrigerator in the first place. I couldn't get by with those same old excuses: "I'll start dieting tomorrow. . . . I'll start exercising next week. . . . I'm only thirty-seven, so I can handle a little extra weight. . . ." I looked at my kids and told myself, "Hey, you want to be around for their graduation."

And so Randy went on a diet and began to exercise—nothing dramatic, just watching what he ate and being sure to get in a brisk walk of a couple of miles at least four or five times a week. He didn't use Opti-Fast or any other product. In fact, he even allowed for treating himself to a very occasional Snickers bar, which he explains this way:

> I did this on purpose. With my all-or-nothing perfectionist mentality, I knew that if I tried to go cold turkey on sweets again, I would eventually fail, and that could send me right back on another weight-gaining binge. And so I've allowed for a little failure, but the basic goal is the same. I don't need to be Fat Butt any more.

Another thing Randy did was take pressure off himself at work by delegating more responsibilities and reminding himself he didn't have to please everybody all the time.

Slowly the weight dropped away, and when Randy hit 180, he even celebrated with a chocolate shake at McDonald's. But now he stays at 180 with self-talk that says, "Your name is Randy, not Fat Butt. You don't need food every time pressure mounts, and you don't have to please everybody and get everything done by yourself. It's okay not to be perfect."

Perhaps the hardest battle for Randy is staying out of that cookie jar. One thing he has tried to stop doing is going to the cookie jar with his three kids and consuming eight or nine cookies (three for them and the rest for him). He used to do that regularly and tell Donna, "Well, *all* of us were eating cookies. . . ."

One of the major benefits of Randy's battle with weight is that it has given him a new sense of empathy for his clients. Now when he tells them they can stay as they are or choose to change, he has a much deeper appreciation for the effort involved. He has learned that change is a *process*, not a final goal that is reached and ends the struggle. "To permanently change a self-defeating behavior," he says, "you must realize the struggle is never over. Your self-talk never stops. You're responsible to monitor that self-talk, and when the lies start whispering or even shouting, it's up to you to change the channel."

## Different Perceptions Lead to Real Change

To recap the principles in Randy's story, here is the "secret" to permanent change:

1. Accept the fact that your memories are lying. More precisely, the perception you have of those memories is not based on reality, but on the interpretation you made when you were very young.

2. Believe the truth instead of those lies that are ingrained into your lifestyle. This is easier said than done. The next step is crucial.

3. Change your perception of the past by reviewing your memories and the feelings you attached to them. Challenge the perceptions you had as a child, which are frozen in your memories, with the rational thinking you are capable of as an adult. As you gain a proper perspective on your memories, you

can change your self-talk. And when you change your self-talk—how you think all day long—you can change your behavior.

The Law of Creative Consistency says people remember only those events from early childhood that are consistent with their present view of themselves and their world. By changing your perception of your memories, however, you can change your present view of things. You are not trapped by remembering feelings that you had many years ago and letting those feelings affect how you act today.

## You Can Rewrite Your Memories

As part of changing your perceptions, try rewriting your early memories from a new perspective. Don't try to change the facts of the memories, but recast them with a more rational adult point of view. For example, Randy could rewrite that memory of the ninety-mile-an-hour grounder that almost removed his front teeth by saying:

> I gave it my best shot, but the ball hopped over my glove and hit me in the mouth. It can happen to anyone. While I quit Little League, I tried sports later and got on the track and basketball teams.

And when he looked back on his second-grade performance in the school play, Randy could say, "I was worried about blowing my lines, but I didn't. I did a good job even though I was scared."

The feelings you attach to a childhood memory may have seemed entirely legitimate then, but they don't necessarily reflect reality for you now. Let's look at some other examples of how revising your memories can work on self-defeating behavior.

## SHARON:  "I just can't let anyone down."

Remember Sharon, the pleaser/perfectionist in chapter 5 who struggled with that memory of a four-year-old who tried to help Dad wash the car and felt "terrible about letting him down" because a few spots had remained? That memory was perfectly consistent with her life theme: "There is so much to do. I can't let people down."

Besides all her responsibilities with two toddlers at home, she was the new president of the Junior League, never said no when the PTA needed help, and had just taken on a part-time job at a day care center run by an old school friend.

Practically stumbling with exhaustion, Sharon came to see Kevin. "What's wrong?" asked Kevin.

And she said: "I'm stuck. I can't make any progress. For every two steps forward, I slip three steps backward into the swamp."

As Sharon described how she hustled from one project to another, constantly falling short of her self-imposed standards, Kevin nodded knowingly. "Shades of Mother Teresa," he said. "With all you have to do at home and in the community, why are you out working, too? Do you need the money?"

"Well, not really. Tom makes an excellent salary and I don't have to work. But when Peggy came and said I was the only one she could trust to help her with all those kids . . . well, what could I say?"

After running through the A and B of truth therapy, Sharon quickly realized that her pleaser/perfectionist lifestyle was based on a distorted picture of reality that started way back when she was a little girl. She also saw the need for dealing with her beliefs about what she thought was true as an adult:

- That she couldn't make any mistakes;
- That she always had to try harder to cover all the bases;
- That she couldn't say no to requests for help.

But changing her self-talk and her behavior was another matter. How could she quit that part-time job when her friend was counting on her? How could she say no to the PTA when so few people were willing to help?

That's when changing her perception of her car washing memory came into play. The feeling she attached to the memory was "terrible for letting Dad down." But her dialogue with Kevin next included this exchange:

KEVIN: But did you really let your dad down?
SHARON: No, I suppose not, for a four-year-old I did pretty well, actually.

KEVIN: Did Dad reject you because of the spots on the car?

SHARON: No, he just smiled and gave me a hug.

KEVIN: Then is it fair to say that thinking you let Dad down is a bit irrational?

SHARON: I suppose.

KEVIN: How could you rethink your perception of that memory? How could you perceive it if you thought about it rationally today?

SHARON: Well, actually I could feel pretty good about helping Dad wash the car. I did the best a four-year-old could.

KEVIN: Then how could you transfer that perception to how you feel today when requests keep coming in for your help and participation and you're just too overwhelmed to fill all of them?

Sharon paused before answering. She was getting the point, but finding it hard to accept the truth because the truth hurts. It is not easy to change a long-held perception.

SHARON: I suppose I should not feel badly about saying no when I really don't have time to do what people ask. And I really should tell myself, "Look at what you're doing already."

For good measure, Sharon rewrote that early childhood memory of the less-than-perfect car wash and came up with this:

When I was only four, I helped my dad wash the car. Part of what I did turned out with some spots on it and had to be done over, but I was glad I could help my dad and do as much as I did.

With her new perceptions, Sharon made slow but steady progress. When her Junior League presidency came to an end, she refused a second term. She started taking fewer jobs with the PTA, and a real breakthrough came when she was able to find a replacement who was acceptable to her friend who ran the day care center.

Sharon is still a pleaser and always will be. But now she isn't an exhausted one, which makes Tom and her two kids a lot happier.

## Controllers Can Change Fast, If . . .

While we don't keep official statistics, we believe it is safe to say that controllers and drivers do better at changing than most of the other lifestyles. The problem with controllers or drivers, of course, is to get them into counseling in the first place. Usually they're busy attending "you can have it all" seminars or organizing something or someone. Once in counseling, however, they are usually quick to recognize the nonproductive aspects of their lifestyles and that their self-talk is telling them fibs.

In chapter 7 you met Allen, the powerful driver/controller who could remember getting whippings from his father when he was very small. Allen responded by fighting back and grew up believing that he had to be tough and in control at all times because he was the only capable one. When Allen changed his basic life tune, he realized that he didn't have to be in charge of everything and that Murphy's Law is right: sometimes things do go wrong, no matter how carefully you plan.

Not surprisingly, Allen had not been getting on well with his second wife. He had remarried quickly and had been destroying his second marriage almost as fast as he destroyed his first with dominating controller tactics. The first self-talk lie that he had to counter in his marriage was, "I have to be in charge around here—that's what a man is for." When he began telling himself, "I don't have to be the boss for my marriage to work," his wife called Randy and thanked him personally for the big change in her husband.

As Allen changed his self-talk, he realized that his ex-wife had not been fully to blame for their divorce. "Carol had a lot of good qualities, and so does Janet," he told Randy. "We can learn to make this marriage work."

Changing his usual self-talk from "*I* can make this work," to "*We* can make it work," was a small but highly significant step for Allen. The controller/driver was slowly learning to back off and work *with* people instead of running roughshod *over* them.

When Allen focused on the feelings he attached to his childhood memories of getting whipped for disobeying, he came up with words like "angry," "rebellious," and "mistreated." Then he tried rewriting those early memories and putting more rational adult perceptions on them. The results startled him. Yes, his father had been strict, but Allen had to admit that much of the blame for the tension was just as much his fault as his dad's. *He began to see that memories of childhood can be perceived in different ways.* A real breakthrough came when he realized his dad's inflexible demands were actually his clumsy way of showing love.

When Allen tried rewriting one of those early childhood memories, he came up with the following:

> I disobeyed my dad and went down to my friend's house on my bike without permission. He punished me harder than he needed to, but he did it out of love for me.

Allen's progress through the A-B-Cs of truth therapy didn't happen in one or two sessions. Thinking patterns that are ingrained from years of habit are never broken easily. Allen will always struggle with the temptation to go back to his old driver/controller ways, but now he has tools and strategies not only to change his self-talk but to change his way of acting and communicating.

You can do the same, particularly if you wrestle with a self-defeating behavior that makes life difficult or unpleasant. Why not go back to the memories you put down in chapter 3 and try running them through the entire A-B-C truth therapy process? Then try rewriting them (see Appendix 1) from a more rational adult perspective. As you change your perception of your memories and permanently change behavior that has been defeating you, you can know the sweet smell of victory.

## Worth Remembering . . .

The "secret" of permanent change
is in your perceptions of your memories.
What you have remembered
from childhood does not have
to be reality for you today.
You can rewrite those memories
and conquer self-defeating behavior.

# Chapter 9

*Learning his parents' childhood memories helped Randy see that parents struggle with the same concerns—expectations, fears, disappointments—their children do.*

# Can You Let Mom
# and Dad
# Off the Hook?

A ctress Patty Duke has childhood memories filled with anger and
alcohol. She recalls her hard-drinking father as a man with pure
white hair, whose handsome Irish face featured blue but bloodshot
eyes and veins that stuck out from drinking too much. Sometimes he
took Patty with him to the tavern, and one of her earliest memories is of
standing on the bar and reciting "The Night Before Christmas," no matter what time of year it was.

She clearly remembers the smell of booze and knowing intuitively
it meant trouble. One part of her wanted Dad there, and the other part
didn't. When he was around, he drank, and when he drank, there was
always trouble. Every Christmas, for example, her father would get angry, get into an argument, and throw the Christmas tree right out the
window into the street.

Patty Duke's revealing autobiography relates a series of personal
struggles including the legacy of an addictive personality. She admits to
drinking too much coffee, smoking too many cigarettes, and going
through periods of drinking heavily, at home or at parties, but never at
work. She realized that when she drank, her personality could easily
become disruptive or destructive.

Her memories are a mixture of loving and admiring her father and
hating his drinking and what it did to all of them. She writes:

Sitting on his lap in the summer while he watched the ball game and drank beer . . . I remember a strong, strong attraction, almost a physical need to be close to him when he was there, and a longing when he was gone. . . .

I have just a few pictures of Dad . . . when I look at those pictures . . . when I talk about him, I still feel the sadness; tears are always very close. And it makes me mad, too; I wonder how long this process has to take.[1]

## Parents Need Understanding, Not Bashing

In recent years, a lot of books and films have contributed to making parent bashing a popular sport. The rules are simple: if you can blame good old Mom or Dad for your emotional and relational ills, you win—supposedly. The assumption says, "Get the anger off your chest and put the blame on those unthoughtful parents of yours. Then you'll feel better."

Patty Duke's memories of her father don't carry the bitter sting of parent bashing, but she does struggle with coming to terms with what his drinking did to her life. In her own words, "How long does the process have to take?"

Our answer is, as long as it takes to change your perceptions of early memories that are painful and discouraging; as long as it takes to understand and forgive. You do not forget, but forgiveness can take the sting out of your painful memories.

If your early childhood memories have left you carrying a big pail of garbage or even a small pocket of resentment, this chapter is dedicated to you. We want to offer you practical steps to letting go of the past so that you can get on with your future.

## Hitler Couldn't Let It Go—But You Can

Adolf Hitler's father was an extremely harsh and violent man. Whippings and verbal abuse were a common experience in the Hitler household. Beating after beating finally brought Adolf to a life-molding decision: he would become hardened against pain and suffering. That decision made a profound impact on the entire world. Later in life, he told his secretary:

I then resolved never again to cry when my father whipped me. A few days later I had the opportunity of putting my will to the test. My mother, frightened, took refuge in front of the door. As for me, I counted silently the blows of the stick which lashed my rear end.[2]

Adolf Hitler carried his unresolved anger toward his father into a life of politics and power, and it finally led to the horror of the Holocaust. His life is an example of the ultimate tragedy that occurs when someone cannot let go of his past. We have shared the early memories of many people in this book. Some of them still harbor anger toward a parent or stepparent who was neglectful or abusive or left some other scar on their lives. They are trapped in bondage to people who, in many cases, are dead.

Perhaps you are trapped in this way, or you may know someone who is trapped. Many clients typically say: "Forgive my parents? After what they did to me? Why should I?"

Our answer is, "Why shouldn't you?" Carrying the hurts and grudges of your childhood memories is exhausting, nonproductive and self-defeating. Instead of continuing to struggle with this unnecessary burden, you can get rid of it by releasing those who have hurt you from your debt. You have the tools to do it. We gave them to you in the last three chapters, especially chapter 8, which talks about changing your perceptions of the past, including memories of your parents' mistakes.

## Sam Had a Lot To Be Bitter About

When Sam came in to see Randy, he was dragging a heavy bundle of pain and regrets. His father had been an alcoholic, and when he was drunk, he regularly beat Sam's mother and occasionally Sam and his little sister.

When Sam was nine, he lost both parents. His mother was killed in a car accident, and his father died of liver cancer. Through deep sobs of pain, Sam told Randy, "I never had a day of peace when my dad was alive, and I have never had a day of security after he died. There is so much I'd like to redo in my life." As Sam told his story, his comment about wanting to redo things made sense. His life had been a series of frustrations and failures:

- Three marriages
- Rebellious runaway teenage children
- Time spent in and out of alcohol rehabilitation programs
- Three jobs lost in one year

And now the final blow had come. At age fifty-seven, he had fallen victim to cancer. His future wasn't sure, his past was a mess, and he felt trapped with nowhere to turn.

Sam's early childhood memories reflected a confused emotional state and vivid images of a damaged life theme:

> My father was very mean to me and my sister. I recall one Saturday night that he came home from the bar about 2:00 A.M. I could hear him and my mother fighting and yelling. I heard some hitting and then a knock against the wall, then silence. My father had knocked my mother unconscious. He got scared and called an ambulance, and they took her to the hospital. I was afraid that she had died and that I would never see her again.

> I was always scared to death of my father. I remember the day that I disagreed with him about some stupid thing. I'm not even sure what it was anymore. All I can recall was being pushed into my bedroom, beaten, and then locked in my closet for what seemed to be a couple of hours. I was scared that he might come back and beat me some more if I yelled for help, so I just sat there and cried until he unlocked the door and let me out.

Sam is a tragic example of how a person's life can be twisted by parental ignorance and selfishness. As an adult, Sam was stuck and in need of help. Randy shared with him the steps of truth therapy, especially rewriting the past in the light of new thinking and a changed perspective.

"Tell me something about your father's background," said Randy. "What was his childhood like?"

"Well, he grew up in a poor family down in Mississippi. His father died when he was only five, and his mother remarried when my father was about ten. My father used to say that his stepfather would whip him and put him down all the time. My father didn't have much good to say about his own childhood."

"So your father didn't get a very good start in life either?"

"I guess he didn't."

"In fact, it sounds as though he only repeated on you what he learned from his own stepdad."

"I suppose you're right, but what does that have to do with me?"

"It's perspective, Sam; I want you to put your childhood and all the bad things that happened to you in perspective. I want you to try to humanize your parents—make them real people with real problems. Free them from being only a series of childhood memories and bad feelings."

At the end of that session, Randy gave Sam some "homework." He was to spend the coming week thinking about and recording some of the real life battles and problems his parents had faced. Sam returned to his next appointment with the following:

1. My father had only an eighth-grade education, which kept the good jobs out of his reach.
2. He became an alcoholic by the time he was fifteen.
3. My mother went only through the third grade and never could read or write well.
4. My mother had a deep faith in God, but my father would never let her go to church.
5. When my father wasn't drinking, he really wasn't too bad of a guy to me and my sister.
6. Every time my parents seemed to get ahead financially, something would come along and shove them back, like the Depression.
7. They both had things they wanted to accomplish in life—like travel to California, pay off the mortgage on the house, and buy a car—but they never were able to do any of those things.

Through this simple process, Sam was able to move his parents from the category of abusive failures to being fellow strugglers, real people with real problems. It didn't excuse their behavior, but it did help Sam. He revised his childhood memories of his parents' mistakes by looking at them with the perceptions of a fifty-year-old adult. His mother and father were no longer locked into the perceptions of a small boy who had lived with fear, anger, abuse, and neglect.

With new perceptions of how his parents struggled with their own weaknesses, shortcomings, and problems, Sam was able to move on to the next important step: forgiveness. Randy said: "Sam, you will always be stuck in that pit of anger and self-pity until you learn to forgive—your parents for their failures, your ex-wives for their insensitivities, your children for their rebellion, and yourself for your imperfections. My advice is to let go of all of it, or its stranglehold will eventually kill you."

First, Sam cut the emotional ties that held him tightly attached to the pain and hurt of his past. Randy had him write out the following statements and then repeat them aloud:

- I release you (my parents) from the responsibility I gave to you long ago to determine how I feel and respond to life.
- I release you from the anger I have felt because of our past relationship.
- I release you from being responsible for my happiness.

Randy also suggested that Sam release his parents spiritually by saying a simple prayer: "God, I put my parents back in your hands. I can't handle the pain any more, so I give them back to You. They were Yours in the first place."

We always encourage clients to exercise their spiritual faith as a part of the forgiveness process. Whenever we mention the spiritual aspect of life, there are clients who respond, "You mean religion?" We try to clarify by saying, "Not religion—your faith in God."

We find that few people have a problem dealing with the physical self or the emotional self. But when the spiritual self is mentioned, questions can arise. In our counseling practices, however, we both view humankind as physical, emotional, and spiritual beings. All three of these areas must come together if anyone wants to deal successfully with the problem of forgiveness.

Randy asked Sam to take one final step in the process of letting his parents off the hook: "It's time to rewrite some of those early childhood memories and use your healthier, more productive perception. How would you describe those memories now that you've forgiven your parents?"

Sam took pencil and paper and rewrote the memory of being beaten and locked in that closet:

> My father was very mean to me when he beat me and locked me in the closet for a long time. But now I understand his frustrations and how alcohol had him in its grip. I feel sorry for him and forgive him for how he treated me.*

## The Key to Letting Go Is Acceptance

Suppose your past was the pits, like Sam's. Your parents may have seemed to do all they could to discourage and put you down. What are you going to do about it? You have three choices:

1. Keep swinging at thin air by carrying the grudges, the pain, and the hurts.
2. Gripe about your past and those who were part of it. Keep opening your own wounds and those of others.
3. Accept your past for what it was and move on.

Oprah Winfrey, America's leading talk show hostess, is an outstanding example of taking step number three. On television, Oprah is poised, outgoing, and totally in control. From watching her each day, one might think she had a positive, encouraging childhood, that perhaps life had been handed to her on a silver platter. But according to a biography written about her, her early years were spent being bounced between ever-feuding parents and being farmed out to a grandmother who often beat her. She says: "When my grandmother used to whip my behind, she'd say, 'I'm doing this because I love you.' And I'd want to say, 'If you loved me, you'd get that switch off my butt.' I still don't think that was love."[3]

At age nine, Oprah was raped by a nineteen-year-old cousin and recalls her false—but very real—fears that she might be pregnant: "That for me was the terror: Was I going to have it, how would I hide it, all the people would be mad at me, how could I keep it in my room without my mother knowing?"[4]

---

*If you wish to try this same process, see Appendix 2.

With childhood memories like those, Oprah Winfrey had reason to be angry and stay angry. She could have chosen to let anger eat her alive and ruin her life. Rather, she chose to accept her past for what it was and those in it for what they were and go on. She saw the folly in being angry with people because it always hurts you more than it hurts them. Instead, she chose to accept responsibility, not for what happened, *but for overcoming what happened to her.* She observes:

> I understand that many people are victimized, and some people certainly more horribly than I have been. But you have to be responsible for claiming your own victories, you really do. If you live in the past and allow the past to define who you are, then you never grow.[5]

## Rebuild Bridges if You Can

The ideal way to let Mom and Dad off the hook is to rebuild relationships with them in person, if possible. In some cases, like Sam's, this was impossible because his parents had died. In other situations, however, parents may still be alive, but it may not be the better part of wisdom to try to contact them right now. Only you can be the judge of that, but if there is any possibility or inclination on your part to make contact, we strongly recommend that you do so. There is nothing like looking a parent in the eye and establishing forgiveness and new lines of communication. It not only frees you, but it frees them as well, usually from feelings of guilt about all the mistakes they made in bringing you up.

There are several keys to rebuilding relationship bridges between you and your parents. You may need to lay a better foundation by reminding them that you are now an adult and would like to establish a *new* relationship built on mutual respect and friendship. You are no longer their little child and you may need to gently remind them of that truth.

You can approach your parents by letter or phone call, but the best way is a personal visit. Plan your contact carefully. Stay positive and *refuse* to get into any arguments or fights with them. Quietly and firmly tell them how you feel. If your first attempt doesn't go perfectly, don't be discouraged. At least you have made a start, and you can try again when the opportunity presents itself.

### Try Swapping Memories with Mom and Dad

Along with establishing new ground rules for a relationship, you will want to establish new patterns of communication. Patterns you learned as a child need to be changed. In most homes, the children are talked down to. Very often, this habit is carried on after the children become adults themselves.

One good way to get on the same communication level with your parents is to ask them about their childhood memories. As they start recalling their experiences, you can gain insights you never had before. For example, the idea for this book came as a result of a stimulating discussion between Randy and his mother and father. As his parents shared their early childhood memories, they became so fascinated with the topic and what they learned about one another that his mother commented that a book should be written to help other people understand the value of early childhood memories.

The most valuable part of that evening, however, was helping Randy put flesh and blood on the two people who had been "bigger than life" for him. He learned a great deal about his mother, his dad, and himself through a casual discussion of early memories. He saw in a new and different light that parents have problems, too, and that they struggle with the same kinds of concerns as do their children: fear, pain, expectations, frustrations, and disappointments.

## "It's Just Another Broken Doll"

The earliest childhood memory of Randy's mother is a vivid example of the Law of Creative Consistency. The event she recalls from her early childhood is absolutely consistent with the view of life she has had throughout her adult years. She was born the youngest in a family of seven children and grew up during dark Depression days. Her family had necessities like food and a warm house, but they had very little else. Clothes were make-overs, and new shoes were a real event.

Christmas was also a special event even though each child received only one modest gift. Somehow, throughout the year, her parents scrimped to put aside pennies, nickels, and dimes so that each child could have something for Christmas. When Randy's mother was only six, she saw a china doll in a shop window a few weeks before Christmas and started dreaming about how wonderful it would be if she could only have that doll. Of course, only rich little girls had such dolls, so she thought all she could do was dream.

Christmas Eve came, the traditional time for the family to open gifts. There were the boxes under the tree, carefully wrapped with last year's paper. Randy's mother opened hers, carefully removing the ribbon and paper so that it could be used again. She peeked into the box and there was the china doll from the shop window! Her dream had come true, and she experienced what she still believes was the greatest joy of her childhood. But her greatest joy led to her most vivid childhood memory, which she recalls like this:

> The doll was beautiful and I loved her so. I could hardly take her out of the box for fear something would happen to her. Often I would carry the doll around in the box, not wanting her to get soiled or have her hair get tangled. I kept the china doll in the box on a shelf, safe from any harm—or so I thought. One day as I reached to take the box down, somehow I dropped it and my beautiful doll shattered into what seemed a thousand pieces. It was the saddest day of my life. I cried for days, and the loss seemed so great I just knew life would never be the same again.

They say time heals all wounds, but not necessarily. Through the years there were other dolls, even prettier and more elegant, but still locked away in her memories was that first china doll beneath the Christmas tree. Randy's mother wrote a poem about the doll, the last stanza of which says it all:

> My shattered dreams are broken dolls
> As years have passed away;
> Locked within my memory chest
> Is my china doll today.

Randy's mother grew up to be a blend of victim and pleaser who became used to disappointments and losses. Whenever she faced any kind of disappointment, she would refer to it as "just another broken doll."

But instead of being a bitter, disillusioned woman, Randy's mother has used the broken dolls in her life to make her sensitive to the needs and hurts of others. Throughout her life she has helped others with their broken doll experiences, joining with her husband to establish nonprofit facilities in Michigan and Arizona that are dedicated to helping disadvantaged children with their physical, emotional, and spiritual needs.

While that memory of the tragedy of her first china doll became an integral part of her lifestyle, she didn't let it overpower her. Raised in a rock-solid, church-going family, she has always stood on the truth of the Scriptures no matter how she felt. Her spiritual faith and values have helped her stand fast, even when those victim voices whisper, "It's just another broken doll." She has literally overcome her basic victim lifestyle by placing faith in what her Bible says. While the grain of her wood often nudges her toward bitterness, her faith helps her choose to be positive, patient, and compassionate.

What does all this tell Randy about himself? It gives him a much better insight into the family atmosphere in which he grew up. Without question, he took after his mother in many ways, becoming a victim and a pleaser himself.

## Test Your Memories on Other Family Members

For a slightly different approach to communicating with your parents, try comparing childhood memories when your whole family is present, particularly any of your brothers and sisters.

Janice came to Randy for counseling because of a lifelong conflict with her mother. Mother-daughter disagreements are nothing new, but Janice, deeply disturbed by her inability to get along with her mother, wanted some help. Randy suggested having the whole family come in and discuss some of Janice's childhood memories together. Early in the session, Janice shared a memory with her mother and father and Bob, her brother, who also took part. Janice said, "I remember the day that Mother wouldn't let me go with my friends on a big beach trip that I had been looking forward to all summer. I was getting ready in my room and Mom came in and simply announced that I couldn't go with them. She never did tell me why and I was really mad at her for that."

"I don't recall it that way, Janice," her mother interjected. "As I remember the incident, you and Bob were playing in the back yard when

I came out and simply reminded you that if you weren't ready to go in ten minutes, you would miss the bus that was taking your group to the beach. You didn't get ready in time, and the bus left. But I didn't make you stay home that day."

"Do you remember that particular situation, Bob?" asked Randy.

Bob thought for a few seconds and then replied, "Yes, I do because I really wanted to go on that beach trip also. But I think Mom is right. I recall that she came out in the back yard and reminded us that we'd miss the bus if we didn't get ready soon. I missed it, too, and I couldn't go either."

Janice gave Bob a dark look, but didn't say anything. Randy continued guiding the discussion, hoping nobody would stomp out. This was a critical time for Janice because she was learning the importance of dealing with the present by deflating her past.

As Janice shared other childhood memories with her family, she was in for more surprises. She quickly learned that no two family members recalled an event in the same way or with the same intensity. In that single session, she gained a new perspective on her family—especially her mother—and got some insights on her present life theme, which centered on being a victim.

You can try this same exercise without the aid of a counselor (although you do need to realize that it won't work if you have people in the family who are really at odds with each other—or ready to go at each other's throats). One possibility is to bring up some early childhood memories while you're having Thanksgiving dinner, or some other get-together for a special occasion.

A modified approach would be to get together with a brother or sister or as many siblings as possible and recall some early memories that all of you might have. You will need to do a little explaining about how memory exploration works, and you can use some of the examples in this book to illustrate the entire concept. Then go around the circle and have each person share an early childhood memory and have everyone compare notes.

If you keep talking long enough, you will probably uncover important pieces of information that will give you insight as to how you fit into your family and how the family perceives you. We caution you again, however, to be sure not to try this if you have people who strongly disagree or just plain don't like each other. Some of the ground rules for sharing memories as a family include: no criticizing, no accusations, no yelling, no put-downs, no walking out, no sharing what is said beyond the family circle.

## Forgive—But Remember

The steps suggested in this chapter need to be taken carefully and gently. Always set the primary goal of being friends with your parents if at all possible. Maintaining a friendship is not like maintaining a car or some other piece of machinery. There are always feelings involved—and perceptions. Keep your parents in a proper perspective by giving them the time, the respect, and the honor they deserve. Strive for flexibility and openness, and always be ready to forgive.

Counselors, therapists, pastors, and others in the helping professions disagree on the old cliché, "Forgive and forget." Some believe this is possible while others say you can forgive but you can never forget. We agree that it is possible to forgive, but once something is in your memory, you do not forget it. It may fade, but it can return at any time.

We also want to suggest that it isn't wise to forget, especially the small victories or tiny steps of progress you have made to take responsibility and let other people off the hook of your blame for what has happened. It's like hitting a great golf shot off the tee and getting out to where your ball landed, looking back and saying, "My goodness, did I hit the ball *that far?*"

So forgive. Let Mom and Dad off the hook, and you will let yourself off the hook as well. And then remember. Sometimes you have to look back to realize how far you've come!

### Worth Remembering . . .

Rewrite bad memories of your parents'
mistakes by using your adult perceptions,
not the hurt feelings of the little child
who is still part of you.
Keeping your parents on the hook
of your blame and bitterness
will gain you nothing.
Forgiving them will gain
you everything.

# PART FOUR

## Where Memories Count Most

# Chapter *10*

*Kevin and Sande prove that opposites do attract. Baby Cub marries Mama Bear.*

# You Date the Adult,
# You Marry the Child

Picture the scene. The handsome prince from the office is on the phone saying, "Listen, I've been wondering . . . would you like to go out to dinner? I'd love to take you to dinner. . . ."

"Why, that would be wonderful," she replies. "But first, may I ask you something?"

"Of course . . . just name it."

"What are your three earliest childhood memories? What can you remember back before you were, say, eight years old?"

At this point, handsome prince may be thinking, "Am I on 'Candid Camera'?" He could easily remember he has an appointment and that he'll call back later—much later.

It's not likely that many women would actually try our crazy idea, but we toss it out at this point for a very good reason. As the chapter title suggests, you date the adult, who is always on best white-knight behavior, but you marry the child, who not only has frogs in his pocket—he may *be* a frog! Our marriage counseling files are loaded with cases of couples who met, fell in love, and got married with high expectations that came tumbling down fast, sometimes even before she had to carry the luggage over the motel threshold.

If nothing else, playing "Let's share early childhood memories"

147

can reveal everyone's expectations. If there is anything that leads to marital strife, it is each person's expectations of what marriage will supposedly be like.

## Wanted:  One Perfect Wife

Following one of our "Today's Family" radio broadcasts, we received a letter from a listener who obviously perceived himself as an "eligible bachelor." He had some definite ideas on what was right and best, particularly in a wife, and he wrote:

> I hope someday to find a good loyal woman to be my wife and to be a kind loving mother to any kids we may have by each other! The woman who becomes my wife must be able to meet the following qualifications:
>
> 1. Must marry for real romance, not just for companionship.
> 2. Must love children.
> 3. Must need me.
> 4. Must care about people, especially people who are hurting.
> 5. Must be further along spiritually than I am.
> 6. Must be able and willing to listen carefully.
> 7. Must have a deep sense of humor so we can laugh a lot.
> 8. Must put God first, me second.
> 9. Must generate true romance (SPARKS).
> 10. Must be an understanding and gentle woman.
> 11. Must love to read.
> 12. Must love poetry.
> 13. Must love to sing.
> 14. Must love horses.
> 15. Must love hockey and baseball.
> 16. Must love roller skating and ice skating and fishing.
>
> Above are the qualifications I require in the woman who becomes my wife!

Now there's a man who knows what he wants! We don't want to go out on a limb here, but we predict he may be looking for a while. And if he ever does find his dream woman and gets married, we wonder what will happen when he discovers his bride doesn't love hockey, fishing, or horseback riding as much as he expected.

We couldn't probe this controller-bachelor's memories, because it turned out that beside his name was a number—he was spending time in a prison. As you read his letter, it's not hard to spot a controller type of lifestyle—someone who knows what he wants and how other people should shape up to match his expectations. Apparently his expectations got out of control, and he wound up behind prison walls.

To our convict friend's credit, at least he was willing to spell out his expectations rather completely. But most people date, fall in love, and get married without doing so. Let's go back to our original suggestion of asking for childhood memories before you ever go on that first date. Suppose the guy who asked the girl for a dinner date answered her question and shared memories about good times with his parents, especially Mom. That would definitely be a green light to go ahead and have dinner because chances are this fellow might have a much better concept of how to treat a woman (note that we said "might"—there are never any guarantees).

But suppose his memories were full of disasters and embarrassments. Then the yellow caution light might be in order. Chances are good you might have found a victim who is looking for a mother.

And if his memories all centered on how he battled to control life and other people, starting with his parents, watch out. The light has definitely turned red. That doesn't always mean that he'll wind up walking all over you, but the signs are not encouraging. If you do decide to go out with him, note if he is quick to get irritated or angry. Does he always have to win? Does he always have to be right? All of these are more red lights that signal trouble.

## How Those Walls Can Go Up

Of course, few people will ever take our suggestions. Instead, they go ahead and get married and then work it all out later. And that's how the walls often go up.

Marriage is supposed to be a joyous experience, a life of discovering and sharing. But for many couples, all those hopes and dreams of the wedding day are now a hollow memory. All those plans for sharing and caring have turned into a life of silence and selfishness.

Over the years, walls have steadily risen, stopping healthy communication. Instead of growing together, you are growing apart. The barriers seem insurmountable. The following poem vividly describes the destructive despair on each side of this barricade.

# WALLS

Their wedding picture mocked them from the table,
　　these two
　　　whose minds no longer touched each other.
They lived with such a heavy barricade between them that
　　neither battering ram of words nor artilleries of touch
　　could break it down.
Somewhere, between the oldest child's first tooth and the
　　youngest daughter's graduation, they lost each other.
Throughout the years, each slowly unraveled that
　　tangled ball
　　　of string called self, and as they tugged at stubborn
　　knots each hid his searching from the other.
Sometimes she cried at night and begged the
　　whispering darkness
　　　to tell her who she was.
He lay beside her, snoring like a hibernating bear, unaware
　　of her winter.
Once, after they had made love he wanted to tell her how
　　afraid he was of dying, but fearing to show his naked
　　soul, he spoke instead about the beauty of her breasts.
She took a course in modern art, trying to find herself in
　　colors splashed upon a canvas, and complaining to other
　　women about men who were insensitive.
He climbed a tomb called "the office," wrapped his mind in
　　a shroud of paper figures and buried himself
　　in customers.
Slowly, the wall between them rose, cemented by
　　the mortar
　　　of indifference.
One day, reaching out to touch each other, they found
　　a barrier
　　　they could not penetrate, and recoiling from the coldness
　　of the stone, each retreated from the stranger on the
　　other side.

> For when love dies, it is not in a moment of angry battle,
>     nor when fiery bodies lose their heat.
> It lies panting, exhausted, expiring at the bottom of a wall it
>     could not scale.[1]

## Some Walls Loom Large and Thick

"Walls" totally captures the pain of some couples we deal with in counseling. Their marriage lies gasping at the foot of a parapet that seems to rise high into storm clouds of hopelessness.

It was that way for Jessica, who had eating problems that would make Oprah Winfrey (before diet) look like a canary. You may remember the fall day in 1988 when Oprah devoted her talk show to sharing the secret of how she lost sixty-seven pounds and got into a pair of size ten Calvin Klein jeans. But on Jessica, sixty pounds was pocket flab. Her husband, she said, described her as a beached whale.

Jessica's self-esteem was in shambles for obvious reasons. Her early childhood memories revealed a critical father who battered her self-image daily. Nothing she could do was ever good enough, and she began finding comfort in food when she was very young. About the only positive childhood memory she could recall was getting a new plaid dress on her tenth birthday and feeling grown up and beautiful, even though she was already quite a bit overweight.

As is often the case, Jessica went on to marry a flaw-picker. Michael was a patent attorney who took up where Daddy left off. She tried her best to please him, but to no avail. Before she ballooned totally out of control, she used to bowl and was very good at it. One night, she bowled 299 for her league team, and what did Michael say? "How could you miss that ten pin? You could have had a 300 game!"

It got so bad that Jessica moved out of the house for a while. During those three months of living alone in her own apartment, she decided she would no longer try to lose weight for her husband who would only take cheap shots at her anyway. She would begin to enjoy life as best she could.

In therapy, her constant life theme was, "I'm not any good, anyway," and variations on that theme.

"Look," Kevin told her, "there's no question life has kicked you squarely in the teeth, but the question is, what are you going to do about this? How are you going to change?"

It wasn't hard to help Jessica identify her lifestyle. She was a blend of pleaser and martyr, who would do anything for the approval of the men in her life. As a child, she literally brought her father his slippers at night. As a wife, she put her flaw-picking husband through law school. As mother of four boys, she worked tirelessly to give them a good home.

But all of them—daddy, hubby, even her sons—had kicked her in the teeth. One Mother's Day, two of her boys didn't even bother to give her a card, a small thing to some Moms who just laugh it off, but not to her. She was crushed. And when life crushed her, she fought back the only way she knew how—by heading for the refrigerator.

Moving out of the house was a turning point. She recognized that her husband had always needed somebody to wipe his feet on, and she had served that need perfectly. As she sorted it out, she was able to start losing some weight, not for her husband, as she had always tried to do before, but for herself. She lost fifty pounds, which didn't even get her close to a size ten, but it was a start.

She moved back home where her husband started treating her a little better (having to be Mr. Mom for three months sort of got his attention). The last time Kevin saw them, she was still struggling, but the struggling was based on the truth, not the lies she had been feeding herself since she was a little girl.

## Some Walls Are under Construction

For other couples, their walls are not as high, but they are going up fast. A wife who is starving for communication drags her husband to Kevin for counseling. Hubby "can't understand what's bothering her," but it doesn't take long to find out.

He is an only child and one of his finest memories is of being eight years old and going fishing, accompanied only by his dog. He opens his lunch and there is his favorite—a peanut butter and jelly sandwich, with a big orange. No Zingers or Twinkies for dessert, though. His mom is always after him to eat healthy. As he takes a bite of his sandwich, he feels the pleasant solitude all around him. He is alone and life is very good.

What does this Norman Rockwell scene have to do with an unhappy marriage twenty-five years later? It turns out the husband is a computer whiz, living with a wife who works and two children who spend the day with a sitter. But solving computer mysteries all day long isn't enough. Every night after dinner Mom has to catch up on parenting their attention-starved kids while Dad heads for the den, which contains his personal Apple 2000. And there he checks out for the evening. Only sixteen feet from his wife and children, he might as well be sixteen hundred miles away.

All evening long, he plays with his computer, and his actions at age thirty-three are consistently in line with his memories from age eight. He was good at amusing himself then, and he is still good at it because it satisfies his need for control in his life. He has always told himself, "You need to be in charge, and the best way to be in charge is to do it alone." That theme served him well until he got married, but now it is causing him all kinds of grief.

Gently but firmly Kevin explained the facts of life with a wife and kids. "Gary, you're married, and you've got two children. Betty works full time. What gives you the right to check out at 6:45 in the evening and not be seen again?"

Fortunately, Gary got the message. His computer-oriented mind clicked in and he started helping more—with the dishes, with the kids, and even trying to talk to his communication-starved wife.

## Marriage Includes Four, Not Two

What every married couple needs to understand is that those walls of indifference are always ready to form. Those lies each spouse brings to the marriage guarantee it. We don't mean lies you tell each other (that's a different problem). We're talking about the self-defeating lies you have been telling yourselves all your lives. Believing those lies leads to behavior that your spouse can't understand—or accept, and then the walls start to go up.

Can sharing childhood memories with each other help? Absolutely. If you know something about your spouse's childhood memories and vice versa, you have one leg up on better communication and better understanding of each other. As Hugh Missildine points out in his best-selling book, *Your Inner Child of the Past,* a marriage means that four, not two, persons must "adjust to one another." Each of you brings your adult self to the marriage, and each brings that "inner child." As we already mentioned, you marry the child as well as the charming, mature adult who was on best behavior while you were dating.[2]

## Use Memories To Enrich Your Marriage

While we both use memory exploration as a counseling tool, Randy takes it a step further into his weekend marriage seminars. Across the country, he teaches couples the value of sharing early childhood memories with each other to gain better understanding and communication. First he asks for a volunteer couple from the audience. After the husband and wife share their childhood memories, the rest of the group helps uncover the secrets found in those memories.

In one seminar, Karen and Joe volunteered to share memories, and Karen led off by recalling the first time—in first grade—when she got a quarter for every A on her report card. She clearly remembered how proud she was when she handed the card to her parents and how surprised and pleased she was when they gave her the money. The "quarters for As" practice became a tradition her parents continued all through her school years.

"What I learned from that," said Karen, "was that if I was good, everyone in my life was glad." Plainly, Karen had become a confirmed pleaser while still a young child. It wasn't surprising that Karen admitted that she was an "overjoiner," always spreading herself too thin by volunteering for too many organizations and duties.

This was an important clue to be matched against Joe's childhood memory, which happened when he was five or six. He remembers being locked out of his bedroom—probably by an older brother or sister—and kicking at the door to get in. He finally kicked a hole right through it and got bawled out by his mother for doing all the damage. His key feeling was one of unfairness. After all, it was his room. What right did anyone have to lock him out, and why was Mom getting so upset?

It didn't take much for the seminar audience to analyze Karen and Joe. She was a pleaser who had a hard time saying no and who found her self-esteem in volunteering and helping other people. But she was doing it for the wrong reasons. She volunteered to make people like her. Her life theme said, "If I make people like me, everyone will be happy, and I will feel worthwhile."

And what lie was Joe telling himself? He admitted that when Karen volunteered for anything, he would often wind up saying, "I want my wife back." There he was, wanting to get into his own room again. And when Karen went out to do her volunteer work, he often pouted and wound up going bowling or doing something else with his buddies. His life theme said, "When you're treated unfairly, don't take it lying down."

With these two memories and the insight they provided, Karen and Joe were able to talk about her need to please and inability to say no, and his need for control and ownership, which left him feeling deserted when she volunteered for anything. What they needed was a better understanding about the time involved and how much of her time he would have to give up. When Joe saw Karen "volunteering again," he didn't need to think he was being "locked out of her life." That little video of being locked out of his bedroom was going off in his head, but he didn't have to let it control him. Instead of telling himself the old lie, he could tell himself the truth: "Karen has volunteered again, and she has a right to do what she wants. She's my wife, but I don't own her."

## Some Ways to Use Memory Exploration

You don't need to attend a seminar to explore memories together. Just go out to dinner sometime, or sit down after dinner and start to share. It's amazing what you can find out about one another that you never knew before. People often tell us, "I learned more about my spouse in a few minutes of memory sharing than I had learned during our entire marriage."

To get the most from sharing memories together, we suggest three basic steps:

1. Discover each other's "life theme." Each of you should try to identify three early memories and the basic feeling you attached to the clearest part (freeze frame) of each memory. From this, try to come up with your life themes—your personal and private views of life.

2. Understand how your life themes may conflict with one another. When you have a life theme for each of you, see what these themes say about the battlefield where you habitually cross swords: money, the children, in-laws, personal insecurities, sexual difficulties, friends, religious beliefs, work, and any number of others. Every marriage has at least one point of potential conflict, and usually several.

These conflicts are inevitable because they result from two unique individuals with two unique life themes joining together and telling each other, "Meet my needs!"

3. Understand how your life themes can complement each other. Memory exploration is a great way to make your spouse a "special study." The better you know each other, the better you can communicate and gain a new level of understanding, compassion, and tolerance.*

The most important point above is number three. In our opinion, too many relationship books suggest "dumping the chump" if he doesn't change. This is terrible advice for two basic reasons: you can't change anyone but yourself; and "dumping the chump" to find somebody else often simply repeats the same old tired cycle.

Whatever happened to accepting each other for what you are— differences, warts, quirks, and all? This is a simple thought that has been around for thousands of years in forms like the Golden Rule and the biblical admonition to "love one another." Nonetheless, it seems like a revolutionary idea to many of our clients: "What do you mean accept him the way *he* is? . . . You've got to be kidding! Accept *her* when she acts *that* way? No way!"

But if you get anything out of this book, don't forget the grain of the wood. Your grain, as well as your mate's grain, is firmly set, which suggests the well-known prayer often quoted by members of Alcoholics Anonymous: "Lord, grant me the serenity to accept the things I cannot change, the courage to change the things that I can, and the wisdom to know the difference." That's a prayer we both use often because our marriages are no different from yours. We also have to work with our wives as we deal with different lifestyles, different expectations, and different personalities.

## At Home with the Lemans

In Kevin and Sande's marriage, opposites did attract. As spoiled Baby Cub of his family, Kevin got used to taking advantage, putting people in his service, and getting special treatment. Kevin recalls how it drove his older brother, Jack, crazy to see him riding that new Roadmas-

*For more complete information on how to cover these three steps with your spouse, see Appendix 3.

ter bike he got for his birthday. No other Leman kid ever had a new bike. Sally and Jack had to settle for walking or something secondhand. And what really burned Jack up was to watch Kevin ride that new Roadmaster up on the driveway, hop off, and let the bike coast on by itself for another twenty feet before it crashed in a heap.

With his record of childhood memories, Kevin was hardly someone he'd recommend today as a good bet for marriage. Except for a couple of important factors. First, his mother and his older sister, Sally, taught him a great deal about women. Kevin remembers being eleven or twelve and hearing Sally say, "This is what girls like, or don't like, about boys." He would shrug and think, "Who cares? I don't like girls anyway." But in just a few short years, he understood the value of her wisdom.

Second, he met and married a woman who is just like his sister. Sande turned out to be just the person he needed to help him get his life squared away and come to terms with the one Authority he could not seem to ignore. Sande's strong faith and trust in a personal God were stablizing factors in helping Kevin make peace with the church upbringing that had turned him off all his life.

That's not to say they don't have their struggles. Sande's early memories clearly picture a tender-hearted pleaser who can be conned rather easily. For example, she remembers the day her parents gave twenty-five cents each to her and her cousin, Denny, who was her same age—six. They went down to the corner store to buy candy bars and Denny fast-talked Sande into paying for both candy bars with her money while he pocketed his.

Sande also has a hard time seeing anyone or anything suffer. Another memory—when she was four—is of her mother cooking lobsters and lifting one out of the boiling pot while it was still wiggling. The feeling she attached to that scene was feeling "so sorry" for the helpless lobster who was being cooked alive.

When they were getting their marriage license, Kevin could not resist having a little fun with his gullible bride-to-be. As they came up to the window, he said, "I know of an old Leman family tradition. The wife always pays for the marriage license."

Sande looked at Kevin for a second and then said, "Oh, how neat!" And she plunked down the five dollars. As they walked down the courthouse steps, Kevin told her, "You've just started a wonderful tradition."

In their first years of marriage, first-born Sande got a little tired of living with a last-born baby. At times, she thought she had simply replaced Kevin's mother. The playful Cub often took advantage of kindhearted Mama Bear who learned about his exotic tastes in food—absolutely *no* lettuce *ever, only* peas and corn for vegetables, and hamburgers *every* night.

Sande also became fed up with her husband's concept of organization. As Kevin dropped his shirt and socks on the floor in little piles, she dutifully followed after him picking them up. This went on until Mama Bear had had enough. One night, Kevin came home and couldn't get in the door because a huge pile of his clothes was blocking it. The Cub wasn't too amused, but his tender-hearted pleaser said: "I'm tired of being your mother. From now on, you hang up your own clothes. And as far as being a short order cook with only three things on the menu, I'm sick of that, too. I'm going to fix what I fix, and you can eat it or go hungry. If you really believe all this child psychology you've been studying, it seems to me you would want to practice it, too!"

The Cub blinked a couple of times, but the message soaked in. It was a turning point in their marriage, which is now in its twenty-second year. Today Kevin picks up his clothes, helps with the kids, and has even learned to eat Hawaiian chicken and most veggies in addition to hamburgers.

Kevin works at not taking advantage of Sande, but at times she still feels she is "the only one who does anything around here." He has to remind her that he is not her fifth child and that he does help—a lot. To make his point, he has worked out the perfect plan. When Sande leaves her coffee cups around the house, particularly in their bedroom, Kevin collects them and walks by her, clinking them softly, but firmly. If she doesn't pay sufficient attention to his little act, he clinks them still louder, which always gets her to respond, especially if some of the cups are her good Norwegian china.

"Okay, okay," she says good-naturedly, "you *do* help. Good man, Leemie. Just don't break my cups!"

## Both Carlsons Are Pleasers

Randy and his wife, Donna, are a good example of reversing the "opposites always attract" syndrome. They are a great deal alike, which poses a different set of problems for their marriage. Like Randy,

Donna is a pleaser, whose early memories include the time she and her younger sister both had chicken pox when they were four and three years old. A lady came to visit Donna's mother, and when she saw both little girls sitting quietly on the couch, she said, "My, look at how good Donna is—so sick, but still being a quiet, good little girl."

Mixed with Donna's desire to please (Randy says she's the type who would throw up and clean it up herself) is a strong need to make a good appearance. Another early memory for her is being five and getting all dressed up in a new frilly pinafore. She came out of the bedroom to show her parents and grandparents, and as she twirled around, she said, "Aren't I a cute little stinker?"

As an adult, Donna still feels appearance is important, not only her own, but those of her family and her home, which has a reputation for being spotless. Donna's life theme is: "Don't upset anyone, never cause problems, and look good doing it." Unlike Randy, she is not a victim, but is more positive and even-tempered, able to roll with life's punches better.

Another area in which they differ is fighting weight. Randy does, but his wife doesn't, never has, and probably never will. Donna is 5'8", weighs 120, and never has carried an extra pound in her life.

Earlier in their marriage, she simply couldn't comprehend why Randy battled the bulge so compulsively. She worried about Randy's health and his lack of energy. She was also not too pleased with his love handles, saying at times, "Hey, Buster, it ain't no fun making love to a fat guy."

Since Randy has taken steps to stop telling himself, "You can eat your way to happiness," no one is happier than Donna. She's his biggest booster and encourager in the battle to lay Fat Butt to rest.

### Is It Okay To Sweat—Just a Little?

Another lie from his past that has affected Randy's marriage is: "Don't let people see you sweat." That memory from age six when his dog Stony got hurt and all he could do was flee to the closet and hide is still fresh in Randy's mind. Over thirty years later, he can still feel the fear that his dog was going to die. But he couldn't let people see him cry. Big six-year-old boys don't cry, and so he tried to hide as best he could.

As he grew up, he continued to hide his emotions. He told himself,

"Don't be vulnerable; don't let people know how you really feel." He knew better, but the grain of the wood is hard to handle for anyone, even a trained counselor. One experience that has helped him confront this lie involved his little daughter, Andrea:

> About a year ago, when Andrea was six, we discovered quite by accident that she was nearly legally blind in one eye. This hit me very hard because, coming from a family of all boys, I had always wanted a daughter, and Andrea was the pride of my life. A routine examination revealed that she had amblyopia or lazy eye. Both eyes were not aligned properly and one had started to shut off because the brain could not deal with conflicting messages. As one eye shut down, the other eye took over, and Andrea wasn't bothered enough by it to say anything to us.
>
> When the doctor discovered the problem, he told us that if he had been aware of it even a few months earlier, he could have done more to restore her sight in the weak eye.
>
> Naturally, my first thought was, "You idiot, you dummy, why didn't you notice the signs?" In retrospect, there were signs of trouble. Andrea was often careless when eating and would drop food or spill. She sat too close to the television set, and the printing on her school papers was sloppy. Why hadn't I asked her about this instead of just correcting her for bad habits?
>
> I was dying inside and I had a choice to make. Did I share my grief with Donna, or did I hide it? Did I try to play the macho role and say everything would be okay, that somehow I would get it all fixed? That is so typical of men, and I was no exception. But Donna could see I was hurting, and I knew that she knew. And so I took a chance, and I shared with her my pain and my agony. And, of course, she didn't think less of me. On the contrary, it was a tremendous release for both of us. Then we could work on the problem together and lean on each other for support.

In this instance, Randy was able to confront a lie he had told himself since childhood and defeat it. It's a lie that many men tell themselves: "Don't be vulnerable in front of your wife. Don't let her see what is really going on inside." And what can this do to a marriage? Many things, and they are all bad. The bottom line is that there is a dehumanizing effect.

You might call it the John and Jane Wayne syndrome. Just tough it out, and whatever you do, don't let Jane see you cry. We see marriages like that all the time. Couples come to our offices, and often the husband tries to act tough and detached. He doesn't understand why he's here, and he dares us to show him anything is really wrong. But inside he is dying. Some husbands finally show cracks in their armor and start trying to communicate, but for many it is difficult. Those childhood memories are hard to cut down to size.

## Using Truth Therapy on Your Marriage

After sharing early memories and identifying each other's life themes, you can take practical steps to improve your relationship. Your memories reveal your weaknesses and needs, but they also say something about the expectations you brought to your marriage. Sometimes two widely different lifestyles can cause tension. And, as Randy and Donna demonstrate, having similar lifestyles doesn't assure smooth sailing.

One exercise we suggest to married couples is to separately list expectations you have of each other. As you describe each of your expectations for your spouse, talk about how you feel when that expectation isn't met. It's a good idea actually to write these out and exchange lists.

Then, while going over your spouse's list of expectations, identify those you can meet most of the time, those you can meet some of the time, and the ones you feel you cannot meet very often, if at all. Ask your spouse why each expectation is important and what kind of compromise you can reach when some expectations can't be met completely.

Another useful exercise is to share the personality strengths each of you brought into the marriage. As Randy worked with a couple named Susan and Herb, they reported that sharing early memories and understanding their respective views of life had been a revelation. Their marriage had been in serious trouble because Susan was a victim desperately needing security and Herb was a driving controller who wanted to live life at full throttle.

Randy's first assignment for Susan and Herb was to spend an evening alone, sharing in detail with each other as many of their early childhood memories as they could recall. Then, from what they knew about memory exploration and how it predicts personality, they made a list of the personality strengths each of them brought into the marriage.

When they returned the following week for their next session, they were greatly encouraged. Herb said, "Sharing our childhood memories was a real help. Now we understand each other's view of life a lot better, and we can even see how we can start using our strengths to help each other and build our marriage."

Almost proudly, they showed Randy their lists of unique strengths and commitments they were willing to make to each other. Susan's included:

> 1. I enjoy taking responsibility, and I am willing to take over the checking account and pay the bills (this had been a sore point in the past).
> 2. I am sensitive to others, and I am willing to be sensitive to Herb's needs when I am aware of them (Herb had complained that Susan had seemed distant and disinterested in his needs and problems).

From Herb's list came these items:

> 1. I'm a hard worker, and I'm willing to provide for my family.
> 2. I like to experience new things, and I am willing to help make Susan feel comfortable in new experiences around new people (Susan had complained of Herb's lack of understanding when she didn't want to go into new situations and meet new groups).

These first steps were only a start for Susan and Herb, but it made the difference in getting their marriage back on track.

Another good way to use early childhood memories is to share how they may have affected your approach to parenting. As you share with your spouse how you gained your view of what parenting is all about, you may get some valuable clues regarding another cause of tension in your marriage. Our case files show that disagreements over how to rear the children are a major cause of tension for many couples. We'll look more closely at parenting traps and what they can do to a family in the next chapter.

# Chapter *11*

*Kevin has early memories of good times with his family. Today he makes time to plant memories his children can savor and pass along to the next generation.*

# Avoiding Those Parent Memory Traps

We want you to meet Vicki, soon to have her first child. At twenty-seven, her life is good. She has a devoted husband, is a member of a loving, supportive church, and has many friends. To look at Vicki you might have trouble believing that just two years ago she entered counseling after:

- Being married and divorced three times
- Having two abortions
- Losing five jobs
- Being hospitalized for drug addiction
- Attempting suicide twice

That's a lot of heavy living, and it began when Vicki was three years old and her stepfather made a relentless attack on her self-esteem and character that lasted until she ran away from home at seventeen. For some reason, probably fear, Vicki's mother never intervened as her husband destroyed a once emotionally happy and healthy child.

When asked to share her early childhood memories, Vicki literally recoiled in a protective reflex response. Those memories were so painful it took several minutes of silent struggling before she was able to speak.

Even twenty years later, Vicki's memories were still vivid pictures of her distorted view of herself and others. She recalled:

> I always had trouble in school. I never could keep up with the other kids. I recall being asked to come up to the chalkboard in third grade to do a math problem. It was multiplication, I think. Well, I made a mistake, and the whole class laughed. I could have died, I was so embarrassed.
>
> My first day of school was awful. I was so embarrassed when my stepfather took me into the class. He was so drunk that he could hardly walk, and it was only 8:30 in the morning.
>
> When I turned six, my mother gave me a birthday party. We were playing a game, Pin the Tail on the Donkey, I think. Well, my stepfather did it again. He didn't think I was doing it right, so he called me a whole bunch of names—stupid, dummy, and vulgar things I really don't want to repeat. He was always putting me down. I hated him.

Vicki's childhood left deep scars on her life. Every area was affected by the destructive memories of those years. As she matured, she fell prey to the traps that await a person trying to run from a past of pain and personal abuse. Because she had no help from her family or any other support system, it was not surprising that she followed a series of trails that led down dead-end streets to divorce, drugs, and on two occasions almost to death.

But then she met her husband, Jim, got into counseling, and underwent an emotional and spiritual renewal that helped her make real progress toward putting her life back together.

During counseling, she learned to change her perception of her memories with truth therapy. She also made slow progress with forgiving her drunken stepfather who had so badly scarred her life by making her childhood a living hell. The Law of Creative Consistency dogged Vicki like a hound on the scent. With her victim/pleaser lifestyle, she believed that to be accepted she had to make everybody happy and never say no. Her life theme told her, "You're no good. . . . You don't deserve a wonderful husband or your friends."

Randy helped Vicki see that the lie in her life theme was being whispered by the little girl she once was, who was still living inside. "But now your rational adult self knows better," Randy told her. "You have to take responsibility for your adult self and keep telling yourself the truth to counter those lies."

As part of her therapy, Randy made it a point to talk about her expected baby and the parent traps that could easily interrupt her journey back to health. When she and Randy explored those early childhood memories, several recurring patterns became obvious, and any of them could threaten to show up in her own parenting unless she remained vigilant. The list included:

*The trap of being too harsh.* Vicki hated how her stepfather treated her. She didn't have a very good opinion of her mother either because she had never lifted a hand or her voice to protect her. Yet Vicki had to realize a hard truth: her mother and stepfather had taught her how to parent. Under stress with her own kids, it would be easy to fall back into the same old unhealthy pattern she had known from childhood.

*The trap of demanding too much—or too little.* Because Vicki's early childhood memories lacked balance, they were full of extremes and overreaction. When she parented her own child, she could easily go either way, becoming very permissive or very authoritarian.

*The trap of discouragement.* Vicki was still struggling with the feeling that she couldn't do much that was right. She struggled with the fear that she would become a bad parent because of her terrible background. After the baby arrived, she was bound to have days when things wouldn't go well. She could easily blame herself, or perhaps others. Either way, discouragements could set in, and with discouragement would come resignation and defeat.

*The trap of all talk and no action.* Yelling and put-downs were the main form of discipline around her house when she was a child. Vicki needed to learn the principles of reality discipline, which is light on words and heavy on healthy action.*

---

*See Appendix 4 for more on reality discipline and how parents can counter the four parenting traps described above.

## Parent Traps Are Everywhere

It was not hard to see why Vicki could have problems parenting her own children, but she has no corner on parent traps. As anyone who has tried parenting knows, the same traps lie in wait for everyone. For example, you don't necessarily have to grow up in an abusive family atmosphere to become authoritarian. All parents can become discouraged, and many parents resort to shouting and empty threats rather than decisive discipline that is fair but swift and firm. When Kevin wrote his first book, he entitled it *Parenthood without Hassles (Well, Almost)* out of empathy for the millions of Moms and Dads who find that parenting comes *with* hassles every day.

In chapter 4 we touched on some familiar family atmospheres that help shape a child's lifestyle and life theme. Two common ones are the authoritarian home where the parents' word is law, and the permissive home where the child's whims and wishes are law and parents dutifully obey.

We counsel a lot of kids from authoritarian homes. Ironically, many of the parents in these homes are regular church attenders doing their best to "train up their children in the way they should go." Unfortunately, they miss or fail to understand the biblical admonition to "not provoke your children to wrath." Their constant criticism and harping, their demand for absolute and unquestioned obedience, and their frequent use of corporal punishment build fear, resentment, and a lack of confidence in their kids.

Please don't get the wrong impression. We're for teaching children obedience and discipline in the home, and that includes a swat on the backside when conditions really warrant it. But those instances are really few and far between. There is a much better way to discipline kids. Rather than depending on threats and punishment to keep children in line, "reality discipline" calls for teaching them to be accountable and responsible.

A constant complaint from kids that we counsel is, "My parents just don't listen to me." This is particularly true in authoritarian homes, which are strong on "shooting first and not even bothering with the question." Authoritarian parents seldom give their children a chance to explain, and their only reason for why they want things done their way is "Because I said so."

This kind of parent often shows up in the memories of adult clients who are now having trouble holding a job, keeping a marriage together, or getting along with the world in general. And even more tragically, they are often rearing their own children just the same way, or in a complete swing of rebellion against their upbringing, they are being permissive. These are typical parenting traps that are all too easy to fall into, especially during the piranha hour—around 5:00 P.M. when you're trying to get dinner on and you have a child hanging on each leg and another one screaming in the jump swing just a few feet away.

## Authoritarians Can Be Overprotective

One of the most subtle authoritarian types of family atmosphere is created by overprotective parents who mean well but completely control and dominate their children with ill-advised "smother love." Their motto is, "We'll do it our way because we know best and we won't let you do anything else!"

Kevin counseled one nine-year-old whose overprotective parents were providing their son with some powerful memory videos. The father regularly brushed his son's teeth for him. He even flossed for the boy!

Getting his teeth brushed was bad enough for Jonathan, but even more frustrating was having dear old Dad get him up in the middle of the night, *every night*, to drain his bladder. Although little Jonathan had never had a bed-wetting problem, he eventually (and predictably) developed one. That's why he ended up in Kevin's office, brought by parents who wanted the psychologist to tell them what was wrong with their son.

Of course there was nothing wrong with Jonathan. It was the family atmosphere his overzealous parents had created. Ironically, these parents, especially the father, were only trying to protect their little Jonathan from end-of-the-world calamities like a toothache or wet sheets. Kevin's unique challenge as their counselor was to help them become "worse" parents. Their extreme parental diligence was almost laughable. But the memories they were creating for Jonathan weren't funny at all. What would these memories tell him when he became a teenager and then an adult? Like many children who grow up in an overprotective atmosphere, Jonathan could tend to:

- Feel helpless, inadequate, or irresponsible

- Demand approval from others to know he's okay
- Constantly attempt to put others in his personal service

When you come out of an overprotective home, you often feel helpless to cope with the world around you. You're hesitant and fearful, and in order to take any risks at all, you need to have clear directions and definitions.

Overprotected children are often insecure and unsure of their ability. They need constant verification of their self-worth. As overprotected children grow older, the source of their needed approval shifts from their parents to their peers. Overprotected children often end up following the crowd and compromising important personal, spiritual, or moral values. That's one answer to why so many kids from "good" homes wind up on drugs.

"Poor me, I can't make it unless I get your help," is a theme song of the overprotected child. Continually asking for help may work while you're a child, but it's a lousy way to live as an adult.

Tom was an overprotected child who thought Christmas was an ongoing holiday. Growing up, he received an endless supply of gifts, treats, and other services from parents who never let him wander far from the warmth and parental protection of home. Listen to one of his memories from age four:

> I remember falling off my bike on our driveway. I hurt my knee, and I couldn't walk back into the house without help from my mother.

Tom didn't say it, but his memory did. He feels weak, helpless, and small. "Poor Tom."

But Tom turned out to be a turkey when marrying time came along. What do you suppose he wanted his wife to be like? Right. He wanted Mrs. Tom to respond to him just as his mom always had. When his bride failed the "Let me do that for you, Honey" comparison test, his marriage headed for the rocks.

## How to Raise a Yoyo

A common trap for any parent to fall into is inconsistency. A typical inconsistent family atmosphere might have one parent who is authoritarian while the other is permissive. Or both parents act permissive part of the time and then crack down with authoritarian vengeance when their patience is exhausted. As Kevin is fond of pointing out, this is a great way to raise a yoyo.

The best way to avoid the trap of inconsistent parenting is through reality discipline, which Kevin describes as "pulling the rug out and letting the little buzzards tumble."[1] Moms aren't always charmed when Kevin refers to their little darlings as buzzards, but it's all in good fun to make a point: when children need disciplining, parents must go into action, not into filibuster. And when you "pull the rug," it's to teach, never to harm. Reality discipline operates on a basic rug-pulling principle: *help the child face the consequences for his actions; help him be responsible for his behavior.* For example:

- When children break a sibling's toy, they buy a new one—with their own allowance.
- When they come home late for dinner, they wait until breakfast to eat.
- When they fight in the car on the way to the soccer game, Daddy pulls off to the side of the road and says, "This car does not move until the fighting stops." (Note: This strategy works better while going to soccer games than it does while going to church or the dentist.)
- When they sleep in and miss the bus, they walk to school and take the consequences for being late.

And so on and so on—one rug after the other. This kind of parenting is obviously not permissive; but neither is it authoritarian. It is *authoritative* and the family atmosphere it builds is one of *mutual respect* between the parent and child.

## The Anatomy of Mutual Respect

Authoritative parents are in charge, but never overbearing or unreasonable. They are just as strong on love as they are on control. Authoritative parents nurture instead of neglect. They are there for their kids, but never do for them what they can do for themselves.

Authoritative parents build an atmosphere of mutual respect that has these characteristics:

- Unconditional acceptance
- Emphasis on positive qualities—what a child does right
- Minimum focus on mistakes—"You'll do better next time"
- Training to be responsible and accountable according to one's ability
- Experiencing of natural and logical consequences
- Encouragement to do one's best, but freedom to be imperfect and even to fail
- A sense of humor
- Setting reasonable expectations and living up to them
- Exposure to being honest about feelings—hearing openly
- Courteous treatment (as if the child were a friend of the family)
- Empathy—learning to see, hear, and feel things from the other person's point of view
- Warmth, affection, and love with emphasis on loving each other as unconditionally as possible[2]

## Grab the Moments—Make a Memory

Above all, authoritative parents seek to make good memories for their kids, the kind that will help them counter the inevitable bad ones that life will bring their way. Almost all of the parents we work with want to make good memories for their families. They worry about being part of the bad ones, but there is no avoiding it; parents do play a major role on the family stage, and sometimes they blow it. It does no good, however, to go on guilt trips for those times you were not perfect. The question is, Where do you go from here? What do you want to do from now on?

Our advice is to relax and do the best you can, and the memories will take care of themselves. A first step is telling yourself the truth regarding commitment. Parents can be committed to all kinds of things besides their children. Jeff, a client of Randy's, summed up memories of his family by saying, "It was like an eighteen-year prison sentence. I got out of there as soon as I was able. The only thing my mother was committed to was getting us kids out of the house and out of her hair."

Jeff wound up in Randy's office because he was struggling with his marriage. Those memories of no commitment at home had followed him through life, and he was having trouble keeping relationships together. One of Jeff's earliest memories gives poignant testimony to why he grew up without sensing the value and importance of commitment:

> I must have been four when my dad split. I mean, he just packed up one day and left. He never talked to me or tried to explain why he was leaving. He never called, and I didn't see or hear from him again until I was sixteen. I hated him for doing that to me.

As for Jeff's mother, she wasn't much better. All he could recall from the time he was four to age ten was being bounced from one baby sitter to another. "It seemed to me," Jeff said, "that she was always more interested in herself than anybody else and that us kids were nothing but a bother to her."

Jeff grew up learning to be committed to himself and no one else: "Me first, and if there is anything left, I might give you a little of it." Jeff's understanding of commitment was precisely opposite of the positive definitions that include dependability, trustworthiness, and always being there when you're needed. Commitment is vital to the success of any organization, particularly the family. Without commitment to each other, the fabric of a family is flawed and will eventually come apart at the seams. When Vera shared some early memories with Randy, she recalled:

> One day when I was about seven or eight, a neighbor accused my brother of stealing some strawberries from his garden. My dad and mom took my brother into a side room and talked to him alone about it. We later found out that my brother was innocent, but my parents didn't know that at first. They took my brother's word that he hadn't done it, and they defended him and supported him against the neighbor's accusations.

Vera also recalled that her parents always treated her and her brother with respect and expected the same from them. "Commitment to one another was important to all of us," she said.

If you want to make good memories for your children, practice sitting down with them on a regular basis and telling them, "I love you, no matter what. No matter what you do or what you become or where you live, I'll always love you."

## It Takes Time to Make Good Memories

To make good memories for his own children, Kevin has always made it a point to take each of them on a special birthday outing. They get to choose—their favorite restaurant or other fun spot—where they can go all alone with Dad, nobody else along. Kevin has turned down speaking engagements and other invitations that conflict with these birthday outings. In one instance, a prestigious group offered him a substantial fee to speak, but he said, "No, I am tied up that day. It's my daughter's birthday."

The spokesman for the group was incredulous. He said, "Well, that's no problem—you can bring her along."

"You don't understand," Kevin replied. "This is my daughter's special day with me and the rest of the family. We never miss—*for anything.*"

Kevin doesn't stop with birthdays. He also takes his children along on talk show tours and speaking trips—to give them memories of what Dad does to help other people. On one occasion, he incurred the disfavor of the principal of Kevey's school because he chose to take his son out of class for a week to go trout fishing back in upstate New York where he grew up.

The trip cost time—Kevey's time in school and Kevin's time taken from his counseling practice (Kevin made arrangements for Kevey to get ahead on some school work and make up the rest when he got back). It also cost a lot of money, but as he totaled it out, Kevin believed that it was well worth it. By taking his son to New York, Kevin knew he was planting memories that Kevey could savor and, more importantly, that he could later recycle to his own children.

## How Memories Go Good or Bad

Without good communication, your chances of making good memories for your kids are nil. There are dozens of books on how to communicate. Basically, it boils down to being interested in the other person and taking time to talk—and listen. From the biography of President Lyndon Johnson comes this warm recollection about his grandfather, who was a master of the art of asking simple but relevant questions:

> I remember that when I was a boy, that I walked through the sand, hot sand, up to see my grandfather. A child of five or six—I would cross the dusty field and walk along the banks of the river.
>
> My granddaddy would ask me questions. He would say, "How many ponies do you have? How many chickens do you have? How many cows are down there at your place? Tell me about the state of the crops—when are you going to start picking your cotton?"
>
> I would stand there and wiggle my toes in the sand with my finger in my mouth. And if I knew the answers and answered all his questions correctly, grandpa would take me in and open a black mahogany desk he had and reach in and get an apple. And I would walk satisfied and quite proudly back across the fields along the bank of the river.[3]

This simple story holds some keys to good communication. First, Grandpa *made it safe to communicate*. Despite being a shy five-year-old, his grandson always felt welcome. Grandpa's questions were about the little boy's life—the things he experienced each day. And although not directly stated, other skills are implied. Grandpa *listened* to little Lyndon and he *didn't interrupt*. Also, it's fairly obvious he never *jumped to conclusions* and put the little boy on the defensive. If he had, little five-year-old Lyndon would not have taken that hot dusty walk to Grandpa's house more than once.

But maybe the real drawing card was that apple. Some might call it a bribe, but there is much more meaning to it than that. Little Lyndon could have asked for apples at home, but instead he would walk all the way to Grandpa's to talk. The apple was a symbol of that priceless communication commodity called *appreciation* (and just maybe it was Grandpa's way of thanking his grandson for coming by).

We have no way of asking Lyndon Johnson for the "freeze frame" of that memory, but it's a good guess it centers around his walk back home, munching on that apple, feeling satisfied and proud about talking with Grandpa and being able to answer the questions.

## Actually, You *Always* Communicate

Communication is often described as a complex and difficult art, but it is really very simple. You are *always* communicating with your kids, and your words and actions either encourage or discourage them.

Forty-year-old Peter recalled how all through his teen years his dad would criticize him for almost everything he attempted to do. Some of Dad's favorite remarks included:

- "You can't do that, so stop trying."
- "That's beyond your capabilities, so why waste your time?"
- "You're as stupid as your mother."

Peter got the message—and some bad memories that only rein-forced the lies he began telling himself at an early age: "I'm no good . . . . I can't do it. . . . There's no point in trying."

Peter's unfortunate memories are a good reminder for parents to deal in potential, not the past, not even the present. It's just too easy to get tired, irritated—and, yes, fed up with your little ankle biter and start telling yourself lies like:

- "That kid will never change."
- "He's just like his Uncle Harry."
- "She's hopeless."
- "I give up on him."
- "Our relationship will never be good."

Helen was more fortunate. Her parents understood the value of encouragement, and her early memories bring back healthy and positive experiences:

> My dad was the greatest. He always encouraged me to do the best I could. I recall that when I tried out for my fourth-grade class play, my dad spent the entire evening before the tryout helping me learn the lines and feel comfortable. He kept saying, "Helen, you can do it. Keep trying. You can do it."
>
> Both my mother and dad were very helpful to me when I tried to do something new. I remember the time I had some

particularly hard spelling words, and Mom was very patient with me, even when I kept missing some of them over and over. I appreciated my mother's patience with me while I was growing up.

Good memories are often centered around an encouraging experience. Some parents encourage their children about as often as plants need water—once a week. But kids need huge daily doses of encouragements like these:

- "You did it all by yourself—great!"
- "I can see you worked hard on that!"
- "Do that again!"
- "I have faith in you!"
- "That's good thinking!"
- "That's a terrific paper—let's put it up on the refrigerator."
- "I appreciate what you've done!"

If you want to make as many good memories as possible, keep in mind that when dealing with your kids you always have two choices: to encourage or put down. Their tremendous need for love and acceptance doesn't leave much middle ground.

## Do You Try to Understand?

St. Francis supposedly said, "Seek not to be understood, but to understand." That's good advice, especially for parents. Rare is the child—especially the teenager—who doesn't say, "My parents just don't understand." We hear that complaint almost every week as we sit trying to negotiate another parent/child impasse.

Parents could argue that there is no way to keep a child from feeling misunderstood, at least some of the time. Because we're parents, too, we have been there more than once and we agree. Sometimes the realities of life—and discipline—run head-on into the heartfelt desires of your son or daughter, and there just isn't any give.

For example, when Randy and Donna discovered their daughter's problem with amblyopia in her left eye, the doctor suggested therapy that Andrea didn't like at all. She was required to wear a patch over her good eye for several hours a day, which would force her weak eye to work harder and get stronger.

Andrea hated wearing that patch. There were many arguments and tears, but Randy and Donna stood firm: the patch was no fun, but reality said, "Wear it or go entirely blind in one eye." Today Andrea's eye is much improved, and she will not be needing the eye patch much longer.

No matter how tough enforcing discipline can be, it doesn't mean you ever stop trying to understand how your child feels. You must take time to watch and listen. You can learn a whole lot that way. For example:

> Not long ago, Kevin walked into a department store with his oldest daughter, Holly, now a teenager. It was just before closing time, and he saw her glance quickly at her watch and look anxiously around.
>
> "Checking to see if they're going to turn off all the lights?" he asked gently.
>
> She smiled a tight smile and didn't say anything. But she didn't have to. She knew her dad understood that memory of the day she was four and was with Mom at the supermarket. Closing time was approaching and to warn all shoppers to hustle to the check-out stand, the manager turned out the lights. It was pitch black for only a few seconds, but it gave Holly a bad memory she carries to this day. Most important, however, is that her dad knows about it—and understands.

## Disagree, Yes; Disrespect, No

But what happens to all those warm fuzzies when children or their parent or both "lose it" and get angry? At Randy's house, they have an unwritten agreement to keep "short accounts" on anger. Granted, the burden usually falls on Mom and Dad to make the agreement work, but when they do, it is a powerful model for their three children to follow.

During the writing of this book, Evan, Randy's ten-year-old son, got frustrated and stepped way across that familiar line called "respect for parents." It was Saturday, and the back yard was a total disaster filled with toys, gravel kicked all over the patio, and other odds and ends that had accumulated over a week of heavy use by everyone in the family.

Randy called Evan and said, "All of us need to get out here and help clean this up—company's coming this afternoon for a barbecue."

Evan responded by saying none of the mess was his, he had other things to do on Saturday, and he wasn't going to help. Randy responded by saying everyone would help and Evan should appear immediately in the back yard. Evan did not, and in Randy's opinion, the reality of the situation called for a few sharp swats and a mini-seminar on the evils of disrespect.

Off Evan stomped to his room, licking his wounds, only to return in about five minutes, rested and ready for Round Two. With his verbal dukes up, he came at Randy again. He still didn't want to admit any of the mess was his, and he couldn't see why he had to work on Saturday. At this point, Randy had to make a decision. This was not like his normally conscientious and cooperative first-born son. Something really had to be bothering him. Randy said, "Evan, enough of this, let's sit down and talk about it."

As they talked it through, it became clear that the main thing on Evan's mind was that his dad should understand that Evan didn't like working on Saturdays, and he wanted to be sure Andrea would do her share. Randy said, "Okay, maybe most of the junk out there is Andrea's, but we all live here and we all make the mess. I know you'd like to do other things on Saturday—so would I. But right now the yard needs cleaning up, and we all need to pitch in and do it together."

That seemed to satisfy Evan, and he willingly joined in helping clean up the yard. But more importantly, father and son learned something about respect that day. Evan learned why it's necessary for "children to obey their parents." And Randy himself got new insights into the truth that we teach our children respect by treating them with respect.

## The Lasting Values Count the Most

What really matters in your family? Whatever it is, it will make the memories that will flicker across the screen when your kids are grown and have families of their own. Recently Kevin was talking with Dr. James Dobson before appearing on his nationally syndicated radio program "Focus on the Family." One of the leading advocates for the family in America, Dr. Dobson has many warm memories of the love he received from his own parents, including a simple scene that happened when he was around a year old. For anyone to remember anything that early is rare, but Dobson clearly recalls being held by his mother as she sat on the front porch of their home. She was feeding him, and someone else was present, but he doesn't remember who the person was. Most important, however, are the feelings he attaches to that memory: warmth, comfort, and security in his mother's arms. It is no coincidence that today, over fifty years later, Dr. James Dobson's life is dedicated to preserving the family and helping parents learn how to communicate the same kind of love to their own children. A warm nurturing family is where children can learn to sink their roots and know what it means to belong somewhere and be a part of something that never really dies.

Every year Kevin takes his entire family back to Lake Chautauqua, near Jamestown, New York, where they spend the summer fishing, swimming, waterskiing, and just enjoying one another, building memories that will never fade. A couple of summers ago, Kevin dragged his entire family over to a tiny community called Gowanda to visit, of all places, the cemetery. We'll let him explain:

> I wanted to have my family see where most of the Leman clan is buried. Sande and the kids kind of gave me a bad time, but decided to humor me and come along for the ride. Gowanda is forty miles from Williamsville, and it took a while even to find the cemetery, which was a lot bigger than I thought it would be. Then it took us another half hour or so to find the huge LEMAN headstone that marked the plot where many Leman family members are buried. When we did come across it, we practically celebrated and stayed for over an hour taking pictures and just talking about family memories my father had shared with me.
>
> The pictures that meant the most, to me at least, were the ones of the kids posing with the grave markers with sort of a then and now effect. There were the Leman names etched in granite—Uncle Val and Aunt Fannie, my great grandfather, John Henry Leman, and my grandfather, Joseph, who froze to death in a snow bank one night when he was drunk.
>
> I know our cemetery excursion meant more to me than it did to the rest of the family, but that's okay. As far as I was concerned, I was planting seeds for memories, giving our kids

some of the substance of life, showing them what's important and letting them know they had roots—that they were part of generations who had gone before.

You may not be into visiting cemeteries to check out the family plot, but there are all kinds of things you can do to pass on lasting values and memories to your children. Make a video or audio tape of your life—a "This Is Your Life" minus Ralph Edwards! Talk about your roots, your positive childhood memories, the values you hold. Share from your heart what is really important in your life. Have the tapes available only at your death. What a treasure you will have to give to your children. The important thing is to start doing them—now; not next month, not next week, not even tomorrow, but now.

We read of a man who was preparing for his wife's funeral after her sudden and tragic death. As he and his sister-in-law went through his dead wife's bureau gathering clothing to take to the mortician, he found a tissue-wrapped package of lovely lingerie that she had bought some eight or nine years before. It was made of exquisite silk and trimmed with lace, the impressive price tag still attached. His wife had never worn the lingerie. She had always said she was "saving it for a special occasion." As he slammed the bureau drawer shut, the grieving husband said, "Don't ever save anything for a special occasion. Every day you're alive is a special occasion."[4]

Don't wait to make memories. Don't wait for some special occasion when you can stop to do what you've been postponing too long already. Remember: tomorrow's memories are being made today.

# Chapter *12*

*A master of fun and games, the Cub finally discovered:*
*"You're better than that!"*

# You're Better Than That!

There are two ways to respond to this book:

    1. You can say, "Childhood memories are interesting, I guess, but they seem to tell me I'm stuck. I can't change who I really am. Even Leman and Carlson admit the grain of your wood is with you for life."

    2. Or you can say, "Maybe these guys have something here. The grain of my wood may be set, but I can change the way I operate. It's up to me to whistle a different tune."

We hope you take route number two because we did and we know it works. If Fat Butt and the Cub can do it, so can you.

Neither one of us, however, is all the way home. Randy still finds himself in front of the fridge when pressure mounts, but now he knows and *believes* he doesn't have to open the door. And he still hears that little voice whisper, "Watch your butt" when tough decisions come his way, but he no longer runs for cover.

# A Shaggy Dog Story

One turning point came when Randy lived next door to a neighbor whose big shaggy-looking German shepherd barked incessantly as he ran along the fence separating Randy's one-acre plot from his neighbor's ten acres. The dog barked at all hours for apparently no reason, and one Sunday afternoon Randy had had it. What happened next was this:

> I had to do something because all that noise and confusion caused by the dog's barking was hammering away at my peace. So I decided to confront him (the neighbor, not the German shepherd). Reverting to my usual nonconfrontive style, I called him on the phone, and when he answered I snarled, "Take care of your dumb dog!" Then I hung up without identifying myself.
>
> But all that did was eat at my insides all the more. The neighbor wasn't about to take care of his dumb dog because of an anonymous call like that. So, after another hour of listening to almost constant barking, I called again, and this time I didn't say anything. I just hung up as soon as he said, "Hello." I was positive he knew who it was. That cautious little man who lived in my head kept assuring me that I didn't have to identify myself and that eventually the neighbor would get the message.
>
> This bizarre dance went on for two or three days: the dog would bark; I would call, hang up, and then march to the refrigerator to find solace from its silent but friendly shelves. It was Pavlov's experiment with salivating dogs in reverse. In this case *I* was the one who salivated when I heard a certain stimulus—that incessant barking.
>
> Finally, I said, "This is ridiculous." Donna already knew that, but she held her peace. We were living in Michigan at the time, and snow was piled everywhere. It was a bitter cold night, but my stomach was on fire for two reasons. The barking was maddening, but so was the knowledge that I was not handling the situation like a mature adult.
>
> I got on my boots and coat, found a flashlight, and plowed through the snowdrifts to my neighbor's front door. I knocked and met my neighbor for the first time. He invited me in, and I got to the point: "I wanted to tell you it's been me who's been calling you and hanging up, and I want to apologize for the way

I've dealt with this. I was wrong. Your dog has been bugging me, but I should have come over and told you about it to your face."

We chatted a few minutes, and, strangely, we never did talk about the dog or keeping him quiet. I simply apologized to my neighbor for not confronting him directly, and then I left. Actually, I hadn't gone over to his house to talk about the dog's barking, but to apologize for my behavior on the phone. Making that simple, but courageous, move gave me a tremendous lift.

Oh, yes, the dog never barked again.

## How Kevin Keeps the Cub on His Leash

As for Kevin, he still struggles with keeping baby Cub on the leash. The charmer/driver/rebel has to remember that there is a big streak of self-centeredness right down the middle of his grain. Being the irrepressible Cub, he gets so excited and involved in what he's doing—his next talk show, his next book—that it can sound to other people as if he's just blowing his own horn. As he says:

> It's easy enough to trace this habit all the way back to that Sunday morning on the front steps when I was pounding on the door to get in. The drive and desire to be heard, seen, and paid attention to still tempt me to take out my little trumpet and toot it as loudly as I can.
>
> I also battle overscheduling. The invitations come constantly to go here and there to speak, to appear, to entertain, to teach. They're all tempting, because I love the excitement, the applause, the laughter. In that sense, I want to go. The grain of the wood comes right to the surface, and that same little kid who wanted to go out and ride his Roadmaster bike while everyone at his party waited for him to get back is right there wanting attention. But another voice is constantly saying: "You can't do them all. You have a family and they count more than pleasing yourself."

Kevin's family also does its bit to keep him in line. For example, on one occasion his wife, Sande, was introducing him to a woman who was new to the community, and Sande said, "I'd like you to meet my husband, Kevin Leman." The woman did a double take and replied, "You mean, *the* Kevin Leman?"

Never batting an eye, Sande responded, "Oh, no, not *that* one."

Kevin also works on taming the rebel who used to pick off priceless Christmas tree ornaments with his BB pistol and nail passing cars with snowballs. Of course, he has had some setbacks—such as the day he couldn't resist the temptation to get revenge on the head nurse who was Sande's supervisor when she met Kevin over a trash basket outside the rest room at the Tucson Medical Center. When the supervisor learned that Sande had begun dating Kevin, she said, "Don't have anything to do with that janitor. He'll never amount to anything."

It was several years and a couple of degrees later when Kevin saw this lady again. By now he had married Sande and was on the staff of the University of Arizona as assistant dean of students. The nursing supervisor had decided to pick up some graduate courses, and she was registering for classes, along with several thousand other students. Kevin recalls:

> I was manning a registration table when I spotted her. I couldn't believe that this lady, out of thousands, would wind up in my line. I had seven students to think it over. Would I be nice to her or would the little rebel from Williamsville come out to play? I couldn't resist. She stepped up for her turn and didn't seem to recognize me.
>
> I looked over her papers and said in my most official tone, "You'll have to get signatures on these over at the TBA Building. That's the one at the far southwest corner of the campus."
>
> She nodded gratefully and disappeared into the crowd on her sixteen-block hike, searching for the TBA Building, the name of which came right out of the registration folder, "To Be Announced." I smiled the rest of the day, picturing her stopping people and asking for directions to the TBA Building.
>
> I know it was a cheap trick, but the grain of the wood isn't reshaped in a day or even a decade. I can safely say I'm not that vindictive today (although I sometimes do get tempted to touch my brakes just enough to scare freeway tailgaters out of their wits).

## We've Saved the Best for Last

We are transparent enough to share our weaknesses with you for a couple of reasons. First, we want you to know there is nothing special about psychologists or counselors. They struggle with fears, childishness, and hang-ups like everyone else. Second, we have saved the most amazing thing about this memory business for last.

As you explore your memory videos, you will not only be able to cut them down to size; you will also be able to change your programming. The good memories start to crowd out the bad or at least balance them out to some degree. And there are all kinds of good memories in there among the disasters, embarrassments, guilt trips, and realizations that you are anything but perfect.

This book has focused primarily on the dark side of early memories—the insecurities, the anger, the fears, the loneliness, and the pain of life. As we work with clients every day and ask them for early childhood memories, the vast majority come up with negative ones. That's logical because they would not be coming to see us if all they remembered were good things. In memory exploration seminars, however, Randy still notes that people come up with negative memories more often than positive ones. There seems to be a natural tendency in many people to recall calamities, sorrows, getting into trouble, and other misfortunes.

Memory exploration is, however, much more than a shovel to dig up negatives from your past. It can also uncover the positive stuff in your life: your creativity, your love for others and life, your concern for the feelings and needs of others, your perseverance, your loyalty to friends and family, your love for God and humankind. And it can turn up those warm moments when someone loved you and made you feel wanted and secure.

## The Good Can Outweigh the Bad

We think it's safe to say all people have a mix of good and bad memories. Comedian Carol Burnett claims that she remembers the following scene from age two. Notice the almost unbelievable detail in this very warm, pleasant memory:

> My earliest memories are being bathed in the kitchen
> sink in the old house. I couldn't have been much over two,
> because I fit in it. Mama kept the door on the stove open, and
> I'd stare at the waves in the air the heat made. I remember her
> drying me, holding me, kissing me and putting me to bed. It
> felt good.[1]

That little memory is full of all sorts of diamonds and roses. Little
Carol felt cared for, and she enjoyed her surroundings. Home was important to her. She liked being held and kissed. There was security there—
the bath, the touching, the bed, and above all, Mama.

But Carol Burnett's life was not all diamonds and roses. After her
description of the bath scene, her memories continue on a different note:

> Sometimes she'd [Mama] wake me up after I'd fallen
> asleep, and she'd pull my thumb out of my mouth. It made
> me mad. She left for somewhere after that.[2]

The "somewhere" Mama left for was California, leaving Carol with
her grandmother in San Antonio, Texas. Carol recalls traveling to Santa
Monica when she was four to visit her mother and her father, who were
still together at that time. Her daddy had a drinking problem, and she
would watch her mother break bottles of liquor he had hidden when
she could find them. When Daddy came around the corner with wobbly
legs, it made Mama mad. Carol didn't stay in California long because her
parents separated, and she was shipped back to San Antonio to live with
her grandmother and great-grandmother.

Despite being deserted by her parents at different times, Carol
Burnett came to understand them and holds warm feelings toward them.
That early recollection of being bathed, kissed, and held occupies a key
place in her memory library. It helps explain why Carol Burnett has such
a healthy, realistic perspective on life today.

Evangelist Billy Graham also recalls a mixture of warm and cold
memories. One of his first recollections was of his father trying to teach
him to walk in a wide grassy field beyond their house:

> It was in the afternoon. I remember him clapping his
> hands, opening his arms, calling, "Billy Frank, come to
> Daddy. C'mon to Daddy, Billy Frank. . . ."[3]

But that loving scene is not entirely representative of the relationship little Billy had with Dad as he grew up. According to one Graham biography: "They never met: they remained forever, in an elusive but elemental way, irrevocably strangers to each other. As Billy stood with his family in the funeral home, he finally turned bleakly to his sister: 'I wish I could cry. I wish I could, but I can't.'"[4]

Billy Graham's mixed memories of his father are a good example of the power of perception. The freeze frame that sticks in his memory is his father's beckoning to him with open arms. It is a symbol of how Billy Graham came to perceive God and the world. The evangelist became famous around the globe for his open-armed pose, bidding people to come forward to commit their lives to Jesus Christ.

Sometimes there can be good things in a memory otherwise filled with horror and trauma. A client named Joseph related this memory from age five:

> When I was five, my mother was killed in a car accident. I recall that my dad picked me up and held me close to himself as he tried to explain to me that Mother was gone and wasn't coming back. I felt sad, but secure that my dad had me in his arms.

Terrible as that memory is, it is not too hard to see positive and healthy ingredients hidden in the loss, sadness, and pain. There are at least three healthy impressions that stand out:

- There was tender touching—"my dad picked me up and held me close."
- There was open communication—"He tried to explain to me that Mother was gone."
- There was a sense of security—"I felt sad but secure in his arms."

## Finding Diamonds in the Coal Pile

Within many early childhood memories, you can find one or two bright spots—something positive about life and one's self. As we have seen in the A-B-Cs of truth therapy, *it's not just what you remember, but how you perceive it that counts.*

Heather is an example of someone who found some diamonds in the coal pile by changing her perceptions. A twenty-eight-year-old mother of three small children, she came to Randy for counseling because of her overwhelming feeling of intense anger. She had no peace and was often angry with others, especially her children. She felt guilty, confused, and afraid that she might harm them.

When Randy asked her to list some of her strengths, she stared blankly and replied, "None that I can think of offhand."

But when Heather shared three of her earliest memories, they were encouraging indications of personality strengths hidden among the obvious indications of the roots of her anger:

> When I was a kid, I did more listening than talking. I remember one day my friend Joan was telling me about her parents' divorce when my mother came into the bedroom where we were and made Joan go home. I was really mad at my mother for doing that when Joan needed to talk to me. I told my mother how I felt—but she didn't listen. She never did.

> I must have been six or seven at the time, and I recall that my grandmother was very ill. She was living in our spare bedroom. One day when everybody was gone except for Grandma and me, she had one of her attacks and couldn't get to the bathroom to get her medicine. She yelled downstairs for help and I remember going up and getting the medicine for her and sitting with her for about an hour before the attack passed. It felt good to help my grandmother when she needed help.

> I remember that my mother and I fought a lot. She never tried to understand me or listen to me. I recall one day I felt really sad that my friend Joan had to move out of state. I was crying and feeling pretty sorry about the whole thing when my mother came in and told me to stop crying, grow up, and get out into the kitchen and get the dishes washed. I was furious and felt really hurt that she didn't try to understand how I was feeling about Joan's leaving.

Obviously, Heather's anger appeared to be rooted in her relationship with her mother. Randy spent several sessions working with her on mother/daughter issues that needed to be resolved. Then, to encourage her to see bright spots in her lifestyle by changing some perceptions, Randy said, "Heather, I see some very positive things in your memories."

"You do?" she responded. "What are they?"

"First, I see evidence that you're a good listener."

"Yeah, I guess I am," she replied. "I enjoy hearing what others have to say and how they feel about things."

"I picked that up as well, Heather—I mean your concern about how others feel. You said in your first memory you did more listening than talking—and you were listening to your friend talk abut her personal problems.

"But I'd also guess from your first two memories that you must be a pretty good 'care giver.'"

"You know," Heather interrupted, "others have told me that, too."

"You see these three little childhood memories that you shared with me are nothing more than three picture-window looks into your adult personality today. Even though so much of your focus is wrapped up in the anger and the conflict between you and your mother, I see in your memories a person who really cares about other people, is willing to listen to their problems, and wants to help others and care for them. And that's a pretty positive picture in my book."

Through tears Heather admitted that she'd allowed her feelings toward her mother to become a cesspool of anger that was threatening to drown out the rest of her life. She saw her need to change her focus from anger to healthy, positive attitudes. As Randy worked with Heather, together they found her positive attributes, hidden in her early memories of angry exchanges with Mom:

- Heather is willing to stand up for what is right. (In her first memory, she says, "I told my mother how I felt.")
- Heather feels strongly about issues. ("I felt really sad that Joan was moving.")
- Heather needs and enjoys lasting deep relationships. (The entire third memory concerns her sense of loss when her friend moved.)

## Put Good Memories to Work for You

One of the chief goals of this book is to help you reach your fullest potential by understanding yourself. You need to allow for your weaknesses and capitalize on your strengths. We've spent a lot of time and space on recognizing and correcting the weaknesses. Here's where we lay out a simple strategy for spotting and building on the positive ingredients in your memories.

Look back over the memories you have been recording and note any evidence of positive experiences and positive personality traits. Here's a little quiz that can help you:

1. Was there healthy touching?   Yes_____ No_____
2. Was there respectful talking and/or listening?
   Yes_____ No_____
3. Were you caring for or giving to others?
   Yes_____ No_____
4. Do your memories produce happy emotions?
   Yes_____ No_____
5. Were you respected by others?   Yes_____ No_____
6. Would you enjoy reliving the memory(ies)?
   Yes_____ No_____
7. Were you comfortable around other people?
   Yes_____ No_____
8. Do the memories make you feel good about yourself?
   Yes_____ No_____
9. Do the memories help you feel secure?   Yes_____ No_____
10. Were you involved with others in a positive way?
    Yes_____ No_____

These are just starter questions to get you thinking about and looking for the positive ingredients of your memories. Each time you answer yes to one of these questions, probe a little deeper with who, what, where, when, how, and why questions to discover any encouraging experiences and positive personality traits even hinted at in your memories.

If you're like Heather, you may be so discouraged and down on yourself that you won't be able to find a blossoming weed, let alone a rose or carnation. If that's the case, you may want to discuss this book and your personal memories with a friend. Ask that friend to help you pick out some positives that you may be missing. Often an objective person can see things that you overlook.

And sometimes it's easier to find roses or diamonds by looking in a better location. If all your memories seem particularly negative, try exploring some of the more positive times. Think about holiday celebrations or some of your early birthdays. Try to recall any special times, special places, or special people.

If you keep looking, you're bound to find some flowers or gems. Some people have to look long and hard before they find even one, but it's been our experience in counseling and in our own lives that they are always there.

## Some Memories Are Life Changers

Sometimes a good memory can help set a person's direction for life. Charlie Chaplin, one of the greatest comedians who ever charmed people into gales of laughter, recalls this experience when he was five years old:

> I remember standing in the wings when Mother's voice cracked and went into a whisper. The audience began to laugh and sing falsetto and to make cat calls. . . . the noise increased until Mother was obliged to walk off the stage. When she came into the wings, she was very upset and argued with the stage manager who, having seen me perform before Mother's friends, said something about letting me go on in her place.
>
>       . . . In the turmoil I remember his leading me by the hand and, after a few explanatory words to the audience, leaving me on the stage alone. And before a glare of footlights and faces in smoke, I started to sing, accompanied by the orchestra, which fiddled about until it found my key . . . .
>
> Half-way through, a shower of money poured onto the stage. Immediately, I stopped and announced that I would pick up the money first and sing afterward. This caused much laughter. . . .
>
> And in repeating the chorus, in all innocence I imitated Mother's voice cracking and was surprised at the impact. . . . There was laughter and cheers, then more money-throwing; and when Mother came on the stage to carry me off, her pres-

ence evoked tremendous applause. That night was my first appearance on the stage and Mother's last.[5]

## The Cub Couldn't Fool Miss Wilson

We have emphasized that the earlier the memory, the more significant it can be in explaining your lifestyle and life theme. But that does not preclude the value of later childhood memories, and Kevin recalls a life-changing experience that happened during high school, when he was confronted by someone who cared about him. Most of his memories from teenage years are a chronicle of rebellious buffoonery done to get attention and to count in the only way he thought he could count. But Miss Wilson, a math teacher, saw through his façade. She stopped him one day in the hall, looked him in the eye, and said, "Kevin, when are you going to stop playing your little game of being best at being the worst?"

Kevin tried to laugh it off, but he knew she had him cold. And when she offered to tutor him in math on her own time to get him through high school, he took her up on it. The fact that somebody believed in him enough to spend her evenings helping him get beyond consumer math is a nice enough memory in itself, but there is more. Many years later, Kevin telephoned Miss Wilson just to thank her and chat about old times:

> I'll always be thankful Miss Wilson offered to tutor me. I might never have escaped from high school if that dear lady hadn't seen through my goof-off/charmer behavior and believed in me.
>
> She moved to North Carolina after she retired from teaching. One day a few years ago, when I was passing through Charlotte, I decided to look her up in the phone book and give her a call to thank her for what she meant in my life.
>
> The phone rang and she answered. I said: "Miss Wilson, this is Kevin Leman."
>
> She just started laughing, and after waiting a moment or two, I went on, "I was going through town and I just had to call and thank you for the special role you played in my life."
>
> She laughed louder. I said, "Miss Wilson, do you realize

I've said two sentences and you haven't said a word? All you've done is laugh."

I could hear her struggling for composure on the other end of the line. Finally she managed her first words: "I'm sorry, Kevin. Just hearing your name makes me laugh."

Kevin could have taken that as a put-down, but he knew why Miss Wilson was laughing. She was undoubtedly recalling some of his antics in high school, but as she explained later in the conversation, another reason she laughed was with sheer delight in hearing from a student she had refused to give up on, when most of her colleagues already had. Some of Kevin's classmates had kept her informed about his career, and she had seen him on TV several times.

Best of all, however, they both had the last laugh together because someone had cared enough to tell a smart-alecky rebel the truth: "Quit playing your games—you're better than that."

Miss Wilson's words are worth repeating. In fact, the whole world should heed her wisdom. We hope memory exploration will help you quit playing your games. Quit telling yourself lies that whisper to you from childhood memories that you haven't been able to put in proper perspective. Change your perception of those memories, and you will unlock the grandest secret of them all:

YOU'RE BETTER THAN THAT.

# Epilogue

*Memories of fishing at Glen Park in Williamsville, New York.*

# A Childhood Memory Revisited

Her letter began with the usual, "Dear Dr. Leman," but it went on to remind Kevin of one of the special serendipities that memories can bring your way:

> Was it really you? Did the author of *Parenthood Without Hassles (Well, Almost)* give me an autographed copy of his book at Glen Park in Williamsville, New York, during the month of March? If it was you who gave me a copy of your book while my son was fishing, I want to say thank you. . . . I feel God had you enter my life. I really need help. I am living in a nightmare and want to know what I can do. If you have an office in this area, please let me know and I will make an appointment to come and see you. Sincerely . . .

Since receiving that letter, Kevin has written to the woman and talked with her on the phone about her problems. As for that day when he saw the woman and her son at the creek, he vividly recalls what happened and what it meant to him:

> I had just done a talk show in Buffalo, New York, and was headed to catch a plane. Williamsville lies just eight miles

outside Buffalo, near the airport, and while it was a little bit out of my way, I took a slight detour to drive through town just for old times' sake. I was headed back to the thruway out of Williamsville, and as I crossed the Ellicott Creek Bridge in Glen Park, I saw them, a woman sitting on the bank, reading a book, and a little boy fishing from a rocky ledge. *They were in precisely the same spot and doing the same thing that my mother and I had done some forty years before.*

As I crossed the bridge, I could almost hear the "Twilight Zone" theme playing in the back of my head. Was it too many plane rides or hotel rooms? I did a U-turn and came back across the bridge again. They were still there. It wasn't my imagination or my memory playing tricks on me. I turned around once more, came back across the bridge a third time, and parked.

I sat there a few moments and remembered those days when the simple pleasures were all our family had. I was around five and liked to go fishing. My mother really didn't have time, but she would pack a lunch, I would grab my pole and bait, and we would walk the half mile from our house to the bridge by the creek. Then she would read a book or knit while I fished happily away, trying to land one of the small-mouthed bass that were plentiful at that time. And when I did catch one, she celebrated with me as enthusiastically as though she had caught it herself.

I was about to drive on when I got the strong feeling I had to give that lady and her son something by way of appreciation for kindling such warm memories for me. I opened the trunk of the car and found a single copy of *Parenthood Without Hassles*. I quickly signed it and added, "Continue to take good care of that little fisherman; you're giving him memories he will remember for the rest of his life."

I walked down the bank and approached the woman. I guess I startled her when I said, "Hello," because she jumped a little. Then I added, "I'd like you to have this," and I handed her the book.

She said, "Thank you," almost automatically, but looked surprised and puzzled. I just smiled, turned away, and walked back to my car. I might have stayed to talk, but I seemed to have something in my eye. . . .

I drove away, headed for another plane, another microwave meal, and more talk shows. But the mantle of nostalgia still held me in its warm embrace. I remember saying aloud, "Gosh, life goes by so fast."

I was feeling my roots, remembering how wonderful life had been in Williamsville many years ago. It had been a simpler life, but such a good one. Our family had very little then, but in another way we had it all. At that moment, I had new feelings of gratitude for my family and my upbringing. I felt special, proud—and happy—just the way I had felt when Mom took time to take me fishing.

And memories don't get better than that.

# Appendix 1

## To Rewrite Your Early Memories

Read chapters 6, 7, and 8 carefully, noting the principles of truth therapy and the different illustrations of how they were applied by the authors and others. Then enter below the personal memories you explored in chapter 3. (Or, you may wish to enter additional memories you have recalled since reading chapter 3.) If possible, try to put down at least three memories:

**MEMORY NUMBER ONE:** _____

_____

_____

THE CLEAREST PART OF THIS MEMORY IS: _____

_____

_____

THE STRONGEST FEELING I ATTACH TO THE CLEAREST PART OF THIS

MEMORY IS: _____

_____

**MEMORY NUMBER TWO:** _____

_____

_____

THE CLEAREST PART OF THIS MEMORY IS: _____

_____

_____

THE STRONGEST FEELING I ATTACH TO THE CLEAREST PART OF THIS

MEMORY IS: _____

_____

**MEMORY NUMBER THREE:** _____

_____

_____

THE CLEAREST PART OF THIS MEMORY IS: _____

_____

_____

THE STRONGEST FEELING I ATTACH TO THE CLEAREST PART OF THIS

MEMORY IS: _____

_____

Next, put each of your memories through the A-B-Cs of truth therapy. Ask yourself:

What are the possible "lies" these memories are telling me out of the perceptions I had as a child?

As you find misconceptions, you will want to replace these lies with the truth as you see it from an adult perspective. Remember that the feeling you attached to each memory is crucial. It is the feeling you remember from childhood that can still dictate how you see that memory (and your life) today.

The next step is the most important: Changing your perception of the memory you remember from childhood to a more rational adult view. To accomplish this, try rewriting each memory below. Don't change the facts of the memory, but change your perception to something more accurate—and usually, more positive and healthy. (Review the material on self-talk in chapter 6, pp. 89-92, and the examples of rewritten memories in chapter 8, and then try it yourself.)

MEMORY NUMBER ONE REWRITE: _____

_____

_____

MEMORY NUMBER TWO REWRITE: _____

_____

_____

MEMORY NUMBER THREE REWRITE: _____

_____

_____

# Appendix 2

## To Let Your Parents Off the Hook
## of Blame and Bitterness

Review chapter 9, particularly the story of Sam, pp. 133-137. Then go through the same steps he did.

1. List your memories of how your parents treated you.

MEMORY NUMBER ONE: _____

_____

_____

THE CLEAREST PART OF THIS MEMORY IS: _____

_____

_____

THE STRONGEST FEELING I ATTACH TO THE CLEAREST PART OF THIS

MEMORY IS: _____

_____

MEMORY NUMBER TWO: _____

_____

_____

THE CLEAREST PART OF THIS MEMORY IS: _____

_____

THE STRONGEST FEELING I ATTACH TO THE CLEAREST PART OF THIS

MEMORY IS: _____

_____

**MEMORY NUMBER THREE:** _____

_____

_____

THE CLEAREST PART OF THIS MEMORY IS: _____

_____

THE STRONGEST FEELING I ATTACH TO THE CLEAREST PART OF THIS

MEMORY IS: _____

_____

2. Write down what you know about your parents' background—the way they were reared, their own battles, struggles, and disappointments.

3. If possible, repeat the following statements aloud. (Note: If this proves extremely painful for you, you may want to consider seeing a counselor or therapist.)

a. I release you from the responsibility I gave to you long ago to determine how I feel and respond to life.

b. I release you from the anger I have felt because of our past relationship.

c. I release you from being responsible for my happiness.

4. Pray your own prayer, forgiving your parents for their mistakes.
5. Rewrite your memories of how they treated you, using the new perceptions and perspective you have gained.

MEMORY NUMBER ONE REWRITE: ⎯⎯⎯⎯⎯⎯⎯⎯⎯⎯⎯

⎯⎯⎯⎯⎯⎯⎯⎯⎯⎯⎯⎯⎯⎯⎯⎯⎯⎯⎯⎯⎯⎯⎯⎯⎯⎯⎯

⎯⎯⎯⎯⎯⎯⎯⎯⎯⎯⎯⎯⎯⎯⎯⎯⎯⎯⎯⎯⎯⎯⎯⎯⎯⎯⎯

MEMORY NUMBER TWO REWRITE: ⎯⎯⎯⎯⎯⎯⎯⎯⎯⎯

⎯⎯⎯⎯⎯⎯⎯⎯⎯⎯⎯⎯⎯⎯⎯⎯⎯⎯⎯⎯⎯⎯⎯⎯⎯⎯⎯

⎯⎯⎯⎯⎯⎯⎯⎯⎯⎯⎯⎯⎯⎯⎯⎯⎯⎯⎯⎯⎯⎯⎯⎯⎯⎯⎯

MEMORY NUMBER THREE REWRITE: ⎯⎯⎯⎯⎯⎯⎯⎯⎯

⎯⎯⎯⎯⎯⎯⎯⎯⎯⎯⎯⎯⎯⎯⎯⎯⎯⎯⎯⎯⎯⎯⎯⎯⎯⎯⎯

⎯⎯⎯⎯⎯⎯⎯⎯⎯⎯⎯⎯⎯⎯⎯⎯⎯⎯⎯⎯⎯⎯⎯⎯⎯⎯⎯

# Appendix 3

## Exchanging Life Themes and Expectations
## (An Exercise for Married Couples)

After reading chapter 10, use the following form to compare your early memories with those of your spouse. You may also want to review chapter 3 and the Six Rules of Memory Exploration. Be sure that each of you includes the feeling you attach to each memory. If possible, try to analyze three memories each, and then see if you can come up with some sort of headline or brief statement that would describe each other's "life theme."

### Memory Number One

MY SPOUSE'S MEMORY:          MY MEMORY:

_____    _____

_____    _____

_____    _____

FEELING ATTACHED          FEELING ATTACHED
TO THIS MEMORY:           TO THIS MEMORY:

_____    _____

_____    _____

## Memory Number Two

MY SPOUSE'S MEMORY:                    MY MEMORY:

_____                _____

_____                _____

_____                _____


FEELING ATTACHED                       FEELING ATTACHED
TO THIS MEMORY:                        TO THIS MEMORY:

_____                _____

_____                _____


## Memory Number Three

MY SPOUSE'S MEMORY:                    MY MEMORY:

_____                _____

_____                _____

_____                _____


FEELING ATTACHED                       FEELING ATTACHED
TO THIS MEMORY:                        TO THIS MEMORY:

_____                _____

_____                _____


SPOUSE'S LIFE THEME AS SEEN            MY LIFE THEME AS SEEN
IN THESE MEMORIES:                     IN THESE MEMORIES:

_____                _____

_____                _____

MY SPOUSE'S EXPECTATIONS
OF WHAT MARRIAGE SHOULD
BE LIKE:

MY EXPECTATIONS
OF WHAT MARRIAGE
SHOULD BE LIKE:

_____        _____

_____        _____

The last part of this exercise asks each of you to list your expectations of what marriage would be like. Try to list at least ten or more expectations each and then discuss them. As chapter 10 suggests, identify expectations that you feel you can meet most of the time, the ones you can meet only part of the time, and the ones you doubt you can meet very often.

Talk about how you can compromise on unmet expectations. For example, say: "This expectation would be difficult for me to meet all of the time. These are the reasons why I don't think I can meet it. Can you tell me why this is so important to you? How does this affect you? What can I do instead?"

## DISCOVERING EACH OTHER'S STRENGTHS

Sit down with your spouse and take a few minutes to answer the following quiz. From what you have learned through memory exploration, list the items that are strengths for you or your spouse by placing an "X" in the proper column. If it is not, leave the space blank. After you list your strengths, discuss together how you can use them to complement each other and build a stronger marriage.

| Strength | You | Your Spouse |
|---|---|---|
| 1. Concerned about others | | |
| 2. Decisive | | |
| 3. Listens well | | |
| 4. Responsible | | |
| 5. Takes good care of self | | |
| 6. Committed to God | | |
| 7. Enjoys children | | |
| 8. Puts marriage first | | |
| 9. Patient | | |

10. Kind
11. Forgiving
12. List others:

# Appendix 4

## DEALING WITH POTENTIAL PARENT TRAPS

Many people experience the frustrating paradox of vowing: "I'll never be like my mother—or my father" and then finding themselves repeating the same behaviors they want to avoid. This often happens when the mistakes you watched your parents make with you show up in the way you treat your own children. (Review chapter 11.) To avoid these traps, take the following steps:

1. *Identify the potential parenting traps in your own memories*. If you can recall any early memories of how your parents disciplined or didn't discipline you, record them below:

MY MEMORY OF HOW I WAS PARENTED:

_____

_____

THE CLEAREST PART OF THIS MEMORY FOR ME WAS:

_____

_____

THE FEELING I ATTACHED TO THE CLEAREST PART OF THIS MEM-

ORY WAS:

_____

_____

THE PARENTING STYLE I MIGHT PICK UP FROM THIS MEMORY IS:

_____

_____

Note: If you want to do this exercise with additional memories of how you were parented, use blank end pages in this book.

2. *Identify the potential parenting traps in your lifestyle.* To review how lifestyles are developed, see chapters 4 and 5. The following are some suggestions of the kinds of parenting traps different lifestyles could face:

If you are a pleaser, potential parenting traps might include:

- Not challenging or confronting your children when they need to be challenged
- Being too permissive
- Being too easy to manipulate because you want your children to like you

Please note, however, that pleasers are not always passive. You may be the kind of pleaser who is more concerned about what friends and neighbors think than anything else. This could lead to:

- Being too strict
- Setting perfectionistic standards
- Discouraging your children with excessive demands

If you are a controller, your potential parenting traps could include:

- Being manipulative
- Being a "loving dictator"
- Being less than a loving dictator
- Being authoritarian and even cruel
- Not taking time to explain your actions or to give reasons why
- Ignoring your children's feelings while concentrating on your goals or desires

If you are a charmer, potential parenting traps could include:

- Wanting to be a kid yourself
- Not playing proper leadership roles
- Being inconsistent—seeming permissive at one time because you want to be one of the gang, and then having to crack down and be more authoritarian to regain control

If you are a victim or martyr, potential parenting traps could include:

- Casting an aura of pessimism over the family
- Teaching your children a glass-half-empty view of life
- Wanting excessive sympathy from your family
- Feeling resentment because you think your children are taking advantage of you

3. *Disarm your parent traps (the lies that may be part of your lifestyle) by replacing them with the truth.* Review the basic principles behind reality discipline, which focuses on helping your children face the consequences of their actions and helping them be responsible for their behavior. A key to using reality discipline successfully is to be willing to apply reality discipline to yourself. Take full responsibility for your own parenting actions. Refuse to fall prey to any parenting trap. Instead, take charge and tell yourself the truth. For example, if you know you are a pleaser who is too permissive or too easily manipulated by your children, replace those lies with the truth: "My responsibility is to love my children, whether they 'like me' or not. Loving them means confronting them and disciplining them when they need it."

If you are a controller who is too authoritarian and dictatorial with your children, replace those lies with the truth: "I can be in authority over my kids without squashing them. I can be aware of their feelings and take time to give reasons why. I want to be a loving parent, not a loving dictator."

Any parent trap can be disarmed by:

1. Realizing you are headed for the trap or that you are about to fall into it.

2. Stopping to think about what you are doing and why it is destructive and unhealthy.

3. Taking a different course of action that is constructive, loving, and healthy.

4. Not getting discouraged if you do fall into a parenting trap. Apologize, forgive, and regroup. Resolve to try again. The grain of your wood is not shaped in a day, but you can change *if you want to*.

# Notes

**Chapter 1.** "*Now* I Remember . . . So *That's* It!"
1. See Kevin Leman, *The Birth Order Book* (Old Tappan, NJ: Revell, 1985), 83.
2. David Seamands, *Putting Away Childish Things* (Wheaton, IL: Victor, 1982), 10.

**Chapter 2.** Why Iacocca Is Still Running Scared
1. Lee Iacocca with Robert Novak, *Iacocca: An Autobiography* (New York: Bantam, 1984), 7.
2. Ibid., 8-9.
3. Ibid., 9.
4. Tad Szulc, *Fidel: A Critical Portrait* (New York: Morrow, 1986), 109.
5. Ibid., 113-114.
6. Cris Evatt and Bruce Feld, *The Givers and the Takers* (New York: Macmillan, 1987).
7. Corrie ten Boom with C. C. Carlson, *In My Father's House* (Old Tappan, NJ: Revell, 1976), 37.

**Chapter 3.** Pick a Memory—Any Memory
1. Don C. Dinkmeyer, W. L. Pew, and Don C. Dinkmeyer, Jr., *Adlerian Counseling and Psychotherapy* (Monterey, CA: Brooks/Cole, a division of Wadsworth, 1979), 30.
2. See Psalm 139:14.

**Chapter 4.** "I Remember Mama—and Daddy, Too"
1. William Shakespeare, *As You Like It*, II.7.139-40.
2. See Dinkmeyer, Pew, and Dinkmeyer, Jr., *Adlerian Counseling*, 19.
3. O. K. Moore, ibid.
4. Carrol R. Thomas and William C. Marchant, "Basic Principles of Adlerian Family Counseling" in *Adlerian Family Counseling*, ed. Oscar C. Christensen and Thomas G. Schramski (Minneapolis, MN: Educational Media Corporation, 1983), 23.

**Chapter 5.** Why Donald Trump Makes His Deals
1. Donald J. Trump with Tony Schwartz, *Trump: The Art of the Deal* (New York: Random House, 1987), 49-50.
2. Ibid., 3.
3. For a more complete discussion of pleasers, see Kevin Leman, *The Pleasers: Women Who Can't Say No and the Men Who Control Them* (Old Tappan, NJ: Revell, 1987; New York: Dell, 1988).
4. See Robin Norwood, *Women Who Love Too Much: When You Keep Wishing and Hoping He'll Change* (New York: Pocketbooks, a division of Simon and Schuster, 1985). See

also Susan Forward and Joan Torres, *Men Who Hate Women and the Women Who Love Them* (New York: Bantam, 1986).
5. James Bacon, *How Sweet It Is: The Jackie Gleason Story* (New York: St. Martin's, 1985), 3.
6. Ibid.

**Chapter 6.** Letting the Air Out of Inflated Memories
1. See David Stoop, *Self Talk: Key to Personal Growth* (Old Tappan, NJ: Revell, 1981), 33–46.
2. Proverbs 23:7.
3. Sid Caesar with Bill Davidson, *Where Have I Been? An Autobiography* (New York: Crown, 1982), 11.

**Chapter 7.** What You and Joe Friday Have in Common
1. Phil Donahue, *Donahue: My Own Story* (New York: Simon and Schuster, 1972), 21.
2. Ibid., 21–22.

**Chapter 9.** Can You Let Mom and Dad Off the Hook?
1. Patty Duke and Kenneth Turan, *Call Me Anna: The Autobiography of Patty Duke* (New York: Bantam, 1988), 10, 12–13.
2. John Toland, *Adolf Hitler* (New York: Doubleday, 1976), 12–13.
3. Robert Waldron, *Oprah!* (New York: St. Martin's, 1987), 13.
4. Ibid., 35.
5. Ibid., 36.

**Chapter 10.** You Date the Adult, You Marry the Child
1. Author unknown.
2. W. Hugh Missildine, *Your Inner Child of the Past* (New York: Simon and Schuster, 1963), 56.

**Chapter 11.** Avoiding Those Parent Memory Traps
1. See Kevin Leman, *Making Children Mind Without Losing Yours* (Old Tappan, NJ: Revell, 1984; New York: Dell, 1987). See especially chapter 4.
2. Adapted from Thomas and Marchant, "Basic Principles of Adlerian Family Counseling" in *Adlerian Family Counseling*, ed. Christensen and Schramski, 25.
3. Merle Miller, *Lyndon: An Oral Biography* (New York: G. P. Putnam's Sons, 1980), 8–9.
4. Ann Wells, "What Are We Waiting For?" *The Los Angeles Times*, April 14, 1985.

**Chapter 12.** You're Better Than That!
1. Carol Burnett, *One More Time: A Memoir* (New York: Avon, 1986), 3.
2. Ibid.
3. Marshall Frady, *Billy Graham: A Parable of American Righteousness* (Boston: Little, Brown, 1979), 40.
4. Ibid.
5. Charles Chaplin, *My Autobiography* (New York: Simon and Schuster, 1964), 20–21.

If you have found this book
to be a helpful resource,
of if you are interested in scheduling
a speaking engagement with either
Kevin or Randy, please write or call:

Kevin Leman
1325 N. Wilmot
Suite 320
Tucson, AZ 85712
(602) 886-9925

or

Randy Carlson
Box 37000
Tucson, AZ 85740
(602) 742-6976

# CHAPTER 55

Gamble took the Super Puma to West Virginia. Technically speaking, he wasn't traveling on Buck Technologies business, but he had bigger things to worry about than shareholder complaints about the use of the company helicopter for personal reasons. He reached FCP Alderson early enough to be among the first visitors of the day.

"I'm here to see Sandra Levy," he told the corrections officer at reception.

The guard checked his ID against the list of approved visitors, and Gamble held his breath. He had an appointment, but it was Sandra's prerogative to refuse to see him up until the last minute.

"Follow the guard into the visitation center," he said, which Gamble took as a good sign.

The guard led him to the same table as the last visit, which had Gamble guessing how long it had been since then. Two days? Three? He suddenly wasn't even sure what day it was. So much had happened in the interim. His need to know had grown exponentially. He wasn't sure how he would increase Sandra's willingness to talk.

She pulled up the chair opposite him and rested her hands on the table. "I wasn't expecting to see you again."

"So soon, you mean?"

"Ever."

He wasn't sure where to go from there.

"That's a handsome suit you're wearing, Christian. Like my outfit? Same one I wear every day. Khaki on khaki. They do let me wear a jacket when it gets cold. Sorry I can't model it for you. They're afraid we might use it to hide contraband, so I can't wear it here."

There was a bitterness about her that she'd managed to hide, for the most part, on the previous visit. Inmates had bad days and worse days, he supposed. Getting her to help him would be an even bigger mountain to climb than he'd anticipated.

"You got a raw deal, Sandra. I get it."

"That's an understatement."

"Not as raw as Patrick Battle's."

His words landed with the desired impact. Some of her resentment peeled away. "What do you want from me, Christian?"

"Patrick's kidnappers made a ransom demand."

"How much is that going to set you back?"

"They don't want money. They want code."

"What code?"

"That's the problem. I don't know. Kate doesn't know. They put Patrick on the phone to make the demand. Jeremy Peel and Kate were on. Patrick called it Code Six."

"Never heard of it."

"It doesn't exist," he said.

She smiled a little.

"What's so funny?"

"That's so Patrick. Mess with his kidnappers and make something up on the fly."

He didn't see the need to discuss his daughter's play. "Just because Patrick came up with a bogus name doesn't mean the code the kidnappers really want isn't real."

Her smile faded. "And you think I can help with that. Is that it?"

He checked left, then right, making sure no one was within earshot. "I have a theory. Do you want to hear it?"

"I have a feeling I'm about to."

"My theory is this: the code these kidnappers want is the same code you tried to steal."

Her expression went stone cold. "I told you before, Christian: I didn't steal any code."

"Cut the bullshit, Sandra. This is life or death for Patrick, and now my daughter's down in Colombia, trying to get him home."

"You're asking me to confess to a crime."

"I'm asking you to help save two lives that shouldn't be lost."

"I'm slated for release in less than two years. If I confess to espionage, I could be stuck here, or more likely someplace much worse, for another ten to twenty."

"Do you really think I came here wearing a wire, Sandra?"

"I don't know. Maybe."

He looked at her from across the table, and the way their eyes locked reminded him of how much he'd once trusted her. Apparently, she'd gotten the same reminder.

"No," she said, in a much softer voice. "I don't think that."

"That's good. Because I came here to have an honest conversation."

Sandra took a breath, and then began.

"The deal I cut was pretty favorable. Plead guilty to three counts of lying to an FBI agent. Minimal jail time."

"You were fortunate. Some people thought the Justice Department was too lenient."

"That's an understatement. Even the Justice Department thought my deal was too lenient. Lucky for me, my deal was with the CIA."

"Federal prosecutors work for the Justice Department, not the CIA. Why were you cutting a deal with the CIA?"

"Three reasons. I uncovered the next phase of Project Naïveté. More important, I knew the CIA was behind it. Most important, I agreed to keep my mouth shut."

"Agreed to keep your mouth shut about the code? Or about the fact that the CIA was behind it?"

"It all boiled down to the same thing. The CIA is Buck's biggest investor. If I decided to be the next Edward Snowden and reveal what Naïveté Two could do, the blowback to the CIA would be astronomical."

"What kind of blowback?"

"The kind of blowback that comes when the public learns that the CIA invested tax dollars in a private tech company to develop technology to use against its own people."

He took a moment to wrap his mind around her words. "You were a management coach. How did you uncover all this?"

"I slept with the founder of Buck Technologies and used his credentials," she said, completely matter-of-fact in her delivery, neither proud nor embarrassed.

"First of all, we never slept together," said Gamble. "And even if we had, the CIA has always kept me dark to its most sensitive projects, so my credentials wouldn't have suited your purpose."

"I didn't mean you," she said. "I meant Jeremy Peel."

A lower level of clearance was something Gamble had been forced to accept, given Peel's connection to Walker and the CIA. But hearing about Sandra with Peel, after living with rumors that had all but destroyed his marriage, was enough to make his head explode.

"You and Jeremy? How could you?"

"He was such an easy mark. I'm only five years younger than him, so I'm obviously way too old for his tastes. But all I had to do was suggest that I was sleeping with you, and of course he bit. If it means taking something from you, Jeremy is all over it."

Gamble was in a state of disbelief. "Are you saying you really *are* a—"

She cut him off before he could say the word "spy."

"It's not what you're thinking. But put that aside. Does everything really need a label? The most important thing here is that I acted with good intentions."

"Meaning what?"

"Like I told you. I did it for my daughter."

She'd said the same thing in their last visit, and again it stirred up the confusion he and Kate shared over the suicide note.

"Did *what* for your daughter?" he asked, speaking in a hushed but urgent voice. "What does this Naïveté Two do?"

"How much time do you have?"

"As long as it takes."

Sandra was about to begin, but the corrections offered appeared at their table, and her voice halted.

"Time's up," he said.

"We were just getting started," said Gamble.

"Sorry," said the guard. "This inmate is limited to just one thirty-minute visit per week."

"Since when?" asked Sandra.

"Since the warden announced your punishment this morning."

Gamble looked at Sandra. "Punishment for what?"

"I smuggled in cigarettes," said Sandra, a bit like a schoolgirl caught smoking in the bathroom.

"Look, Officer," said Gamble. "I've traveled a long way. Can we have a few more minutes, please?"

"Sorry, sir. Rules are rules. Come back next week, and the two of you can have another thirty minutes."

Sandra rose. "Hope this can wait a week, Christian."

"I hope so, too," he said, watching as the guard escorted her away.

# CHAPTER 56

Patrick watched and waited as his kidnapper laid Javier's cellphone aside. He and Olga were chained to an exposed metal stud in the wall, seated on a concrete floor.

They were in a warehouse, presumably in Cali. The box truck had pulled up sometime that morning. Patrick had heard the steel garage door open and close before the rear doors of the cargo box swung open, and Liu had ordered them out at gunpoint. Theirs was the only truck in the warehouse, but there were about a dozen cars and SUVs in various states of disassembly. Shelves lined the walls, twenty feet high, and they were loaded with harvested automobile parts. It reminded Patrick of the chop shops he'd seen in the Grant Theft Auto video game he'd played as a kid. Liu had his own desk, though the nameplate read LOPEZ, which Patrick assumed was the name of the actual warehouse manager. The hostages were to his right, near a closet-sized room marked EL BAÑO. Patrick thought the sign should have read "desperate," as no one in his right mind would have used it if he weren't.

"Your friend Kate is trouble," said Liu.

He spoke with none of the screams of anger they would have heard from Javier. His was a wholly different temperament, but it made Patrick even more fearful. He had the eyes of a killing machine, like the soulless black eyes of the great white shark before it tears off your arm.

"If she pulls another stunt like that on the next call, we'll have to demonstrate the virtue of a healthy fear of burning alive."

He was looking at Olga.

"It wasn't a stunt," said Patrick. "I know Kate. She's not a loose cannon. She'd take control like this only if there was no other way to make sure you get what you want."

Liu checked the clock on the wall. "Sounds like you're willing to bet your life on it, which is good. In six hours, either we have an exchange or we have a dead hostage."

He took a seat in the desk chair, put his feet up, and escaped into some form of electronic entertainment on his cellphone.

"I told you he was going to kill me," Olga whispered.

"I'm not sure he meant you," said Patrick.

"He can't kill you. You're the goose that lays the golden egg."

"I can still lay eggs as long as Kate *thinks* I'm alive."

"He needs you to make an exchange."

"I don't think the actual delivery of a live hostage is part of his plan."

"Why do you say that?" she asked.

"Remember those two phone calls you told me about? It was the day I disappeared in the mountains, and you overheard Javier talking on his satellite phone."

"Yes. It was like Javier had two bosses."

"One was Jeremy Peel, who sounded concerned that I disappeared."

"Yes. Apparently, Mr. Peel just wanted to keep you happy enough to stay in Colombia for a good long while. Not lose you somewhere in the jungle."

"But the other caller had a different agenda."

"Totally. It sounded to me like he wanted you dead," said Olga.

Patrick's gaze drifted toward the kidnapper. "I think that other caller was Liu. He hired Javier to push me off the mountain. Javier screwed up the hit, and Liu had to come all the way to Colombia to finish the job himself. And take care of Javier."

"It's like the good book says," said Olga. "No man can serve two masters."

"For he shall hate the one, and be shot in the head by the other," said Patrick, putting his own spin on Matthew 6:24. It was his best attempt at humor under the circumstances, but he had a serious follow-up. "I didn't figure you for someone who knew her Bible."

"Religious education five days a week and Mass every Sunday. Until I was fifteen," she added, and her voice trailed off. "Until Javier took me."

It made Patrick glad that scumbag was dead. It made him hate men like Jeremy Peel even more.

Liu rose from the chair and walked around the desk to the hostages. He stared at Patrick with those shark-like eyes and held the phone up before him.

"On the count of three, I'm going to hit the RECORD button. I want you to say the following: 'Kate, it's me, Patrick. I'm fine. Do exactly as the man says.'"

The kidnapper counted to three and hit RECORD. Patrick repeated the message exactly as instructed.

"Well done," said Liu, and he walked back to his desk.

Patrick and Olga exchanged a nervous glance, and no words were needed. Each could see it in the other's eyes:

*Escape is our only hope.*

A phone rang on the desk. It was Javier's cell, sitting right where Liu had left it. Liu checked the incoming number and answered in a voice loud enough for Patrick to hear.

"Hello, Jeremy."

Peel held the satellite phone a little closer to his ear. He'd placed the call at an altitude of 39,000 feet from Buck's corporate jet. Perhaps the reception was bad, or maybe the roar of the jet engine was making it hard to hear, but the voice on the line didn't sound at all like Javier.

"Who is this?"

"You know who this is."

Peel did. And he didn't dare hang up. "Where's Javier?"

"Javier can't come to the phone. Ever."

The news wasn't shocking, but it chilled him nonetheless. "I want you to know that I had nothing to do with the stunt Kate Gamble pulled in the last call."

"I believe you. You don't have the stones to deliver the code yourself. Never in a million years would you agree to that plan."

"But you're not expecting me to show up with a flash drive and—"

"That's exactly what I'm expecting, Jeremy. I like Kate's idea. Don't you?"

Peel didn't like it in the least, but he knew his preferences were irrelevant. "We'll do it the way you want."

"Good. How soon can you be in Cali?"

"I'm in the air now on my private jet, but we can't possibly land in time for the six-hour deadline Kate put on the next call."

"Call her from the plane and let her know you're on your way. Tell her you talked to Javier and agreed the next call will be tonight at eight p.m. Cali time. Don't mention me. Don't you *dare* mention me."

The call ended. Peel collapsed in his chair, emotionally spent, dreading the coming night in Cali. Then he dialed Kate's encrypted phone.


The call from Jeremy Peel lasted two minutes. Kate agreed to make herself ready for a phone call with the kidnapper at the new time of 8:00 p.m. Beyond that, it was like a game of liar's poker.

"Do you have the ransom?" asked Kate.

"I'd prefer not to have this conversation by phone, even if it is encrypted."

"I need an answer from you before the eight p.m. call."

"Let's meet at your hotel and talk."

"That's impossible. There's not another person on the planet who knows where I'm staying, and I'm certainly not going to tell you. Nothing personal."

They agreed to meet in the lobby of a boutique hotel in one of Cali's wealthiest neighborhoods, Ciudad Jardín. Kate hung up. She looked at Enrique, who was sitting in the armchair in her hotel room.

"I'm worried," said Kate.

"Stay cool," he said. "You took control in this morning's call. Kidnappers hate it when negotiators do that. So it's no surprise that Javier would try to reestablish control by pushing off the next meeting to eight p.m.—to a time selected by him, not you."

"I agree with all that," said Kate.

"Then what worries you?"

"From the previous calls, my impression of Javier is that he's impulsive and quick to react. I would have expected him to call me right back, immediately after I hung up, and retake control. He didn't. Instead, he waited two hours, called Jeremy Peel on a line that I'm not even privy to, and asked him to pass along a message to me. Doesn't that strike you as odd?"

"I hear what you're saying, Kate. You think he hurt Patrick."

"I can't live with myself if my plan backfires."

It was a cumulative effect: Patrick's disappearance, meeting Sandra Levy, her negotiations with Noah, the calls from the kidnappers, standing up to Jeremy Peel—all in the wake of her mother's suicide. Kate needed a tissue.

"Hey, it's okay," said Enrique, handing her a whole box of them.

"I'm so sorry," she said.

"Not a problem. If it means anything, I cried like a baby when I lost my interpreter."

Kate gathered herself and said, "I'm really glad you're here."

"Me, too," he said.

# CHAPTER 57

Christian Gamble arrived at the Washington office of BJB Funding before noon. He was there to see David Walker.

The CIA headquarters is in Virginia, but the agency fastidiously guards against any claims of overlap between its national security operations and its venture capital arm, so BJB operated out of a nongovernmental building on the other side of the Potomac River. The George Bush Center for Intelligence is too far north to be seen from the District, but Walker seemed to have gone the extra mile to assert his independence from the agency by choosing a corner office facing the National Mall to the south, his back squarely to the CIA while seated behind his desk.

Gamble hadn't spoken to Walker since the meeting at Peel's house, where Kate had told the chairman of the board and the CIA to fuck off and announced that she was "going private" to negotiate for Patrick's release. Gamble had phoned ahead from the helicopter on the flight back from FCP Alderson to set up what he described as "a critical follow-up meeting," just the two of them in Walker's office.

"I went to visit Sandra Levy," said Gamble.

"I know," said Walker.

Smug remarks like that one, the air of omniscience that Walker conveyed, made Gamble question the actual degree of separation between the agency and its venture capital arm.

"Then am I correct that the prison guard's sudden decision to cut my visit short was no coincidence?"

"It was my understanding that her visitation privileges have been restricted due to a rule infraction."

"I'm sure. The fact that you know so much about it tells me that's bullshit."

"Christian, if you've come here to give me a tongue lashing, I have far more important things to deal with."

"Then allow me to readjust your priorities. My conversation with Sandra Levy gave me serious cybersecurity concerns. The DOJ's security audit is ongoing. I came to you because I wanted to discuss my concerns with you first. But if you don't have time," he said, rising, "that's unfortunate."

"Sit down, Christian. Before you embarrass yourself by going to the DOJ, what do you know about Sandra Levy?"

Gamble settled back into his chair. He didn't want to divulge too much of his conversation with Sandra, but it was simply a good negotiating tactic to show Walker that he wasn't there on a fishing expedition—that he had some critical level of knowledge.

"I know that the CIA played a key role in structuring what appears to be a very favorable sentence for her."

"Yes, that's true. You do realize Sandra Levy *works* for the CIA."

"What?"

"She was a plant, Christian. The CIA was concerned about a possible leak at Buck Technologies, and to protect its investment in the company, the agency sent in Sandra to find it. 'Management coach' was her cover. We wanted her close to you."

Gamble did a double take. "Wait. Are you saying *I* was the suspected leak?"

"Your wife, to be more precise. Using credentials she stole from you."

There was no use in denying that Elizabeth had compromised his credentials. "She never actually used them to access anything."

"Your wife was an alcoholic who dialed nine-one-one and falsely accuse you of abuse. Who really *knows* what her intentions were?"

"She wasn't a criminal. Sandra's investigation must have confirmed that, right? If Elizabeth was actually using my credentials to steal company secrets, this wouldn't be the first time I'm hearing about this."

"Yes. Sandra Levy concluded that neither you nor your wife were the problem. And then she went badly astray."

"In what way?"

"She shifted her focus to Jeremy Peel without authorization. To make matters worse, she violated some cardinal rules about methods of extracting information from a target. I will spare you the lurid details."

Gamble had already heard it from Sandra, but hearing it from Walker put it in a new light. "Is that why she's in prison?"

"Very astute observation, Christian. She pled guilty to three counts of lying to investigators. Most people think those lies relate to espionage. In actuality, she had sex with Jeremy Peel in violation of CIA rules, and she lied about it. The CIA did her a favor by not making that public."

"All that aside, Sandra must have had a reason to target Jeremy. Has anyone ever followed up on that?"

"I can't discuss the status of an investigation with you."

"Forget the status of the investigation. Here's all I really want to know: What would make a person throw away her career like this? What was driving her?"

"I'm not at liberty to discuss her motivations."

"Well, fuck your liberty. Sandra discussed them with Kate. She said, 'I did it for Megan'—her daughter. Call me crazy, but that sounds an awful lot like the suicide note my wife left: 'I did it for Kate.' So I'd like to know what the hell is going on here!"

"Could be a coincidence."

"I'm not asking what it could be. What do you know?"

"I wish I could say more. I really do."

"Damn it, David! Your firm is the largest shareholder in Buck Technologies. My daughter's in Colombia right now negotiating with kidnappers to get one of Buck's key employees released. If you won't say it for my benefit, say it for hers. What does this all mean?"

"I have no idea what was in your wife's head."

"Fine. What was driving Sandra Levy? What did she mean when she said she did it for her daughter?"

Walker glanced out the window. It seemed that Gamble's plea was getting through to him. Finally, he spoke.

"I'll say this much. Whatever she thought Jeremy was up to, Sandra saw it as particularly dangerous for girls and young women."

Gamble froze. It was as if he'd been in a dark room for months, with the answer sitting right beside him, and someone had finally switched on the light.

"I'm sorry, Christian. I can't tell you more than that."

"I got it," said Gamble. "You don't have to say another word."

Gamble showed himself out, rode the elevator to the lobby. A black SUV was waiting outside the building. He dialed Kate's number as he climbed inside, but she didn't answer. He thought carefully before making the next call, but decided it was the right thing to do.

"Noah, it's Christian Gamble," he said into the phone, leaving the prosecutor a voicemail message. "Call me back immediately. It's important."

# CHAPTER 58

Diego picked up Kate and Enrique at the Hotel InterContinental to take them to the planning meeting with Jeremy Peel in Ciudad Jardín.

"Safety on?" asked Enrique. He was talking about the gun in her purse, and it was the third time he'd reminded her since leaving the hotel room.

"On," she said.

South Cali had some sketchy areas, but Ciudad Jardín was not one of them. Caleños called it a "city within a city" or, perhaps more accurately, a city apart from the city. Mansions lined the lush green avenues. The best high schools and universities were nearby, and an array of fancy restaurants and upscale bars made this wealthy neighborhood a pleasant and safe place to live. On the downside, Ciudad Jardín was a long way from the livelier and equally safe areas along the river to the west and north, where Kate was staying, and it was closer to the massive hillside neighborhood known as Siloé. Diego pointed it out on the ride south.

"Never go there," he said, pointing from the driver's seat. "If you get into trouble, even the police are afraid to go there."

The rule of thumb in Cali was to avoid the east, but gangs also controlled Siloé and other pockets of turf to the south.

They reached the hotel in plenty of time to talk strategy before the 8:00 p.m. call. Diego waited with the car. Peel's bodyguard was in the lobby and took them to a suite on the third floor so they could speak in private. It was Kate and Enrique on one side of the rectangular table, with Peel and his bodyguard on the other. The encrypted phone on which Kate received the kidnapper's calls was resting beside the centerpiece of white and purple orchids.

"Did you bring the flash drive?" asked Kate.

Peel laid it on the table. "Coke Zero," he said, confirming that he wasn't giving up the "secret formula," as Kate had called it.

"In terms of communications," said Kate, "I don't like you having separate phone calls with Javier. I need to be part of all negotiations going forward."

"I didn't initiate the last call. He called me. After you hung up."

"I was asserting control."

"You may have watched one too many *Die Hard* movies."

Kate had been second-guessing herself all day, so she couldn't push back too hard. "What's done is done. Going forward, we should speak with one voice, and that voice should be mine."

Kate's encrypted phone vibrated on the table. It was not yet time for the 8:00 p.m. call, but it wasn't a call anyway. It was a text that contained no message, just a voice recording. Kate played the voice message on speaker. It was Patrick.

"Kate, it's me, Patrick. I'm fine. Do exactly as the man says."

Kate looked at Enrique, who seemed equally bemused. "That's our proof of life? A voice recording? How do we know that's not from a week ago?"

Her phone vibrated again. This time, the text bubble contained a message:

Negotiations are over. No more voice calls. My orders to follow.

Kate stared at the message bubble, then looked at Peel. "This doesn't sound like Javier."

Peel didn't answer, but Kate didn't drop the matter.

"Who did you actually speak to on the phone earlier, Mr. Peel?"

"I told you it was Javier."

"I know what you told me. But I want the truth. Who did you talk to?" she asked, her voice rising. "I need to know who has Patrick!"

The phone vibrated. Another text message:

Mr. Peel: Take the flash drive to Café de Mariscos on Calle Obispo at 9 p.m. A table is reserved in your name. Sit and wait. One bodyguard is allowed. No one else.

Enrique googled the location. "He chose a public place in a good neighborhood to make you feel safe. That's a constructive first step."

"But what about Patrick?" asked Kate. "This has to be a simultaneous exchange."

The telltale moving ellipses appeared below the previous bubble message on Kate's phone, indicating another text was on the way.

"There's more," said Kate, and the message appeared.

If I'm convinced you were not followed, I will join you. The girl will be with me. I take the flash drive. You keep the girl.

"By 'the girl,' I assume he means Olga," said Enrique. "The one you told me about?"

"Yes," said Kate, shooting dagger eyes in Peel's direction. "The girl in the white string bikini."

Another text bubble quickly followed.

As soon as I verify that the code is genuine, I will release Patrick.

"Looks like he's not settling for Coke Zero," said Enrique.

"Shit," said Kate. She grabbed the phone and fired back a quick text.

Not acceptable. Simultaneous exchange only. Both Patrick and Olga.

It took more than a minute for a response to come. It was a phone call this time. Kate answered on speaker, so all could hear, but she didn't even get the chance to speak.

The sound of Patrick's scream filled the hotel suite.

Silence followed. The call was over, short but with the desired impact, as it had made Kate's skin crawl. A text bubble followed.

Final warning. Don't fuck with me.

Kate buried her face in her hands. Enrique laid a comforting hand on her shoulder. "We can work within his rules," he said.

"What choice do we have?" she said, her voice quaking.

# CHAPTER 59

Patrick breathed deeply, in and out, trying to quell the pain in his left biceps.

Liu the pyromaniac had apparently left his napalm science experiment back at the ship, but he'd managed to improvise. A welding machine was standard equipment in any chop shop. He'd spared Patrick the direct and potentially lethal flame of the welding blowtorch—possibly an act of mercy, but more likely he was just too lazy to carry the entire machine from one side of the warehouse to the other. Instead, he'd selected a steel welding rod—one-sixteenth of an inch in diameter, by Patrick's estimate—and held it to the flame until the tip glowed like a sparkler on the Fourth of July.

"This is really going to hurt," he'd said, whereupon the white-hot tip had burrowed into Patrick's arm like a lit cigarette, but so much hotter.

The pain was utterly disproportionate to the freckle-sized mark left behind. He worried where his scream into the cellphone must have led Kate's imagination.

"It's showtime," said Liu. "Olga, you're coming with me."

The hostages were chained to the same post but with separate padlocks. Liu unlocked Olga with the key, removed the chains, and pulled her to her feet. The gun to her head served to remind them who was in charge.

"Patrick, your life is in Olga's hands. If she obeys me, all will be fine. If she doesn't, then here's something you should know. That welding rod I jabbed into your arm was probably five hundred degrees Celsius. A welding arc is about fifteen *thousand* degrees. Tell Olga you don't want to go there."

Patrick noticed that the rod was still resting on the hood of the car nearest to the hostages, where Liu had left it to cool.

"Tell her she needs to be a good girl," said Liu.

"You're an animal," said Olga.

"You have to do as he says," said Patrick.

"How 'bout that, you're both right," said Liu. He led Olga away at gunpoint, wending between vehicles toward the side door to the warehouse. Patrick kept one eye on them and the other on the welding rod that Liu had left on the car hood. A foot-long rod of stainless steel was just a few feet away from him. He was padlocked to a pole, making it impossible to reach it, making it all the more imperative that he find a way to get it.

The rod was about the same thickness as a bicycle spoke, and the fact that Patrick's mind drew that comparison was no coincidence. Once, as a kid, he'd biked to the beach and, when it came time to pedal home, discovered that he'd lost the key to his bike lock while building a giant sandcastle complete with a moat, drawbridge, and three-foot-tall turrets. He had thirty minutes to get home or be grounded. For Patrick, it was just another episode in the long-running series *Internet to the Rescue*. His smartphone pulled up a YouTube video on how to pick a padlock with a reshaped paper clip. As it turned out, a 1.8-millimeter bicycle spoke worked even better.

With a stainless-steel welding rod, this job would be a piece of cake.

The side door opened and closed. A car engine started outside the building, and Patrick could hear the vehicle pull away. Olga and Liu were gone. He was alone in the warehouse. It was time for action.

Patrick would call this episode, "Harry Potter and the Quest for the Rod of Steel."

One end of the chain was fastened to a post. The other end coiled around his wrists and was secured behind his back with a padlock. His most comfortable position was seated with his back to the post, but the chain was long enough for him to lie flat on his back, if he could put up with the pain of a padlock pressed between his lower back and the floor. He concentrated on making his spine as long as possible, taking up every millimeter of slack in the chain. With his body fully extended, he finally managed to brace the crown of his head against the post and plant his feet squarely on the front bumper of the nearest vehicle—the car on which the metal rod rested.

Patrick pushed with his legs and released. It was like doing leg presses at the Buck fitness center. *Push. Release.* He built a rhythm, and before long, the car was rocking like a baby carriage.

He heard the steel rod move. Liu had left it near the windshield. It had rolled forward, halfway down the hood, following the sloped design toward the front bumper. Patrick pushed harder, legs pumping and heart pounding. The worst-case scenario was that the rod would turn sideways and get caught in the slit between the hood and side panel. He couldn't let that happen. He dug deep inside himself and pushed with all his leg strength. The rocking sensation built to a lurch, and Patrick heard the sweet *ping* of a steel rod hitting a concrete floor.

He stopped pumping, exhausted. The car was motionless. Patrick trapped the rod beneath the sole of his shoe and dragged it toward him. It required some contortion-like finagling, but he worked the prized rod all the way up along his leg and into his hands. He was almost giddy with excitement, until he realized that the hard part was still ahead of him.

*Hard. But not impossible.*

It had taken twenty minutes for a twelve-year-old Patrick to pick a lock with his bicycle spoke. Following the instructional video, he'd broken it into two pieces, one bent into the shape of an Allen wrench to apply tension to the wide base of the keyhole, like the flat edge of the key; the other bent at a forty-five-degree angle to "rake" the pins, like the jagged edge of the key.

This job would be no different, though it was his first attempt with his hands behind his back.

*First time for everything.*

Patrick snapped the rod in half and got to work.

# CHAPTER 60

Christian Gamble spent the entire day on the Buck campus, exploring the depths of his own darkness.

The fact that certain Buck projects were dark to the CEO was not something Gamble talked about openly. The investment agreement with BJB Funding actually prohibited him from saying so publicly. But a twenty-year-old contract with the CIA's venture capital arm was not the sole, or even most important, reason to keep quiet about the limitations on his security clearance. It was beyond embarrassing. His own daughter had found it shocking.

*Willful blindness, Dad. It's a corporate disease. Sometimes fatal.*

His phone conversation with Noah had been short and to the point. "I need to know what I don't know," Gamble had told him. Noah balked and said he'd check with his supervisor. Gamble tired of waiting for a response. He showed up at the U.S. Attorney's Office in Judiciary Square to talk face-to-face, behind closed doors, just the two of them in Noah's office.

"I'm sorry," said Noah. "I can't share any preliminary conclusions of my cybersecurity audit with you or anyone else outside the department."

"I don't want your 'conclusions.' I want to verify some facts with you. That's your job, as auditor, correct? To base your decision on facts?"

"Of course."

"Then stop squirming like the spineless wimp my daughter dumped and answer my questions."

"You don't have to make this personal."

"My employee was kidnapped for ransom, and my daughter is risking her life, as we speak, to get him home. How is that not personal?"

"I don't see what that has to do with my audit."

"Can we just verify a few facts? *Please?*"

The "dumping" remark was harsh, but Gamble was in no mood to apologize. To his credit, Noah seemed willing to put it aside.

"Okay. I'm listening."

"Buck has a project called Naïveté Two. It grew out of Project Naïveté."

"I can't talk to you about Naïveté Two. You don't have clearance."

"But I do have clearance to numerous operations that feed in to Naïveté Two."

"How would you know what feeds in to Naïveté Two?"

"Process of elimination."

"I don't understand," Noah said.

"I know Jeremy Peel heads Naïveté Two. After twenty-five years, I know Jeremy's vision. I know which company assets he would draw upon to actualize that vision. I made a list. I spent all day pushing the limits of my clearance in each of those silos until I hit a brick wall."

Noah nodded, seeming to get it. "And you want me to tell you if that brick wall is Naïveté Two."

"No. Don't *tell* me anything. I'm simply going to read you my list of silos that I think feed in to Naïveté Two. If I'm wrong, there's nothing more to do. If I'm right, I would imagine you would want to shoot off an immediate email to your supervisor advising that it is highly possible that the kidnapping of Patrick Battle has compromised the security of Naïveté Two."

The two men locked eyes. Gamble pulled up his list on his smartphone.

"I'll spare you the obvious," said Gamble. "We all know that screen-related sentiment data is part of virtually everything Big Data does. Browsing history, social media connections, online purchases, likes, emojis, emoticons, LOLs and other sentiment-related acronyms, pre-ferred slang, how often you type in all caps, how many fractions of a second you let your cursor linger over the image of a puppy as opposed to the image of a Kardashian.

"My list puts a finer point on the project. It focuses on non-screen data that tells Big Data how you think and feel. Ready?"

No answer from Noah, but he was clearly listening.

"One: smart speakers. By this I mean all the data collected from everything that operates on voice command. Your phone, your car, your house, your microwave oven—everything.

"Two: all those telephone conversations that are recorded with the caller's consent 'for training purposes,' which Big Data buys up so our algorithms can measure what your voice or syntax reveals about your emotions, sentiments, and personality—essentially, 'hear' what you say and how you say it when you're angry or trying to get a stranger to help you, so that you can be coded as 'logical and responsible,' 'creative and playful,' or 'tense and aggressive.'

"Three: personal health monitors, which can be linked to the GPS coordinates on your phone, so we know how fast your heart beats while you're watching the next James Bond film.

"Four: surveillance and security camera images, in case we also want to see the expression on your face when Mr. Bond removes his shirt, or when you run the red light on the drive home from the theater.

"Five, digitally captured internet videoconferencing, which never dies and, unlike General MacArthur and other old soldiers, doesn't just fade away. Six—"

Gamble paused and looked up from his list. "You get the idea. I believe Naïveté Two combines every non-screen data silo at Buck's disposal with traditional screen-sourced data to create a digital profile on every man, woman, and child in America. I'm talking about a massive collection of personal, psychological, and emotional dossiers that would make J. Edgar Hoover ejaculate in his grave."

He waited. Noah showed no reaction, verbal or nonverbal. Thirty seconds passed in silence. Finally, Noah turned in his swivel chair to face his computer monitor.

"Excuse me," he said. "I need to send an email to my supervisor."

He placed his hands on the keyboard and began typing.

Gamble rose and exited the office, Noah having "told" him nothing.

Kate's phone rang. It was her father. Calling to talk her out of danger, no doubt. She decided she should answer. Then changed her mind. Then changed it back.

"Dad, I can't talk now."

"It's a scraping tool," he said.

"What?"

"Code Six, or whatever you want to call Patrick's ransom demand. It's a scraping tool."

Kate was in the backseat of the car, and Enrique's friend Diego was driving. It was a safe neighborhood where people walked to bars and restaurants at night, so Kate and Diego circled the neighborhood while Enrique blended in with the crowd on foot, casing the restaurant where Peel was to make the exchange. The kidnapper had said "no followers" and only "one bodyguard," but it hadn't taken much in the way of persuasion for Peel to see the benefit of having Enrique nearby in case something went wrong.

"I don't even know what that means—a 'scraping tool.'"

"It could be a browser extension. It could be a lot of things. The bottom line is that it's a tool for outsiders to harvest data from platforms like TikTok, Facebook, Instagram, and all the other places where users give up way more than they should."

"And the platforms allow this?"

"No! That's the point. Facebook sends out cease and desist letters all the time. They even threatened the NYU Observatory for scraping data on political ads for academic research."

"So if scraping tools aren't allowed, why is Buck's so valuable?"

"Because no one knows it's there. It's the *stealth bomber* of scraping tools. We can scrape anything from any platform, and no one will know it. Do you understand how powerful that is?"

She did. "Are you sure about this?"

"Jeremy has talked about this for years. Today I pushed my credentials as far as possible in every data silo. Each time, I eventually hit a brick wall. On my side of the wall is the data we collected with proper consent. On the dark side of the wall, I believe, is the data we scraped."

"Illegally," said Kate.

"Without consent. It's a gray area. I wouldn't say illegally."

"Immorally," said Kate.

"We can debate that with Sir Thomas More in the next life. But here's the important thing."

The car stopped, and the passenger-side door suddenly opened, which sent Kate's heart into her throat. Enrique jumped in the backseat.

"Hold on, Dad," she said, relieved to see it was her bodyguard and not a carjacking.

"Peel is moving," said Enrique. "Kidnapper changed the drop site."

"To where?"

"Peel's bodyguard texted and said he'll send me a pin when they get there."

"What do you think happened?"

"Nothing," said Enrique. "I'm sure the kidnapper is just watching to see if anyone follows Peel to the new location."

"Like the police?"

"No, like us," said Diego, offering the insight of a local. "The kidnapper already knows we didn't involve the police. You can't call the police in Cali without the kidnapper getting tipped off."

Kate returned to her call. "Dad, I have to go."

"Wait. There's more."

"Dad, we're about to make the exchange!"

"Kate, I need to know: Is there any chance you're handing over the tool. The *real* tool?"

"No."

"Because this tool is dangerous in the wrong hands."

"This tool is dangerous in the *right* hands. But no, Dad, you don't have to worry. I'll call you when it's over."

Kate hung up. The car started forward. "Where we headed?" asked Kate.

"Club Siloé," said Enrique.

"Siloé? Diego, isn't that the place you told us never to go?"

From the driver's seat, Diego made eye contact in the rearview mirror. "The club's not technically in Barrio Siloé. But it's close."

"How close?"

"It's perfectly safe once you get inside," said Diego. "The fact that it's literally on the edge of danger is what makes it the cool spot in Cali. So you don't want to walk the area."

"We don't have to go, if you don't want," Enrique told her.

Kate hadn't come all this way to hang out with tourists and expats at her hotel while the exchange went down without her. On the other hand, there was a reason her father's kidnap and ransom insurance policy covered immediate family members.

"Just don't park the car," she said. "Circle the block. That's the plan."

"That's a good plan," said Diego, with a little more local insight.

# CHAPTER 61

Peel's driver stopped outside the entrance to Club Siloé. His body-guard, Jaime, was beside him in the backseat.

"I don't like this," said Peel.

"We want a public place, so he doesn't pull anything. But a five-star restaurant in Ciudad Jardín was a safer choice."

Peel had the kidnapper's number from their phone call on the jet. He dialed, was somewhat surprised to get an answer, and stated his position firmly.

"This location is not acceptable."

"I can see you. Go inside."

He'd assumed he was being watched, but until that moment, Peel hadn't felt it. "I'm not going in."

"Do I have to call Mr. Walker at the CIA?"

Technically, Walker wasn't "at the CIA," but that didn't diminish the threat. "You wouldn't do that," said Peel.

"I definitely will. And he'd be very upset to learn what bullshit it is that Buck Technologies only does business with Western allies. Unless you think he considers China a friend."

It could have been a bluff, as it wasn't in the interest of the Chinese government to "out" someone like Peel, a secret source of data on foreigners. But Peel couldn't take that risk. He had no choice but to fold.

"Ten minutes. In and out," said Peel.

"Your table is under the name Cruz. Wait for me there."

Not very imaginative of him to use the Spanish version of Smith, but Peel didn't quibble. The call ended, and with a quick nod to his team signaling "go," the driver opened Peel's door and his bodyguard whisked him inside.

Peel was no stranger to clubs of this sort, where naked young women worked on drunk businessmen, and the old song about a fool and his money was perpetually at the top of the charts. But it was his first time with only one bodyguard. It was risky behavior on his part, but it fed his macabre sense of curiosity to test the limits of what beautiful young women would do for money. Even more fun was to wager on it. "I'll bet you fifty thousand dollars the blonde will drink the redhead's urine for five hundred dollars." Not that he would ever have sex with one of these dancers. For that, men like Javier hooked him up with women like Olga.

*Javier, you should have stuck to business as usual.*

"Table for Cruz," he told the hostess.

"This way," the young woman said.

It turned out that the pole-dancing lounge was a small part of the action. Peel and his bodyguard followed the hostess through a set of chrome-clad double doors that led to the heart and soul of Club Siloé.

A salsa band was playing onstage, and a parquet dance floor was packed with couples making it clear that Shakira wasn't the only Colombian who could dance. Above the stage, stretching wall to wall, was an enormous rectangular meme of Leonardo da Vinci's *The Last Supper*, with whiskey replacing wine, and popular salsa musicians and their groupies replacing Jesus and His apostles. It was beloved by patrons, no doubt, but to Peel, this was art on the order of dogs playing poker. The hostess led them to a booth away from the band, a somewhat quieter section of the club where it was possible to have a conversation without shouting. She laid two menus on the table, and Peel checked the list of drinks. *Cervezas* were on the left; *tragos fuertes* on the right. The words in bold across the top of the menu made him curious.

"*Viva la vida, mira que se va y no vuelve,*" he read aloud in bad Spanish. "What does that mean, gorgeous?"

The hostess smiled. "No can say *en inglés*. Your waitress comes soon."

She left, and Peel put his bodyguard's Spanish to the test. "Do you know what it means?"

"The literal translation loses it. Basically: 'Live it up, 'cause, hey, life goes away and doesn't come back.'"

Peel laid the menu aside, and his gaze drifted toward the empty seats for their guests. "Good advice," he said.

Kate was on her second turn around the block. The plan was for Enrique to go inside the club and monitor the exchange while Kate and Diego circled Club Siloé. As the car stopped outside the club entrance, the voice of Peel's bodyguard came through in real time over the car's sound system, which was linked by Bluetooth to Diego's cellphone.

"Basically: 'Live it up, 'cause, hey, life goes away and doesn't come back.'"

"That's actually a decent translation," said Diego.

Enrique had the cellphone number for Peel's bodyguard, and Diego had used it to hack the phone's microphone so that they could eavesdrop on Peel's conversation with the kidnapper. Technologically, it wasn't difficult to do, especially for a former DEA agent. Diego had busted many a drug dealer who didn't realize that his phone simply had to be powered on, not in use, for hackers to use the microphone as a listening device.

"A lot of background noise," said Kate.

"It's a nightclub. I can't help that," said Diego.

"That's why we still need eyes on the table," said Enrique. "I'll text you with updates."

"Good luck," said Kate.

Enrique got out, and the car pulled away. Diego hung a left at the traffic light, and they continued east, toward the luminous moon above the hilltop.

"That's Siloé," he said, indicating.

Glittering lights dotted the habitable portion of hillside, from street level to an elevation of about one thousand feet. At the very top, jagged granite edges bathed in the moonlight.

"It's actually beautiful at night."

"*Sí*, at night."

Kate noticed a strange glowing dot in the distance. It moved slowly up the hill, like a meteor light-years away from earth, seeming to divide Siloé in half.

"What's that moving dot?" asked Kate.

"That's the new gondola public transportation system," he said, and then he hung a right. "The idea is that if people have transportation, they can get a job and build a better life. That's the station right ahead."

The car slowed, and Kate looked out the window as they passed the station at street level. About two dozen commuters were in line.

"They're all women," said Kate.

"Yeah, mostly housekeepers. The 'have nots' who serve the 'haves.' They work a twelve-hour shift, seven days a week, in Ciudad Jardín and other nice parts of Cali. Then it's back to Siloé. The gondola gives them some hope of getting home to take care of their families without getting robbed."

"Sad."

"Yeah. It just amazes me, though."

"What does?" Kate asked.

"What mothers will do for their children."

Kate couldn't have said it better, but her mind raced beyond the point of mere agreement.

*I did it for Kate.*

She glanced again at the women in line. Diego made another left turn, and as they continued down the street, heading straight toward the gondola rising toward the moon over the hilltop, Kate shook off the confusing thoughts of her mother's death. She was instead thinking of Sandra Levy.

*I did it for Megan.*

Kate had at first dismissed Sandra's words as a snarky comment about her mother's suicide note. Something else was afoot, and her father's explanation of the scraping tool behind Naïveté II was bringing it all into focus.

*The bottom line is that it's a tool for outsiders to harvest data from platforms like TikTok, Facebook, Instagram, and all the other places where users give up way more than they should.*

It was well known that the "users" who gave up the most on social media were between the ages of thirteen and twenty—and female. Studies proved it. Facebook, TikTok, and the other platforms admitted as much. Self-esteem, self-confidence, and self-worth were down; anxiety, depression, and suicide were up. The victims were mostly girls—daughters with mothers who would do anything to protect them.

Kate reached for her phone and was about to call her father when it vibrated with a text message. It was from Enrique on the inside.

They just sat down. Asian guy with the girl.

Kate put her phone away.

"Diego, turn up the volume on the audio feed," she said.

"If I turn it any louder, there's too much static from the background noises around them."

Kate put her ear to the car speaker. As they made their third trip around the block, she listened to the conversation at the table inside Club Siloé.

# CHAPTER 62

Liu entered Club Siloé with a beautiful woman on his arm. If Olga was going to accompany him, she had to look the part. A backless dress would have been sexier, but Javier's knife had done its own brand of salsa dancing there. She looked hot enough in his second choice. Red was her color. A little makeup went a long way to hide the worry lines of captivity.

"Say nothing," he reminded her, as the hostess led them to the Cruz booth.

Liu had reserved this particular booth with purpose. Its proximity to the fire exit, an avenue of escape, had made it narcos' table of choice in Cali's drug-trafficking heyday.

"Speak only if *I* ask you a question," he said. "Understand?"

"Yes."

Ten steps from the booth, he made eye contact with Peel. He didn't recognize the man beside him, but his instructions had expressly allowed for "one bodyguard," and he had no doubt that Peel had chosen a capable one. The hostess placed two more menus on the table. Liu slipped her a hundred-dollar bill and said they wanted to be left alone. She smiled and stepped away.

"Don't sit," said Peel, before they could slide into the booth. "Your old friend here hasn't seen you in a while. He wants to give you a hug."

The bodyguard rose and embraced Liu. It was a patdown, in actuality, and Liu went along with it.

"Great to see you again," said the bodyguard, satisfied. He returned to his seat. Olga took a seat directly opposite Peel. Liu followed, sitting across from the bodyguard.

"Doesn't Olga look terrific, Jeremy? All grown up, just for you. I mean *dressed* up. Freudian slip."

"Can we get on with this," said Peel. "We agreed on ten minutes. I've been waiting at least that long. You're lucky I didn't leave."

"And you're lucky you're still alive," said Liu, and then he addressed the bodyguard. "Just so my old friend here is in the loop, this is our second go at this transaction. The first time, we paid in full, but Mr. Peel didn't deliver in full. He left something out. Patrick Battle calls it Code Six. I don't know if that's a real name or not. But whatever was missing the first time better be on the flash drive the second time."

"Don't threaten Mr. Peel," said the bodyguard.

"What're you gonna do, shoot me? Then what, genius? You keep the girl, and nobody ever sees or hears from Patrick Battle again? Tell him, Olga. Even if your life depended on it, could you find your way back to Patrick?"

She hesitated, as if making double sure she was allowed to answer. "No. I couldn't."

"There you have it," said Liu. "That's why I'm not afraid to come here unarmed. And why you, pea brain, shouldn't even think of reaching for that pistol you have strapped to your ankle."

Peel and his bodyguard didn't deny he was armed. "Let's all just take a breath and relax," said Peel.

"How 'bout the two of you shut up and listen," said Liu. "Here's the deal. You give me the flash drive. Olga stays here. I take the flash drive to Patrick. If he can show me it's real, I let him go, and all is cool. If it's bullshit, I come for you, Jeremy. And next time, I plan to bring my benzene, gasoline, and plenty of Styrofoam cups."

"Bring *what?*" asked Peel.

"Homemade napalm," said his bodyguard.

"I fucking burn you alive," said Liu. "Not a pleasant way to go. Hurts just to have all that gel smeared on your skin. Right, Olga?"

A moment of hesitation, and then she responded. "Yes. It hurts a lot."

"Especially around the eyes," said Liu. "After a few minutes, most people end up begging me to light them up just to get it over with."

Peel laid the flash drive on the table but kept it close, covering it with his hand. "I'm not betting my life on Patrick's ability to convince you this is real."

"Because it's *not* real?" asked Liu.

"No."

"You screwed me once. Why should I believe you this time?"

"I didn't screw you. It was a mistake."

"A mistake? Hardly. You took our money and changed your mind."

"You got what you bargained for."

"What we bargained for was the same set of tools you delivered to the CIA. What happened, Jeremy? Did you suddenly get patriotic? Oh, sure, it's okay for Uncle Sam to scrape the digital world and build personal-sentiment profiles on each and every American who uses social media. But put that same power in the hands of a foreign government? No way. That's where Jeremy Peel draws the moral line."

"That's enough," said Peel.

"It was pointless to screw us, Jeremy. You said it yourself. If you didn't sell it to us, we'd steal it from you."

Peel wrapped the flash drive in his fist. "Fuck you. The deal's off."

"Don't make us steal it, Jeremy."

"You're gonna have to."

"Suit yourself."

In a sudden blur of motion, Liu reached under the table, grabbed the pistol he'd fastened to the underside with Velcro an hour earlier, and squeezed off two quick shots. The first hit the bodyguard, and the second was for Peel. The silencer muffled the gunshots, and before Olga could scream, Liu covered her mouth with his hand.

"Scream and you die."

Out of the corner of his eye, he saw a man running toward him like a charging bull, and Liu quickly surmised that Peel had violated the "one bodyguard" limit. He pulled Olga out of the booth, used her as a human shield, and fired a shot that dropped the charging bull in its tracks. The silencer kept the matter quiet, but the splatter of blood on the dance floor triggered screams of panic. The salsa music continued as men and women ran for their lives, stampeding toward the exit. Liu grabbed Olga by the arm and ran to the fire exit, setting off the alarm as they pushed through the door.

"I'm hit!"

Enrique's words came loud and clear over Kate's phone, hitting her like a punch to the gut. "How bad?" she asked.

"Got me in the shoulder. No major organs. He took Olga down the fire escape. Red dress. Alley behind the building. Go!"

"Are you sure you're okay?"

"Yes, go! Don't lose them! If they make it to Siloé, even the police won't follow!"

Diego hit the gas, and as the car whipped around the corner, a topless Jeep shot out of the alley in front of them. Olga's red dress was unmissable.

"That's them!" shouted Kate.

The Jeep sped up, and Diego was in pursuit.

"They're heading for Siloé," he said.

"Just like Enrique said they would."

"You have to decide right now, Kate. Let them go, or stay with them."

The Jeep continued toward the hillside barrio, speeding along a narrow street that ran beneath the gondola to Siloé.

"Follow them!" said Kate.

# CHAPTER 63

Patrick was starting to lose feeling in his fingers.

Picking a padlock behind his back was much harder than picking his bicycle lock. At least a dozen times he'd felt on the verge of success, only to find repeated disappointment. He recalled Javier, back at the freighter, telling him not to "get all Houdini" on him and try to escape. He was beginning to wonder if the Great Houdini himself could have picked a lock with a bent welding rod and his hands bound behind his back.

Patrick opened and closed his hands several times, working out the cramps in his fingers, and then made a fresh attempt. Tension rod in the widest part of the hole, like the base of the key. Raking rod in the narrower slot, like the jagged edge of the key. Rake the pins from deepest to shallowest—and turn.

*Click.*

"Yes!"

The open lock dropped to the floor, and Patrick shook free of the chains. That first taste of freedom made him almost giddy with excitement. He climbed to his feet, ran to the side door through which Liu had taken Olga, and pushed at full speed. It opened a crack but no more, and Patrick was knocked to the floor by his own momentum, feeling as though he'd run smack into a wall. The door was padlocked on the outside. He jerked his shoulder back into place and searched for Plan B, his gaze sweeping the warehouse.

No windows. No other door, except the main garage door. It, too, was probably locked from the outside. But he had to try. He hurried past the line of chopped vehicles to the front of the warehouse. An electric garage door opener would have been nice, but there was just a rope hanging from the track above him. He pulled hard. The door jerked upward an inch, but it caught on the latch. Locked.

"Shit."

He released the rope and reassessed. He knew from the last call with Kate that Liu was coming back to the warehouse after getting the flash drive. Patrick had to either be gone by then or be able to defend himself. But with what? He counted nine cars, at least one of which had to have gas left in the tank. But a fire was risky. He could end up burning himself alive, trapped in a warehouse. And a Molotov cocktail was no answer to the pistol Liu was packing, only slightly less stupid than the old joke about the knucklehead who brings a knife to a gun-fight. Patrick needed equal firepower. It seemed like wishful thinking, but not really. Chop shops were never in the nicest part of town. To be on the wrong side of Cali meant survival of the smartest, and anyone with a brain knew better than to cruise through the Warehouse District of Cali without protection. There had to be a gun in one of those cars.

Patrick started down the line of vehicles, throwing open the passenger-side door and popping the glove box. Nothing in the first. Or the second. Or the third. The fourth box was locked, which got his heart pumping. He ran to the work bench and grabbed a screwdriver, which made quick work of the shitty little lock. The box popped open.

*Pay dirt.*

Patrick smiled as he wrapped his fingers around the butt of the pistol. It was just like the one his father had taught him to use at the range. He released the magazine. Fifteen rounds of 9-millimeter ammunition. He had all the firepower he needed.

There was a noise outside the warehouse, the sound of a vehicle pulling up in the alley. The engine stopped, and the door opened.

*Liu?*

A second door opened. Someone was with him, which confused Patrick. The deal was that Olga would stay if Peel delivered the flash drive.

*Something went wrong.*

Patrick crouched behind the car, switched off the safety on his pistol, and waited for the door to open.



Kate's wild ride into Barrio Siloé was uphill, a race past one redbrick building after another along narrow streets. Most of the streetlamps were unlit, either burned out or broken, but there was enough moonlight for Kate to read the endless string of graffiti messages on the walls, fences, and shuttered doorways along the way. One word caught her eye. It was eight feet tall and painted in the Colombian colors of yellow, red, and blue: *Orgullo.* Colombians truly were a proud people, even in the darkest corners of Siloé.

"They turned into that alley," said Kate, pointing from the backseat.

Diego steered to the curb and stopped the car just short of the alley entrance. The entire street was nothing but warehouses, not a pedestrian in sight. Directly overhead, a good fifty feet in the air, were the moving cables that carried the commuter gondolas up and down the hillside. Two blocks ahead, Kate could see the elevated platform for the nearest station. Not a soul on it.

"I don't feel safe here," said Kate.

"We're not," said Diego.

"What's the plan?"

"If I was alone, I'd find my way into that warehouse and do what needs to be done. But I can't leave you here."

"Then I'll go with you."

He shook his head. "Not gonna happen. The best we can do is call the police and circle the block until they get here."

"But you said the police won't come into Siloé."

"I have a few friends in the department."

"Friends who would come here?" she asked.

"How much would your daddy pay for the cops to show up right now?"

Kate stole a quick glance of the neighborhood. "Honestly, whatever they asked for."

"Perfect," said Diego, dialing. "Your old man's about to make a very generous donation to Colombian law enforcement."

"No," said Kate.

"What do you mean, no?"

"Patrick is like a brother to me. If your little brother was in that warehouse, would you drive around the block and wait for the police, who may or may not come?"

Diego lowered his phone. "No. I wouldn't."

"Then don't ask me to."

Their eyes met in the darkness. "All right," he said. "We're going in. Check your weapon."

Kate opened her purse and removed the pistol Diego had given her. "Loaded, safety on," she said.

"Keep the gun pointed at the ground, and stay at least ten steps behind me at all times. Stop when I stop. Move from a position of cover only when I wave you forward. When we get to the alley, remove the safety."

Removing the safety had never been a big deal in target practice. Outside a dark warehouse in the heart of Siloé, however, her heart pounded at the mere thought of an active lethal weapon in her hand.

"Ready?" he asked.

Kate swallowed hard. "Ready."

The car doors opened, and they stepped into the night.


Patrick pointed his pistol straight at the side door to the alley. He was on his knees, with his arms fully extended and the butt of the handgun resting on the hood of the car to steady his shot. He knew he had just a few seconds to act. The pole to which he'd been chained would be in Liu's plain view, and Patrick's escape would be immediately obvious. His plan was to take the first open shot as soon as Liu walked through the door.

A clanking noise came from the other side of the door, which sounded like the padlock coming off. Patrick took aim. He had enough experience with guns to know that he was a better shot using the dominant-eye method. The pistol had standard iron sights, front and rear, which he'd been taught to think of as a teed-up football in the front and the goal post in the rear. The goal was to get the football squarely through the goal posts. He closed his left eye and, using only his right eye, aligned the sights, making sure the front sight was directly in the center of the rear sight notch. His target was an imaginary bull's-eye, chest high in the dead center of the door. He focused on the rear sight, leaving his target slightly blurry, which he knew was right. His finger covered the trigger, and Patrick took a deep breath. The door opened. Patrick applied a small amount of pressure to the trigger but held his fire.

Olga was squarely in his sights.

Liu was behind her. Patrick had no shot. His heart was pounding. Precious seconds were being lost. A more skilled marksman might have taken a shot, but as much as Patrick had loved the movie *American Sniper*, he was no Chris Kyle.

Two steps into the warehouse, Liu stopped and suddenly pulled Olga back against his body like a human shield, pressing his pistol against the base of her skull. He'd obviously spotted the loose chains around the poll. He knew Patrick had freed himself.

"Dumb move, Patrick!" he shouted.

Patrick wanted to squeeze the trigger but had no opening. Liu backed his way out, through the doorway, pulling Olga with him into the alley.

Patrick didn't hesitate. He jumped to his feet, ran to the door, and stopped, planting his back to the doorframe. Running blindly and with abandon into the alley was a good way to get shot, but if he lost sight of Liu he'd forever lose Olga. He pivoted, using the doorframe to protect his body, and peered down the dark alley.

A shot pierced the darkness, and Patrick hit the ground.

# CHAPTER 64

**K**ate was at the entrance to the alley, ten feet behind Diego, when the shot rang out.

"Down!" he said, in a hushed but urgent voice.

Kate hurried to the brick wall and hid behind a tall stack of freight pallets. The warehouses were much deeper than wide, nearly the length of a football field from front to back. The alley was barely wide enough for two vehicles, and as far as Kate could tell, the only way out was the way they had come in. There was no streetlamp, or at least not a working one, and the moonlight did little more than create confusing shadows in what seemed like an endless black tunnel. But as Kate's eyes adjusted, she could make out Diego's silhouette ahead of her. He was hiding behind a Dumpster, pistol at the ready. He signaled for her to be quiet, which made her even more aware of how heavily she was breathing.

Kate calmed her nerves and listened. It had sounded as though the gunshot had come from the alley, outside the warehouse, but it wasn't easy to pinpoint a single gunshot. Diego signaled her forward with a wave of his hand. His hiding spot behind the Dumpster was better than hers, and she eagerly came to join him, moving as quickly and keeping as low as possible.

"I want you to stay right here," he whispered.

Kate nodded in agreement.

Diego raised his pistol and stepped out from behind the Dumpster. Through an opening between the wall and the Dumpster's edge, Kate watched him move deeper into the alley, his every move like a trained law enforcement agent. Roll-down steel shutters covered the windows and doors that faced the alley. Corrugated boxes, flattened and stacked for disposal, one on top of the other, rose in cardboard towers. Diego took cover behind one of the stacks about twenty feet ahead of Kate. He listened. Kate listened harder. There was only silence. Diego stepped out carefully from behind the cardboard tower and started forward.

A shot rang out. Diego went down, dropping to the pavement somewhere on the other side of the stack of crushed boxes. He was completely out of Kate's line of sight, making it impossible for her to know if he was alive or dead. Kate had to make a decision, but the possibility that Diego was only wounded, in need of help, eliminated one option.

She couldn't turn and run.

With her back pressed to the brick face of the building, Kate poked her head around the corner, peering cautiously down the black alley. She took another step forward, then stopped. There was a noise from the other side of the stack of flattened cardboard boxes, where Diego had fallen. If Diego was alive, she couldn't tell; and if his shooter was lying in wait on the other side, she couldn't tell, either. She took cover behind the stack, her heart pounding.

A chorus of sirens whined in the distance. Police were on the way. Diego must have called. That meant he was alive on the other side.

Two more quick shots rang out, which popped in the stacked cardboard. Kate hit the deck and saw a man running away from her. The woman in the red dress was with him. He turned and fired again in Kate's direction, still running. Kate log-rolled across the alley, and she didn't stop rolling until she bumped right up against Diego's body. She was looking directly into his eyes.

"How bad?" she whispered.

He tried to speak but didn't answer.

Kate checked his pulse. Weak, but still beating. The wound was to his upper thigh. He'd had the initial presence of mind to rip a rope-like fastener from the stacked boxes and make a tourniquet, but the blood loss had pushed him into near unconsciousness. Kate checked the tourniquet. Another gunshot pierced the darkness, the bullet whizzing overhead. Kate braced for more gunfire, but she heard only the echo of footfalls on asphalt. The shooter was making a run for it.

"Go," said Diego.

"I can't leave you here!"

Ahead, in the darkness, a stack of boxes toppled to the pavement. Kate took aim with her pistol, ready to fire.

"Kate?"

She recognized the voice, and Kate's heart leapt into her throat. "Patrick?"

He hurried toward her and immediately saw the gravity of the situation.

"It's my friend Diego," said Kate. "He's hit but alive."

The police sirens in the distance grew louder.

"I chased Liu toward you," said Patrick, using the name he'd given him. "But I never fired a shot. He has Olga."

"No one ran past us," said Kate.

"There's no other way out of this alley, except—"

They raised their eyes toward the sky at the same time. Liu was four stories above them on the fire escape ladder. Olga was with him.

"You stay with your friend until the cops get here," said Patrick.

"Patrick, you can't—" she started to say, but the look in his eyes said the matter was not debatable.

"I promised Olga I wouldn't leave without her," he said.

Kate squeezed his hand, so proud and yet wanting to tackle him and make him stay put.

"Please be careful," she said, and he was on his way.

# CHAPTER 65

Patrick ran to the fire escape ladder, grabbed a rung, and started climbing the warehouse wall. As he stared up into the night sky, with countless rungs to go, the long and narrow ladder triggered a childhood memory of a picture book Kate had read to him as a toddler, *Papa, Please Get the Moon for Me.* For one scary moment, he wondered if his life was flashing before his eyes.

He was halfway up. Liu was at least three stories above him, and Patrick looked up just as he pushed Olga up onto the roof of the building. Patrick kept climbing. Liu fired a shot from the top of the ladder. The bullet skipped past Patrick against the brick wall. He pressed his body as close to the ladder as possible and looked up. No sight of Liu. The moon was above him, but this was definitely no children's book. Patrick shook off the distraction and summoned the courage of the U.S. Army Rangers who stormed the cliffs at Pointe du Hoc in support of the Omaha Beach landings on D-Day in the face of enemy fire.

*Patrick, lead the way!* he told himself, borrowing the Rangers motto he'd heard a thousand times in his Call of Duty video games.

Holding a gun was slowing his climb, so he tucked it in his belt. Hand over hand he ascended the ladder, reaching the top in a minute or so, stopping just below the roofline. Only at this height did he realize that the back of the building was built on the edge of a steep gorge in the hillside. Death was likely if he fell from the ladder into the alley; it was an absolute certainty if the fall were from the roof into the ravine.

Patrick removed the gun from his belt. With pistol in hand, he slid himself up and over the top rung, slithering onto the roof on his belly to avoid making a target of himself. The roof was flat and barren as a desert, save for a few exhaust vents and pipes protruding from the tar-and-gravel surface. His gaze swept the entire roof, or at least as much as he could see from his worm's-eye perspective. He saw no sign of Liu or Olga. Slowly, he raised his head for a better look.

The roof was tiered, he discovered, with two levels, both flat. He was on the lower tier, alone. Another ladder led to the higher tier, toward the rear of the building—where Olga had to be with Liu. Patrick jumped to his feet and ran to the second ladder. He kept his gun in hand this time, climbing as quietly as possible. There were only ten rungs, and he stopped when his eyes were level with the second-tier roofline.

"That's far enough," said Liu.

Patrick froze. The elevated tier of the roof ran the entire width of the building, but it was a mere ten feet from Patrick's place on the ladder to the back of the building. Liu was standing at the very edge of the roofline. Olga was in front of him, looking terrified with the barrel of his pistol burrowing into her right cheek.

"Hurting Olga gains you nothing," said Patrick.

"Lay your pistol on the roof or she gets a bullet."

"Don't!" shouted Olga. "He got what he wanted! He got the flash drive!"

Patrick didn't move.

"Now!" said Liu, as he pressed the gun harder against Olga's face.

The utter terror in her eyes left Patrick no choice. He rested his weapon on the roof.

"Let her go," said Patrick. "Keep the flash drive and go. I won't stop you. I don't care if you get away."

"You and I both know that whatever is on that flash drive is worthless."

"That's not Olga's fault."

"No. It's yours."

"I had nothing to do with what Mr. Peel delivered on that flash drive."

"You're the one who said to bring Code Six as ransom. Code Six is made-up bullshit, isn't it, Patrick? You *told* him to deliver bullshit code."

Patrick was silent.

"Don't get me wrong," Liu said with sarcasm. "I can see why you'd want to play hero and keep the real code out of the hands of the Chinese government. As if it's any less dangerous in the hands of your own government."

"You're never going to get it," said Patrick.

"Not from Peel, that's for sure."

"Not from anyone," said Patrick.

"That's where you're wrong. Like I told Jeremy: we could buy it, or we could steal it. Might as well make a buck."

"Your logic may have worked with him. But I'm not for sale."

"That's a shame."

The police sirens he'd first heard in the alley were getting closer. All he had to do was keep the situation stable for a few minutes more.

"Just let her go. Please."

"I have every intention of doing so," said Liu. "And in case anyone asks, be sure to tell them: I did it for Kate."

Before Patrick could react to those words, Liu pivoted, flung Olga around, and pushed her off the building.

"Olga!"

Patrick pulled himself up over the top rung and grabbed his pistol. Liu took one last look at him, and Patrick braced himself for the explosion of gunfire, but there was no sound at all. Liu turned and faced the deep gorge in the hillside behind the building.

And then he jumped.

Patrick ran to the roof's edge. The gorge behind the building cut even deeper into the hillside than he'd thought—so deep that the warehouse roof was actually above the moving cables that ran the gondolas. Another hundred feet below the cable, at the very deepest point of the rocky ravine, beneath the glowing lights of a passing gondola, Patrick caught a glimpse of a red dress. His heart ached, and he could barely believe his eyes. Slowly, his gaze shifted to the gondola that had just passed below the roofline, and he saw the most sickening sight.

Atop the car, riding to the safety of the next gondola platform, was a cold-blooded killer who deserved to die.

# CHAPTER 66

Kate rode with Diego in the back of the ambulance to the emergency room.

Imbanaco Grupo Quirónsalud clinic was ten minutes away from Siloé, so the hospital's surgical staff and seventeen operating rooms were no strangers to gunshot wounds. Enrique was coming out of surgery as Diego was going in. Kate called her father from the hospital waiting room. She told him that she and Patrick were safe, that Peel was dead, and that Enrique was on the mend. He had just one thing to say.

"I want you on the first flight out of Cali."

"I'm already booked. It leaves at eight a.m."

"That's not soon enough. I'll hire a private jet."

"Dad, it's almost eleven o'clock here."

"I can have you out of there by midnight."

Kate hesitated. "I can't leave yet. Patrick is still at the morgue. He wants to say a proper goodbye to Olga."

"Fine. Then he can stay. You're coming home."

"Said the father to his eleven-year-old daughter."

"I just want you safe," he said.

"I risked my life to come here and get Patrick. I'm not leaving without him."

"This is getting silly. All this for a prostitute?"

Kate swallowed her anger, but not entirely. "She was a victim of sex trafficking. A victim of *your* ex–business partner. So I'm going to hang up now, Dad, and try to forget what you just said. I'm flying home tomorrow with Patrick, after he says goodbye to Olga."

"I'm sorry, Kate."

"Good night," she said, and the call ended.

A text message came a few minutes later. Patrick had left the morgue and purchased a prepaid cellphone so that Kate could reach him. Diego was just about to come out of surgery, but with the general anesthesia, both he and Enrique would probably sleep through the night. Kate was exhausted and had yet to check out of her hotel. She texted Patrick back to let him know that Enrique's adjoining room was available, if he wanted to catch some sleep before their flight in the morning. He swung by the hospital via Uber, and they shared a ride to the hotel.

"I'm so sorry about Olga," said Kate.

He was casting an empty gaze out the car window. "Thanks."

Kate wanted to say more, but she remembered all too well how she felt after seeing her mother at the morgue. She decided to let him bring it up, but he didn't. At least not directly.

"Have you figured out what Project Naïveté Two is?" he asked.

"I know it includes a scraping tool to collect personal information."

"Not just information. It collects virtually every form of human expression, verbal or nonverbal, and translates it into code. The code is personalized to every technology user and becomes a personal sentiment library. The goal is to have a personal sentiment library for every person under the age of thirty who uses technology."

"For what?" she asked.

"Somewhere in those libraries is the future CEO of Buck. The future chief justice of the Supreme Court. The future president of the United States. And on and on."

"So the idea is, what? Blackmail these people when they grow up and reach positions of power?"

"This isn't about extorting or embarrassing someone for something stupid they did as a child. We're talking about knowing what that person fears. What that person values. What makes that person tick. That kind of window into the adult psyche starts by building a personal sentiment library in the formative years."

"Let me guess: the more expressive a user is on social media, the more robust his or her personal sentiment library will be."

"Yep."

"And we all know that the more expressive user isn't going to be a '*him*.' It's a '*her*.'"

"That's a fact. Teenage girls, especially, are way out in front of boys in sharing what the industry calls sentiment data."

Kate was beginning to connect the final dots, but it wasn't easy to say it. "After my mother died, I visited Sandra Levy to find out why she was trying to steal code. If I were to tell you she said she did it for her daughter, what would you say?"

"I'd say she told me the exact same thing."

"When?"

"Right before she was arrested. She knew the FBI was closing in. She needed to line up someone on the inside to take the baton from her and stop Naïveté Two. She chose me."

"How did she expect you to stop it?"

Patrick turned his gaze away from the window and looked at her directly. "Expose it. Give people hard proof of how their own government intends to handle the next generation of leaders. Make them understand how it would be even worse in the hands of a hostile nation."

"Do you think Peel was on to you? Is that why he sent you to Colombia?"

"Probably. My only regret is getting your mother involved."

The car entered the hotel motor court and stopped. "What did you just say?" asked Kate.

Patrick climbed out of the backseat. Kate followed him into the lobby and to the reception desk.

"Getting my mother involved in *what*?"

"This mess."

The receptionist gave them an extra key to Enrique's room, and Patrick started toward the elevator. Kate continued after him.

"Patrick, you're not nine years old, and I'm not your teenage baby-sitter. You can't just drop a bomb like that and walk off. Talk to me."

He stopped midway through the lobby, looked at her, and spoke in a voice mixed with anger and apology—but the anger was at himself. "I screwed up, Kate."

Kate wasn't sure she could handle what he was trying to say, but this was Patrick, and she forced herself to be patient. "Tell me what it is. Nothing is unfixable."

"It's not that I wanted to hide anything from you. It's like I'm figuring out I screwed up in real time—as I'm talking to you right now."

Kate was about to lose it. "Patrick, just tell me."

"I was in a tight spot," he said. "To stop Naïveté Two, I needed the highest credentials in the company. I could think of only one way to get them."

"You stole them?"

"'Borrow' was the word I used with your mother."

"My mother never had any credentials to borrow."

"I know. I figured that if your father's mistress was able to access his credentials, so could his wife."

Kate looked away in disbelief, then back. "There's so much wrong with what you just said. First of all, my father didn't have credentials to Naïveté Two. And Sandra Levy was *not* his mistress."

"I know that now. That's where I screwed up. I went to your mom. I told her what I *thought* was going on."

"Told her *what?* I want to know exactly."

Patrick struggled, then answered. "I told her that Sandra was using your father's credentials to access Naïveté Two."

"Oh, my God. You made her think my father was sleeping with Sandra Levy."

"I'm sorry. Sandra told me she got the credentials by 'playing the boss.' I assumed she meant your father."

"She meant Jeremy Peel."

"Yes. We all know that now. But back then, I was just thinking the same thing everybody thought about Sandra and your father."

"That they were having an affair."

"Yes. I didn't even realize what I'd done until *now*. That's not an excuse. You have every right to be furious with me. But I want you to know that your mother was so brave, Kate. I told her how awful this project was, especially for girls and young women. I told her Sandra was doing it for her daughter. And you know what she said?"

"What?"

"She said, 'Well, then, I'll do it for Kate.'"

Kate's knees nearly buckled. "I have to sit down," she said, and she found a couch. Patrick sat beside her.

"Here's the weirdest thing," said Patrick. "When Liu pushed Olga off the building, he said the same thing. 'I did it for Kate.' How could he possibly have known that's what your mother said to me—'I'll do it for Kate'?"

"He got it from the note my mother left: 'I did it for Kate.'"

"Don't take this the wrong way, but that's a really strange suicide note."

Kate's expression turned very serious. "That's because it wasn't actually a suicide note."

"Then what was it?"

"I think my mother wanted it to look like a suicide note. But she chose those words so that you would recognize them and know that it wasn't."

"Why?"

Kate hesitated to say it, but it was where her thoughts had led her. "Maybe it was her way of letting us know her death wasn't really a suicide."

"Whoa."

"Yeah. Whoa."

Kate rose. Patrick joined her in the walk to the elevator, and they rode up together.

"When's the last time you showered?" she asked.

"I don't remember."

"Get cleaned up in Enrique's room. I'm sure he has clean clothes that will fit."

The elevator doors parted, and they stepped off at the seventh floor.

"You're acting funny," said Patrick.

"I just discovered my mother may have been murdered. How do you expect me to act?"

"What are you going to do?"

"Call my father. He needs to know all this."

They stopped outside Patrick's room, next to Kate's.

"What if he already knows?" asked Patrick.

"Knows that she was murdered?"

"Yeah. I mean, what if—"

"I know exactly what you mean."

"Don't be mad. I'm just thinking out loud."

"My head is spinning."

"Mine, too," said Patrick. "I'm going to shower. If you need anything, I'm in the next room."

"Thanks. Be ready to leave for the airport at five a.m."

"No problem. I'm dead tired, but I'll be shocked if my mind shuts off long enough for me to actually fall asleep."

"You and me both," said Kate.

Patrick disappeared into his room. Kate dug her key from her purse, the light on the electronic lock flashed green, and she opened the door.

Kate knew perfectly well what Patrick had meant, and the thought of her father having some connection to her mother's death—her *murder*—had her stomach in knots. It seemed impossible and contrary to everything she believed about him. But what if her mother's call to 911 wasn't a revenge call? What if Patrick knew something she didn't? It was too much to think about. She closed the door and stepped inside.

The room was a typical hotel layout with a short entrance hallway, and Kate passed the bathroom on her right and the closet on her left before entering the bedroom and living area. She switched on the light and froze. The sliding glass door to the balcony was open, and the way the lace curtain moved in the breeze was eerily reminiscent of that horrible moment of discovery in her parents' penthouse.

A hand came over her mouth, and she felt the cold barrel of a pistol beneath her chin.

"Not a peep," a man said.

# CHAPTER 67

Kate recognized his voice as the one she'd heard through Diego's phone while circling the block around Club Siloé. It was the man who'd shot Jeremy Peel, his bodyguard, and Enrique. The man who'd pushed Olga off the roof and said, "I did it for Kate." The man Patrick called Liu.

"Is that your mother's perfume I smell?"

Kate wasn't wearing any, and she knew he was messing with her, but she returned the volley. "How do you know my mother's perfume?"

"She just couldn't leave well enough alone, could she, your mother?"

The anger wasn't just in his voice, but in the way he shoved the gun up under her chin. Kate was afraid to say the wrong thing and set him off.

"I don't know what you mean."

"Even Sandra Levy stopped at the point of finding out that the CIA was behind Naïveté. Your mother got dangerously close to finding out that Peel was about to sell it to the Chinese. Sandra got jail. Your mother, of course, got worse."

"My mother took her own life."

"Did it ever occur to you how easy it is to climb from the balcony of your apartment to the balcony of your parents' penthouse?"

It was two stories. And a way to avoid security.

"What are you saying?"

"You know what I'm saying. I brought my own vodka, which was totally unnecessary. That should have been clue number one to you that something wasn't right—that she was dead drunk and hadn't touched the vodka from her florist."

"You made her drink?"

"I didn't make her. I gave her a choice. She could drink up and jump. Or the two of us could sit there and wait for you to show up. And then I'd toss you both over the railing. She made the right choice. I even let her leave a note."

Kate nearly gasped at the realization.

*I did it for Kate.*

"What do you want from me?"

"The code on Peel's flash drive turned out to be shit. So you're going to text Patrick and tell him to come over."

"He won't give you the code you want."

"He risked his life to save a whore. Imagine what he'll do to save you. Where's your phone?"

"In my purse."

"I want you to remove it, nice and slow. And then you're going to text exactly what I say. Got it?"

Kate swallowed her fear. "Got it."

# CHAPTER 68

**P**atrick stared at his image in the bathroom mirror.

Even in periods of raging hormones, he had about as much facial hair as a teenager, but he hadn't shaved since setting foot in Colombia. The last time he'd needed a shave this badly he was a teenager with a caterpillar on his upper lip. He borrowed Enrique's razor and hoped he wouldn't mind.

Kate's room was directly on the other side of the bathroom wall. He didn't mean to eavesdrop, but the hotel was far from soundproof. He couldn't make out what was being said, but he definitely heard voices—male and female, not just Kate's. If she was talking to her father on speakerphone, it was none of his business. But to be curious was human, and Patrick's time in captivity had made him an expert at overhearing conversations in the next room. He leaned closer to the wall and listened. The man was talking, and the voice chilled Patrick so deeply that he nicked his chin with the blade. It sounded strangely like Liu.

*No way.*

Patrick wondered if this was the first sign of PTSD and of many sleepless nights to come—hearing the voice of his captor when it couldn't possibly be him.

As he dabbed away the blood, his burn phone chimed with a text message, which was odd, since the only person who had his prepaid number was Kate. He checked the display:

Need to talk now. No phones. Come to the hotel. IMPORTANT.

Another chill came over him, but it was no harbinger of PTSD or other psychological trauma from the kidnapping. This time, the fears were grounded in real and present danger. Kate was in the next room. Why would she text him? Why would she tell him to come to the hotel? Why wouldn't she just knock on the door that connected their rooms?

Why did that man's voice on the other side of the wall sound like Liu?

Patrick hurried from the bathroom, went to the door that connected his room to Kate's, and stopped. The lock on his side of the door was bolted. He assumed there was also a bolt lock on the other side, allowing either occupant of the adjoining rooms to keep the other out. Patrick stared at the doorknob and wondered:

*Did Kate have the bolt on?*

As things stood, Liu was expecting Patrick to come to the hotel and knock on Kate's door. The side door offered the element of surprise, but all advantage would be lost if his entry weren't sudden and overwhelming. There could be no fiddling with locks to tip off Liu.

Quietly, Patrick stepped to the opposite side of the room and braced his foot against the baseboard. His last attempt at busting down a door had not gone well, but this was not a steel-encased warehouse door with a kickass padlock. Even so, he grabbed a pillow from the bed for the benefit of his shoulder.

The risk was high, and the probability of success was low, but the options were few. He was certain Liu was in the next room. He'd stood and watched as Liu threw Olga off the building. He wouldn't make the same mistake twice. Liu might have something even worse in store for Kate, as witnessed by his fascination with burning flesh and his homemade napalm concoction. Kate had put everything at risk to come to Colombia and help him. He had to act, and quickly.

On the mental count of three, he pushed away from the wall and charged at the door with all the force he could muster.

# CHAPTER 69

The side door flew open. Splinters of wood from the shattered door-frame sailed into Kate's room. It sounded like an explosion, and almost simultaneously, Kate felt Patrick's body slamming into her side. The impact took her down and Liu with her.

A gunshot rang out, shattering the full-length mirror on the wall. Kate wasn't hit, and she managed to extricate herself from the tangle of flailing arms and legs rolling across the carpet. The two men were suddenly on their feet, and in a sudden burst of motion, Patrick slammed into the flat-screen television and Liu pointed his pistol. Maybe the gun had jammed, or maybe Kate had actually reacted that quickly, but before Liu's trigger finger could squeeze off a shot, Kate kicked the pistol from his hand and sent it flying out of the open sliding glass door onto the balcony.

The men sprinted to the gun, pushing and shoving each other, and knocking the sliding door from its track on their way out. Shattered glass showered over them, as the struggle for the gun continued out onto the balcony. Kate felt like she was watching in slow motion, but even in her surreal frame-by-frame view, the two men only seemed to gain speed, like a boulder rolling downhill, as their momentum carried them across the balcony and into the aluminum railing.

Kate screamed as the railing gave way.

Liu went over the edge with the first section of battered aluminum balusters. Then Patrick.

"Patrick!" Kate cried, and she ran to the balcony's edge.

Patrick was hanging on by one hand to a piece of metal railing that was still fixed in the concrete floor of the balcony. His feet dangled in the air, high above the motor court below. Patrick had managed to grab Liu on his way over the railing, and his left hand clung to Liu's forearm.

Kate was standing at the balcony's edge, looking down. Liu looked up, and their eyes met. He was twisting in midair like a kite tail, his life literally in Patrick's grip.

"Tell him to pull me up!" shouted Liu.

Kate said nothing.

Patrick said something. He spoke in a soft voice, as if his words were not intended for Kate, Liu, or any other living person. It was possible, Kate would later tell police, that Patrick was running out of strength and said something like "I can't hold on any longer." But the more likely scenario would forever remain a secret between her and Patrick.

"I did it for Olga," was what Kate heard.

Liu slipped from Patrick's grip, his scream piercing the night until his body slammed into the pavement below.

# CHAPTER 70

January. A blanket of white covered Washington, D.C. Kate had butterflies in her stomach. Giant butterflies. Pterodactyls, even. She hoped that snow on opening night was the theatrical equivalent of rain on a wedding day, a sign of good luck.

The theater held about two hundred, and every seat was taken. Kate chose to sit among strangers, not with family or friends. She preferred to surround herself with the unvarnished reactions of real theater go-ers, not the obligatory praise of folks who were kind enough to come but probably hadn't seen a live play since their middle school's produc-tion of *Annie*.

Patrick was seated a couple of rows behind her. He'd brought a date, which Kate was happy to see. Her father was seated on the aisle in the next section over from her.

Minutes before curtain, she received a text message from Irving Bass.

Break a leg.

She smiled to herself and texted back. Wish you were here.

It was unusual for the director not to attend opening night, but the production of *Code 6*—she finally had a title—had been anything but "usual." It had felt rushed from the beginning. A completely rewritten script. Casting before the script was even finished. Irving's collapse and hospitalization. Hers should have been the first play of the coming season in September, not the first play of the new year in January. Not until December did Irving come clean with her and explain the fast track.

"I have pancreatic cancer, Kate. There isn't going to be a next season."

At first, she'd refused to believe it. Half joking, she'd even accused him of stopping at nothing to get her to accept his revisions to the script. But he was seriously ill, and the fact that her play would likely be his last became their secret. They drew closer over the following weeks, though disagreements were still intense. Irving had even thrown her out of rehearsal one afternoon in front of the entire cast. And, for the most part, Irving did get his way, including his "non-negotiable" item: one act, ninety minutes.

Kate watched the first seventy-five minutes with fingernails digging into the armrest. Some of the "humorous" lines she'd absolutely refused to cut from the script had fallen flat with the audience; Irving had been right, after all. Nonetheless, the audience seemed to be enjoying it. The real test was the final scene—the volcanic point of conflict between an aging Thomas J. Watson, Sr., and his up-and-coming son.

The setting was the 1950s. Watson was grooming his son to replace him as CEO. It was the dawn of the computer age, and IBM was transitioning from electromechanical technology to fully electronic. It was also the height of the McCarthy era, and Tom Junior had made the mistake of speaking out publicly against it. His father had harsh advice for him, leading to another one of their epic confrontations after work at the Watson town house on the Upper East Side.

"A businessman sticks to business," said Watson.

"That's the most narrow-minded view of the world I've ever heard."

"'Shoemaker, stick to your last.' It's the best advice I ever got."

"Which explains how you kept quiet and just kept making shoes, even as German boots were trampling all over Europe."

"You're such a smart-ass, Tom."

"You're such a coward."

"I am not a coward!"

"You don't know what courage is. Did you not learn anything

from the way Hitler played you? Spineless suggestions that he follow the Golden Rule didn't exactly do the trick, did they?"

"I did more than any businessman in America to keep war from coming."

"You did more than any businessman to treat Nazi Germany like a business problem. It wasn't. You can't appease men like Hitler and just hope they'll come to their senses."

"I haven't appeased anyone!"

"If you don't work against them, you're appeasing them. A flat condemnation of Hitler could have made a difference."

"You have no idea what you're talking about. One wrong word from New York and the Third Reich would have nationalized Dehomag. What would that have accomplished?"

"You would have taken a stand. It would have shown the world that 'world peace through world trade' wasn't just a catchy slogan."

"You're never going to let that go, are you?"

"No. You can retire and turn the page. I have to deal with this for the next ten, twenty—who knows how many years. I've only been president since January, and reporters are already breathing down my neck, trying to get records from Europe."

"Records of what?"

"The Nazis' use of Hollerith machines and punch-card technology."

"Why is that a story? Herman Hollerith licensed his patents to Willy Heidinger in 1910. Punch cards were part of the German economy long before the Nazis even existed."

"The story isn't about the German economy. It's about Nazi concentration camps."

"Then it has *nothing* to do with IBM."

Tom paused, his gaze tightening. "Who is Harold J. Carter?"

"Carter? The name doesn't ring a bell."

"I'm told he visited IBM headquarters in July 1943."

"Carver, you say?"

"Harold *Carter*. Damn it, Dad. Don't pretend like you don't know! He's an investigator with the Economic Warfare Section of the Department of Justice." Again he paused, and then he asked in a louder voice, "Did he visit IBM headquarters in July 1943?"

Watson breathed deep, then answered. "Yes. He was here."

"And I have to hear this from a newspaper reporter," Tom said with an angry chuckle. "You didn't think to tell me?"

"Nothing came of it."

"What was the Justice Department investigating?"

"Our German subsidiary."

"What about it?"

"Making sure we played no part in our subsidiary's support for the German military."

"In other words, making sure we weren't in violation of the Trading with the Enemy Act?"

"And we weren't," said Watson.

"That's not the point! Why didn't you tell me about this?"

"It wasn't even an investigation. The Justice Department looked into dozens of companies during the war. Companies as red, white, and blue as Standard Oil."

"There's a difference. Oil isn't refined to process personal information. Hollerith machines were invented for that very purpose— for the Census Bureau."

"It was a big nothing! Harold J. Carter visited and left. He never came back. *Nothing* came of it."

Tom faced his father squarely and assumed a more challenging posture. "Let me ask you a simple question: When did it occur to you that the Nazis might use Hollerith machines against Jews?"

"I—I don't know if it ever occurred to me."

"Hitler's election in 1933?"

"It never even crossed my mind in 1933."

"The Nuremberg racial laws in 1936? Kristallnacht in 1938? Hitler's invasion of Poland in 1939? The creation of the Warsaw Ghetto in 1940? When, Dad? *When?*"

"I don't know when."

"You must know! When did it finally dawn on you that Hitler might use Hollerith machines against Jews?"

"What do you want me to say, Tom?" he asked, shouting.

"After our German subsidiary went from three hundred employees in 1930 to *three thousand* in 1940? After the record profits of 1939?"

"I said I don't know!"

"You do know! When did you know?"

"When it was too late!" he said, his voice booming. "All right? Is that what you want to hear me say? When it was too *damn* late!"

There was utter silence. Father and son were completely still.


The stage lighting changed. Kate glanced across the auditorium in her father's direction. He looked back with an expression that asked the question Kate should have expected:

*Is that what you think I am? A coward?*

She wanted to explain, but she wouldn't get the chance. At least not that night.

He got up from his seat and left before the final curtain.

# EPILOGUE

I rving Bass died a happy man. His final world premiere was a sellout.
The reviews were not what they had hoped for, but if Kate had
gained anything since her mother's death, it was perspective. "An am-
bitious effort from a promising young playwright," one critic wrote,
"but a story too big for the stage." Kate would never say Sean the
Snake was right, but she was getting serious interest from Hollywood.
"Send me ten pages," an agent at CAA had told her. Thanks to Irving
Bass, she didn't have to ask what made a great ten pages.

*Do you want to get to page eleven?*

The big story was Jeremy Peel. He'd fallen from "boss of the boss"—
Buck's chairman of the board, to whom CEO Christian Gamble
reported—to working for a foreign boss, better known as the Chinese
Ministry of State Security. The man Patrick called "Liu" was identified as an agent of the Chinese state-sponsored cyberespionage group
Red Apollo, acting under the direction of the Tianjin field office of
the MSS. The DOJ cybersecurity audit, led by Noah, confirmed that
Peel never did transfer the key code to the Chinese, though it was up
to Swiss banking authorities to reveal how many millions Peel had
taken before reneging on the deal. It was unquestionably Peel who
had hired Javier to keep Patrick out of the country until the DOJ's
audit was over. It was Patrick's theory that "Liu"—*el jefe del jefe*—then
hired Javier to push him off the mountain and connect Peel to Patrick's murder, placing him firmly and forever under the thumb of the
Chinese government. The world would probably never know if Peel
double-crossed the Chinese because he found patriotism, or because

even he couldn't find a way to sneak Buck's most secure code out the door without exposing himself as a traitor.

Strangely, what Kate considered the most important part of the story was, to everyone else, a nonstory. It brought to mind her research trip to see the Hollerith machine, Irving's hundred-year-old aunt who'd survived the Nazi concentration camp at Buchenwald, and his warning about "Holocaust fatigue." Social media was newer to the planet than Kate, or even Patrick, but already the world was suffering from Big Data fatigue.

"Privacy, schmivacy," to coin an Irving-ism.

But Project Naïveté II wasn't just another story about the loss of personal information. It was the CIA's use of taxpayer dollars to fund Buck's development of technology that capitalized on all that was wrong with social media. Its "stealth" scraping tool—the key code that Peel withheld from the Chinese—could scrape (read: steal) data from every imaginable source, without detection by Google, Facebook, or other platform that collected the data in the first place, and package all that disparate and disconnected information into a single and ever-evolving personal sentiment dossier on every American who didn't live under a rock. Jeremy Peel showed how easily that top-secret technology could fall into enemy hands. Perhaps the wake-up call would come twenty years down the road—"Too damn late," as Kate's Watson had put it—when the president of the United States was eyeball to eyeball with a foreign dictator, world peace hanging in the balance, and America's enemies could calculate that her tough talk was merely a bluff, thanks to the personal sentiment data they'd been scraping from her every encounter with both on- and off-screen technology since she was a child. Some members of Congress were calling for an investigation. Change was possible, but Kate wasn't holding her breath.

One change was immediate: the stated manner of death for Kate's mother was no longer suicide. Elizabeth Gamble was officially the year's twelfth homicide victim in Fairfax County, Virginia.

"I think of her as a hero," Kate told reporters. A hero with baggage.

The funeral service for Irving Bass was small, in accordance with his final direction. It was a cloudy day, which all agreed Irving would also have wanted, cold enough for conversations to vaporize in the air, but just warm enough for some of the fallen snow to begin melting. Kate was one of about a dozen invited guests at the mausoleum. Kate's father was not invited, but as Kate walked to her car after the service, he was waiting on the shoveled walkway that led from the mausoleum to the parking lot.

They hadn't spoken since opening night.

"I've been thinking a lot about your play," he said.

She stopped. They were standing near a seventy-year-old gravestone, beneath a seventy-foot blue spruce that was the same age.

"Dad, I don't want to get into it here."

"It was terrific."

"Oh," she said. Not the words she'd expected.

"You were right," he said. "I did turn a blind eye."

"That wasn't the point of my play."

"Isn't that the point of *any* historical work—that history repeats itself?"

She hadn't really thought of that. But he had a point. "I suppose."

"Tell me again. What was the name of the president of IBM's German subsidiary?"

"Willy Heidinger."

"Heidinger, yes. I remember his line: 'Might as well do business with the Nazis, because if we don't, they'll just nationalize the company and take it, or get it from someone else.'"

"I don't know if he actually said it. But that was pretty much his approach, at least in my interpretation."

"It made me think of Jeremy."

Kate couldn't disagree. "Not a bad comparison."

"Watson made me think of me."

Kate glanced back at the mausoleum, recalling how her interpretation of Watson had clashed with Irving's. "It all depends on how you think of Watson."

"I think he lived with regret."

"That's one interpretation," said Kate. "Others would say he was too much of an egomaniac to admit a mistake, even to himself."

"By 'others,' you mean his son?"

Again, she glanced toward Irving's final place of rest. Visions of red ink came to mind, the felt-tipped pen shaking in a hand that grew weaker with each passing day. *Conflict, Kate! We need more conflict!*

"Like I said. It's all a matter of interpretation."

Silence hung between them. Kate knew what he was wondering, and she hadn't prepared to discuss a certain daughter's interpretation of her own father. But in some ways, she'd been preparing all her life.

"You know, I still think Irving had it wrong," said Kate.

"Had what wrong?"

"Tom Junior didn't hate his father. The old man infuriated him to no end. But he didn't hate him."

"So he tolerated him?"

"More than that," said Kate, looking him in the eye. "I think he loved him very much."

The air around them seemed to lose some of its chill.

"Hmm. That's an interesting view."

"People don't have to agree all the time in order to love each other," she said.

"Right. They can agree to disagree."

"Of course, it helps if they agree at least some of the time."

He smiled a little. "I agree with that."

The wind blew, and a few needles from the blue spruce dropped to the snow around them.

"Hey, you want to get a cup of coffee?" he asked.

"Sure," said Kate. "I'd like that."

They started walking toward the parking lot together.

"Capitol Roasters is pretty close," he said.

"Mmm. The coffee at White's House of Bagels is so much better."

"Okay, if we're talking quality, not convenience, then we should go to Brews by Benjamin."

"Ugh! Really, Dad? How do you drink that stuff?"

# ACKNOWLEDGMENTS

The legal disclaimer says "any resemblance to actual persons, living or dead, is entirely coincidental." It's in all of my books. This time, there's a twist.

The friendship between the Battle and Grippando families goes back more than two decades, predating the birth of Patrick Trowbridge Battle, Jr., in 2002. To his mother and all those who knew him in diapers, he was "Baby Patrick." Patrick received a cancer diagnosis in 2017, and despite the love, prayers, and optimism of the "Battle Strong" movement, he passed away on December 11, 2018, at the age of sixteen. In a moment of love, compassion, and perhaps temporary insanity, I promised his parents I would write Patrick into one of my novels. A seamless appearance of a teenage boy in a Grippando novel would be no easy task, and I came up empty in my next two releases—no Patrick. Then, when the seeds for *Code 6* were just taking root, it occurred to me that by the time the book would be in bookstores, Patrick would have been a young man in his twenties. It was a lightbulb moment: I would age Patrick in real time. I owe a huge debt of gratitude to his godfather, Walter Strump, for helping me imagine Patrick as a twenty-something-year-old whiz kid in the tech industry. Walter, your input was invaluable, and your endless love for Patrick is inspirational.

I am also deeply grateful to GableStage and its founding artistic director, Joseph Adler. Joe developed and directed my first play, *Watson*, which made its world premiere at GableStage in 2019. Based on events in the life of IBM founder Thomas J. Watson, Sr., *Watson* is the story of the Nazis' exploitation of IBM technology during the Holocaust and the world's first personal information catastrophe: the systematic identification of Jews for extermination. Sound familiar? If you're wondering how Kate's play turned out, check out *Watson*.

Thanks also to my editor, Sarah Stein, for helping me stretch myself as a writer and create something special for my thirtieth novel, a play within a novel. Thanks also to my agent and friend, Richard Pine, who has been at my side for all thirty creations (thirty-one, if you count the one that crashed and burned), and to my beta reader, Judith Russell, pinch-hitting for her friend Gloria.

Finally, my biggest thank-you is to my wife, Tiffany. Thirty rides on a roller coaster is a lot to ask. You don't even like roller coasters. Thanks for keeping it fun. Thanks for laughing even when it wasn't fun. Thanks for *not* laughing every time I thought I could throw my hands in the air and ride standing up. I'll be loving you . . . always.

# ABOUT THE AUTHOR

JAMES GRIPPANDO is a *New York Times* bestselling author of suspense and the winner of the Harper Lee Prize for Legal Fiction. *Code 6* is his thirtieth novel. He lives in South Florida, where he is a trial lawyer and teaches Law and Literature at the University of Miami School of Law. His play *Watson* is now available in bookstores.